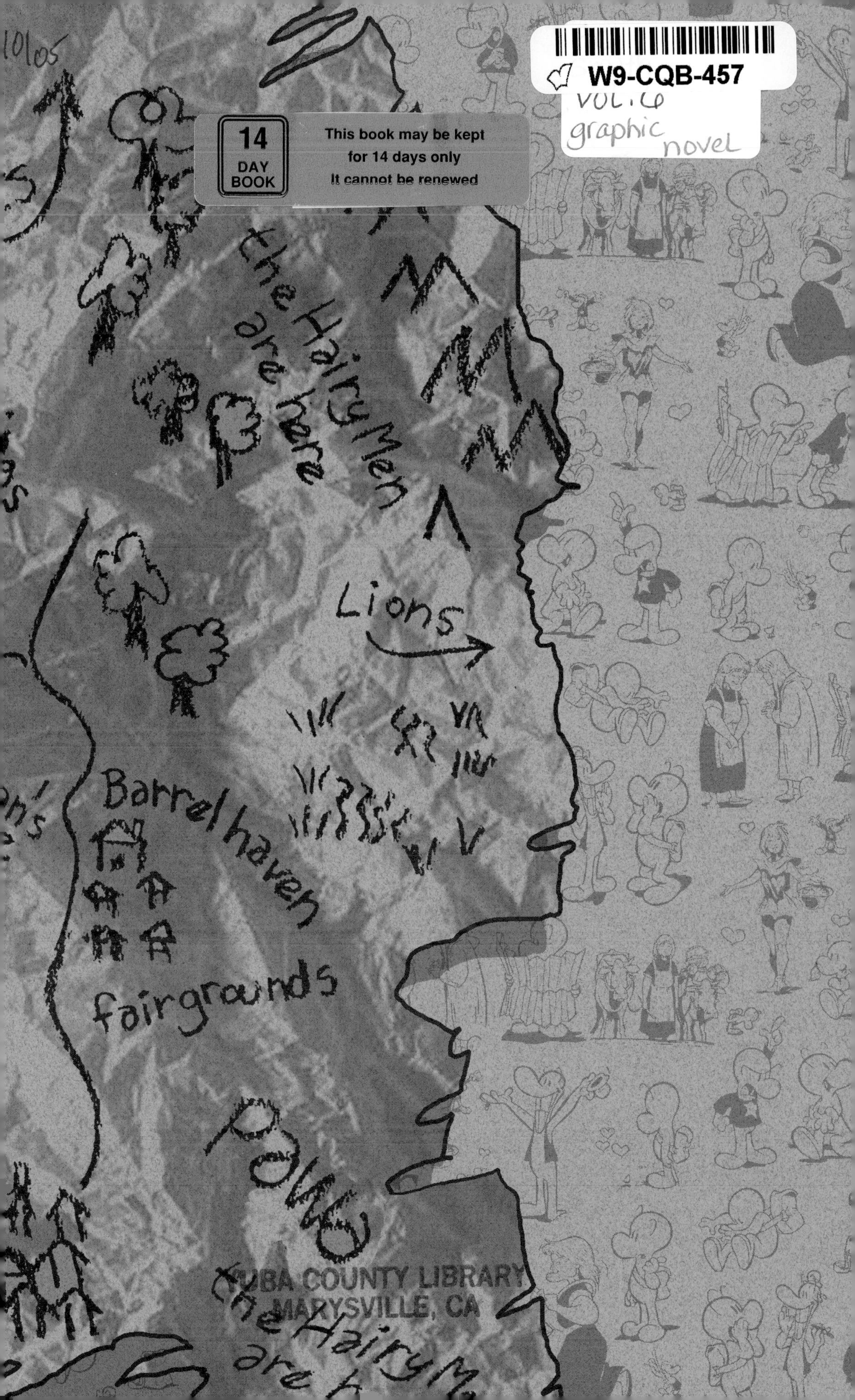
the Hairy Men are here
Lions
Barrelhaven
fairgrounds
pond

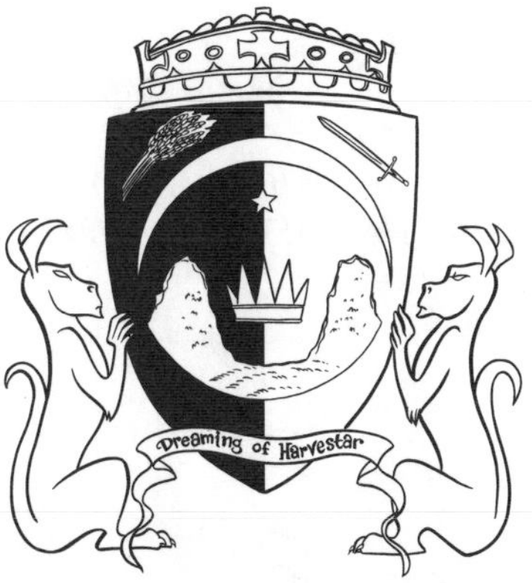
Dreaming of Harvestar

OTHER BOOKS BY JEFF SMITH

THE FIRST TRILOGY

BONE VOLUME ONE: OUT FROM BONEVILLE

BONE VOLUME TWO: THE GREAT COW RACE

BONE VOLUME THREE: EYES OF THE STORM

THE SECOND TRILOGY

BONE VOLUME FOUR: THE DRAGONSLAYER

BONE VOLUME FIVE: ROCKJAW, MASTER OF THE EASTERN BORDER

BONE VOLUME SIX: OLD MAN'S CAVE

(COMING SOON)
BONE VOLUME SEVEN: GHOST CIRCLES

OLD MAN'S CAVE

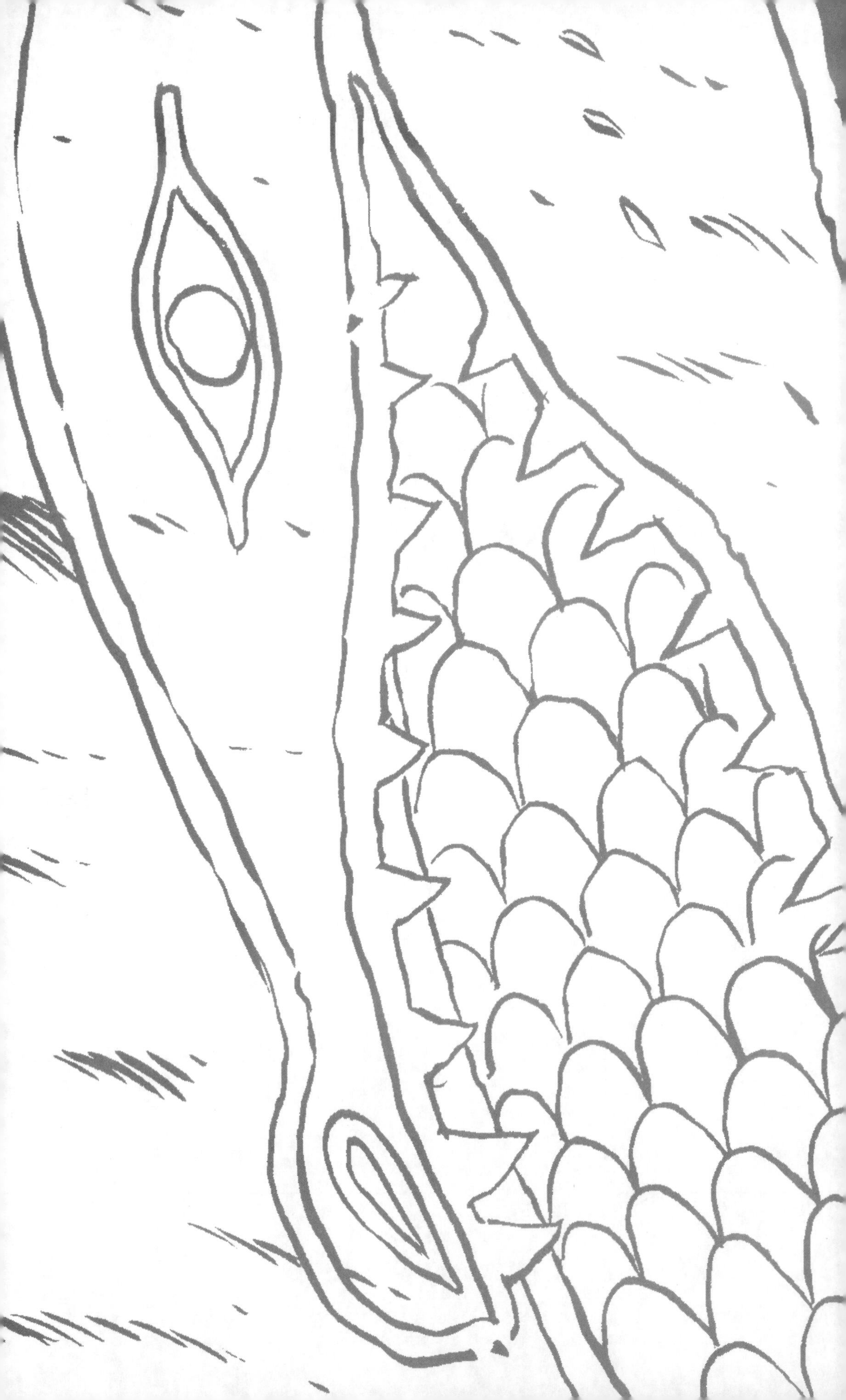

VOLUME SIX:
OLD MAN'S CAVE

JEFF SMITH

CARTOON BOOKS
COLUMBUS, OHIO

THIS BOOK IS
FOR
JIM KAMMERUD

BONE Volume Six: Old Man's Cave copyright © 1999 by Jeff Smith
All rights reserved. No part of this book may be reproduced or utilized in any form or by any means, electronic or mechanical, includ-
ing photocopying, recording, or by any information storage or retrieval system, without written permission except in the case of reprints
in the context of reviews. The chapters in this book were originally published in the comic book BONE and are copyright © 1998 and
1999 by Jeff Smith. BONE® is © 1999 Jeff Smith. Acknowledgements: The Harvestar Family Crest designed by Charles Vess.
Artwork on cover by: Jeff Smith and Elizabeth Lewis.
For information write:
Cartoon Books
P.O. Box 16973
Columbus, OH 43216

Hardcover ISBN: 1-888963-04-2
Softcover ISBN: 1-888963-05-0
Library of Congress Catalog Card Number: 95-68403

10 9 8 7 6 5 4 3 2

Printed in Canada

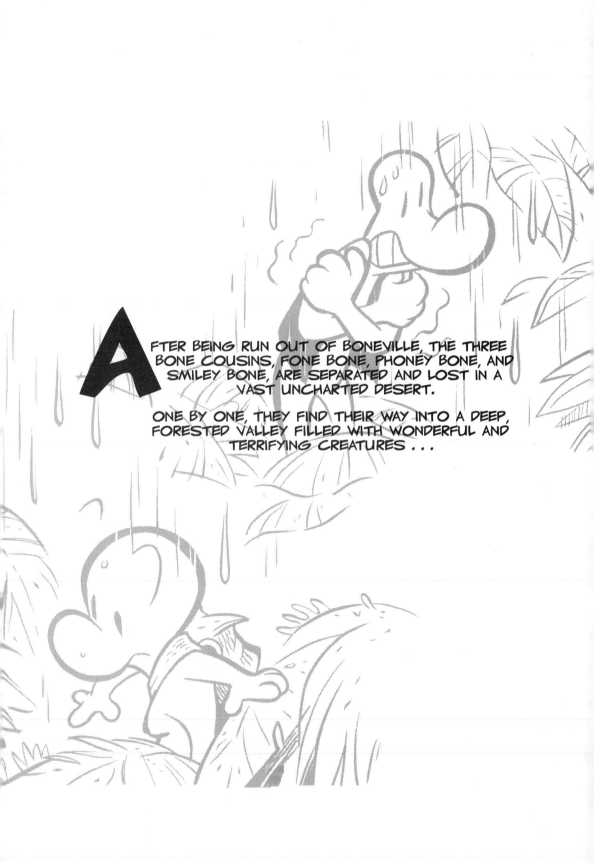

AFTER BEING RUN OUT OF BONEVILLE, THE THREE BONE COUSINS, FONE BONE, PHONEY BONE, AND SMILEY BONE, ARE SEPARATED AND LOST IN A VAST UNCHARTED DESERT.

ONE BY ONE, THEY FIND THEIR WAY INTO A DEEP, FORESTED VALLEY FILLED WITH WONDERFUL AND TERRIFYING CREATURES . . .

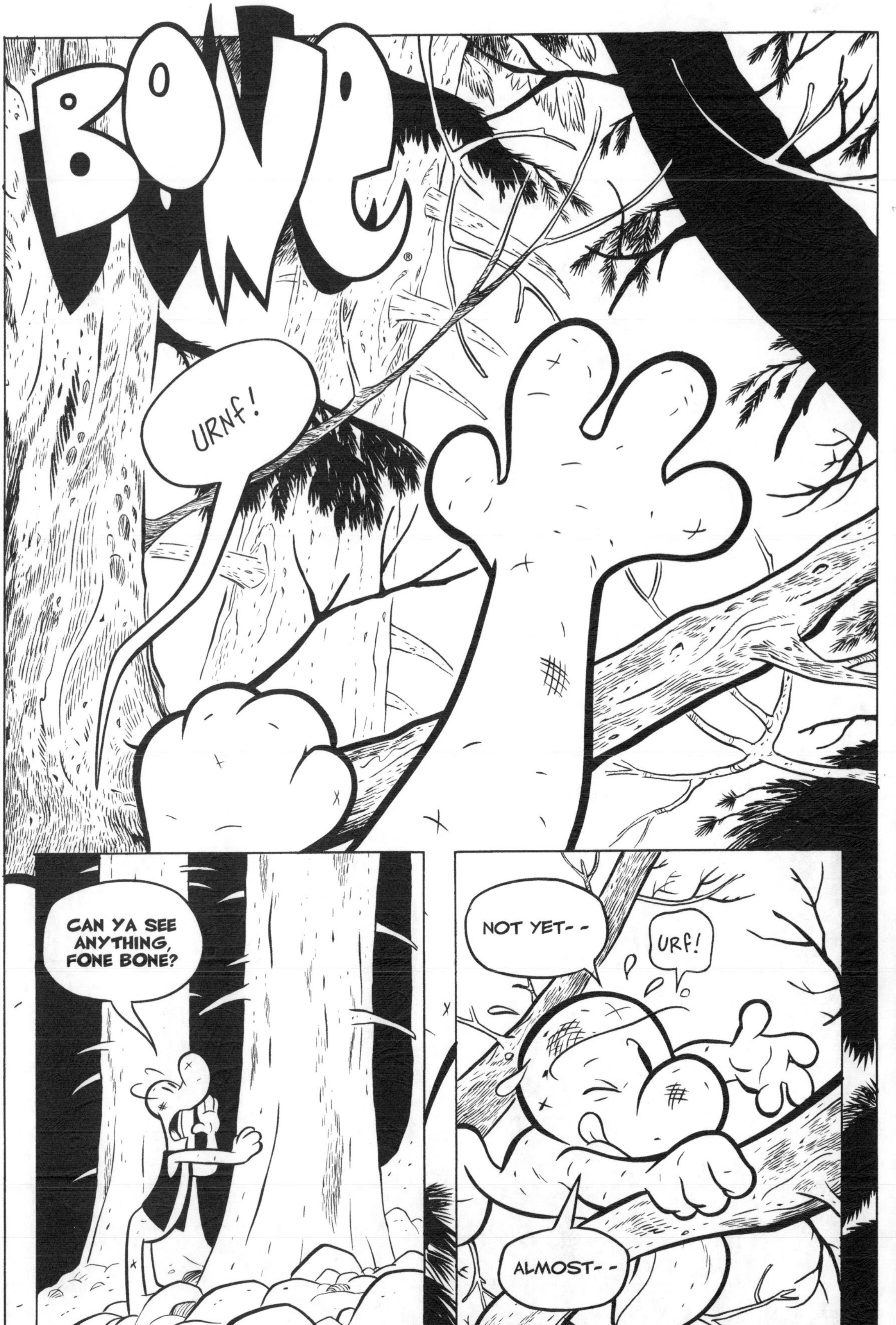
BONE®
URNf!
CAN YA SEE ANYTHING, FONE BONE?
NOT YET- -
URf!
ALMOST- -

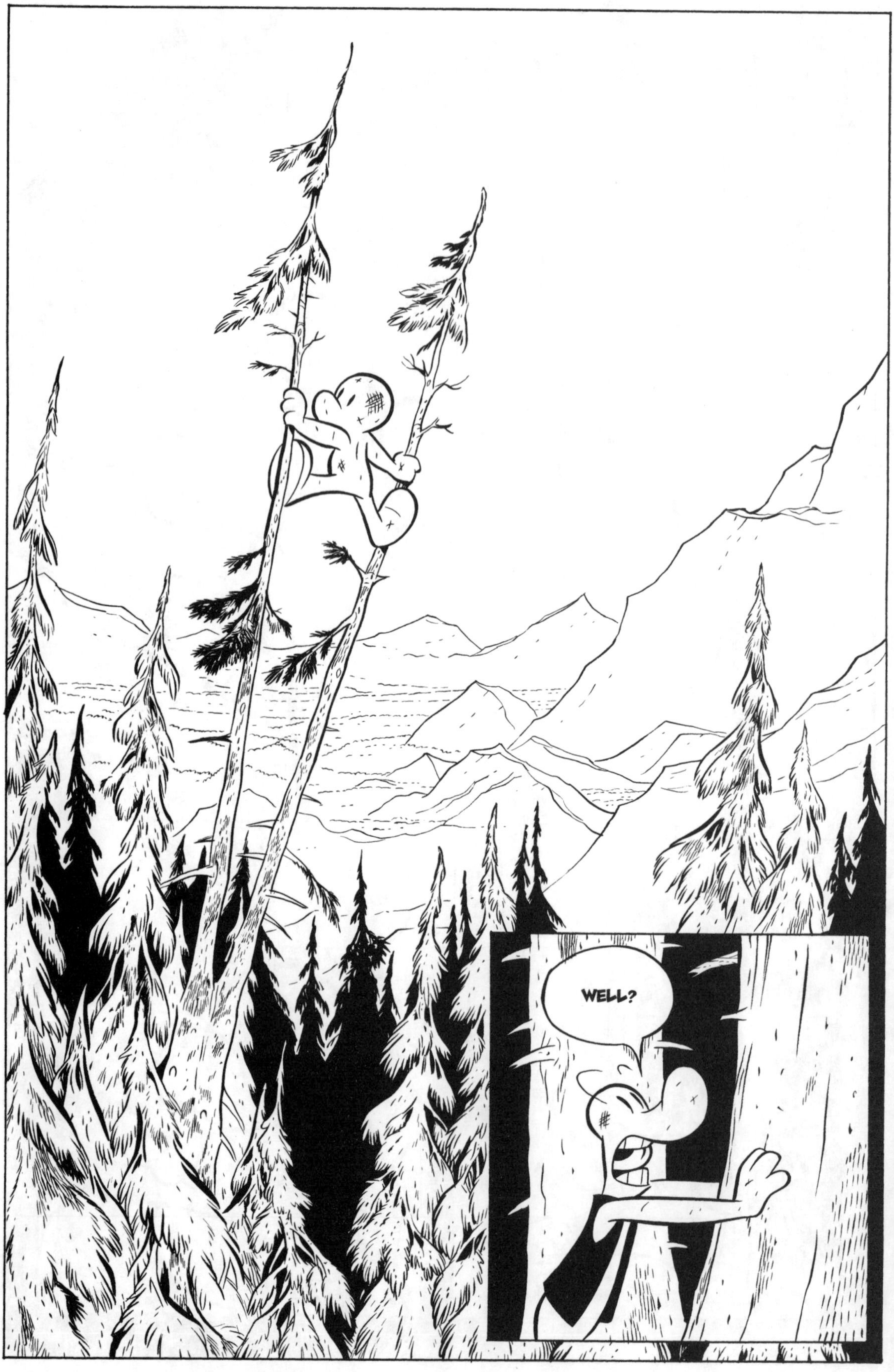
WELL?

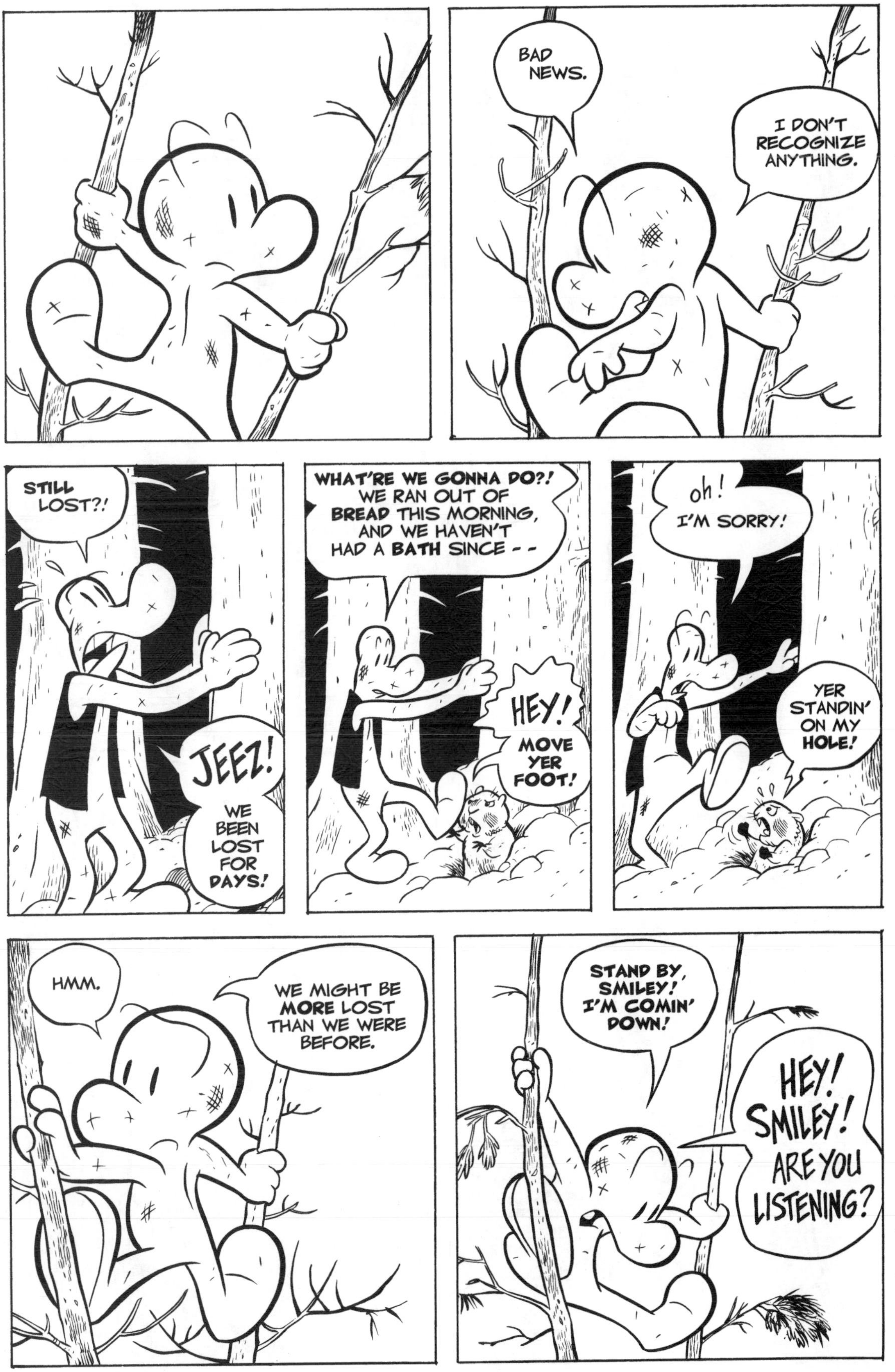

BAD NEWS.
I DON'T RECOGNIZE ANYTHING.
STILL LOST?!
JEEZ!
WE BEEN LOST FOR DAYS!
WHAT'RE WE GONNA DO?! WE RAN OUT OF BREAD THIS MORNING, AND WE HAVEN'T HAD A BATH SINCE - -
HEY!
MOVE YER FOOT!
oh! I'M SORRY!
YER STANDIN' ON MY HOLE!
HMM.
WE MIGHT BE MORE LOST THAN WE WERE BEFORE.
STAND BY, SMILEY! I'M COMIN' DOWN!
HEY! SMILEY! ARE YOU LISTENING?

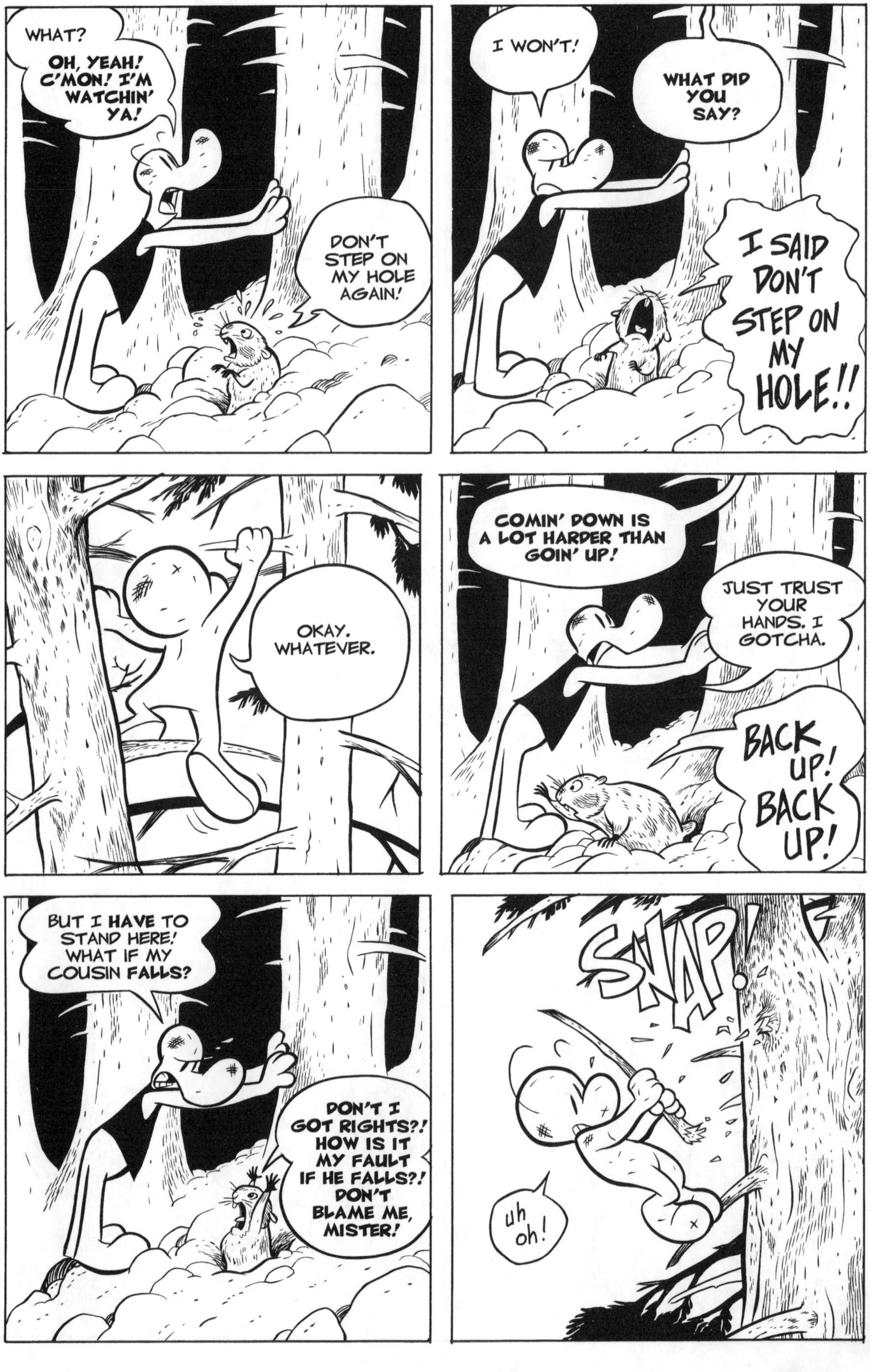
WHAT?
OH, YEAH! C'MON! I'M WATCHIN' YA!
DON'T STEP ON MY HOLE AGAIN!
I WON'T!
WHAT DID YOU SAY?
I SAID DON'T STEP ON MY HOLE!!
OKAY. WHATEVER.
COMIN' DOWN IS A LOT HARDER THAN GOIN' UP!
JUST TRUST YOUR HANDS. I GOTCHA.
BACK UP! BACK UP!
BUT I HAVE TO STAND HERE! WHAT IF MY COUSIN FALLS?
DON'T I GOT RIGHTS?! HOW IS IT MY FAULT IF HE FALLS?! DON'T BLAME ME, MISTER!
SNAP!
uh oh!

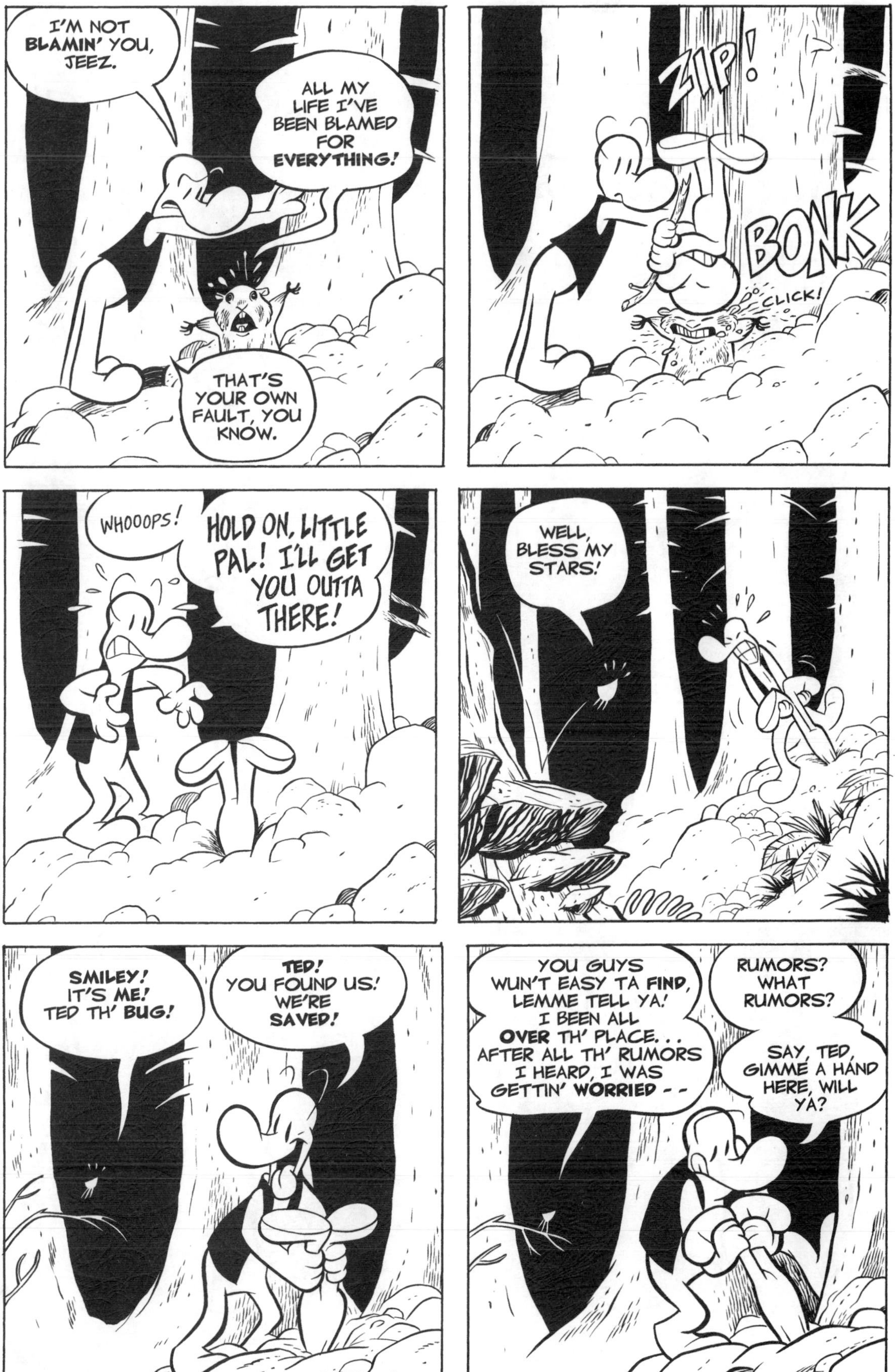
I'M NOT BLAMIN' YOU, JEEZ.
ALL MY LIFE I'VE BEEN BLAMED FOR EVERYTHING!
THAT'S YOUR OWN FAULT, YOU KNOW.
ZIP!
BONK
CLICK!
WHOOOPS!
HOLD ON, LITTLE PAL! I'LL GET YOU OUTTA THERE!
WELL, BLESS MY STARS!
SMILEY! IT'S ME! TED TH' BUG!
TED! YOU FOUND US! WE'RE SAVED!
YOU GUYS WUN'T EASY TA FIND, LEMME TELL YA! I BEEN ALL OVER TH' PLACE. . . AFTER ALL TH' RUMORS I HEARD, I WAS GETTIN' WORRIED - -
RUMORS? WHAT RUMORS?
SAY, TED, GIMME A HAND HERE, WILL YA?

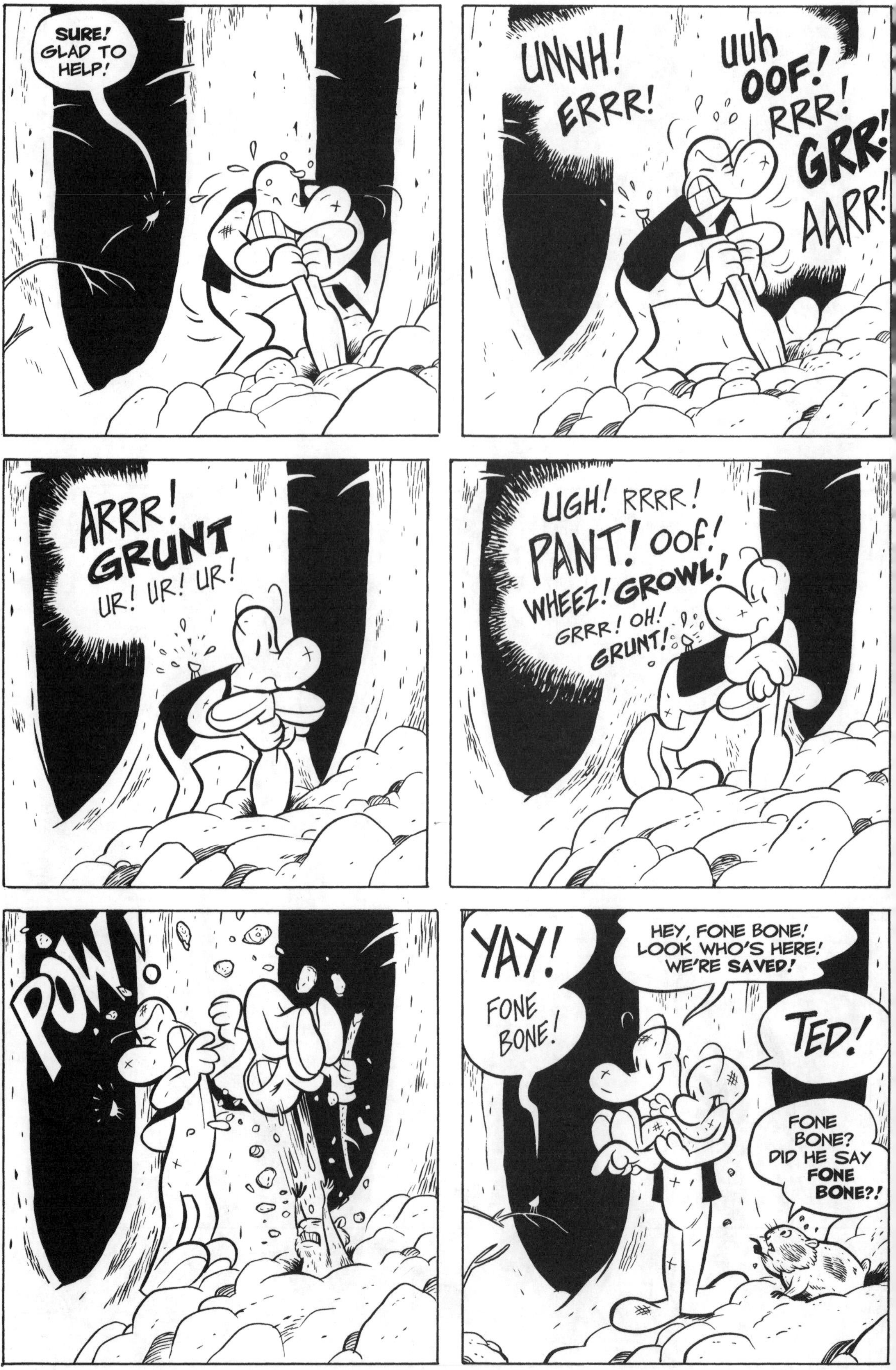
SURE! GLAD TO HELP!
UNNH! ERRR!
uuh OOF! RRR! GRR! AARR!
ARRR! GRUNT UR! UR! UR!
UGH! RRRR! PANT! OOF! WHEEZ! GROWL! GRRR! OH! GRUNT!
POW!
YAY! FONE BONE!
HEY, FONE BONE! LOOK WHO'S HERE! WE'RE SAVED!
TED!
FONE BONE? DID HE SAY FONE BONE?!

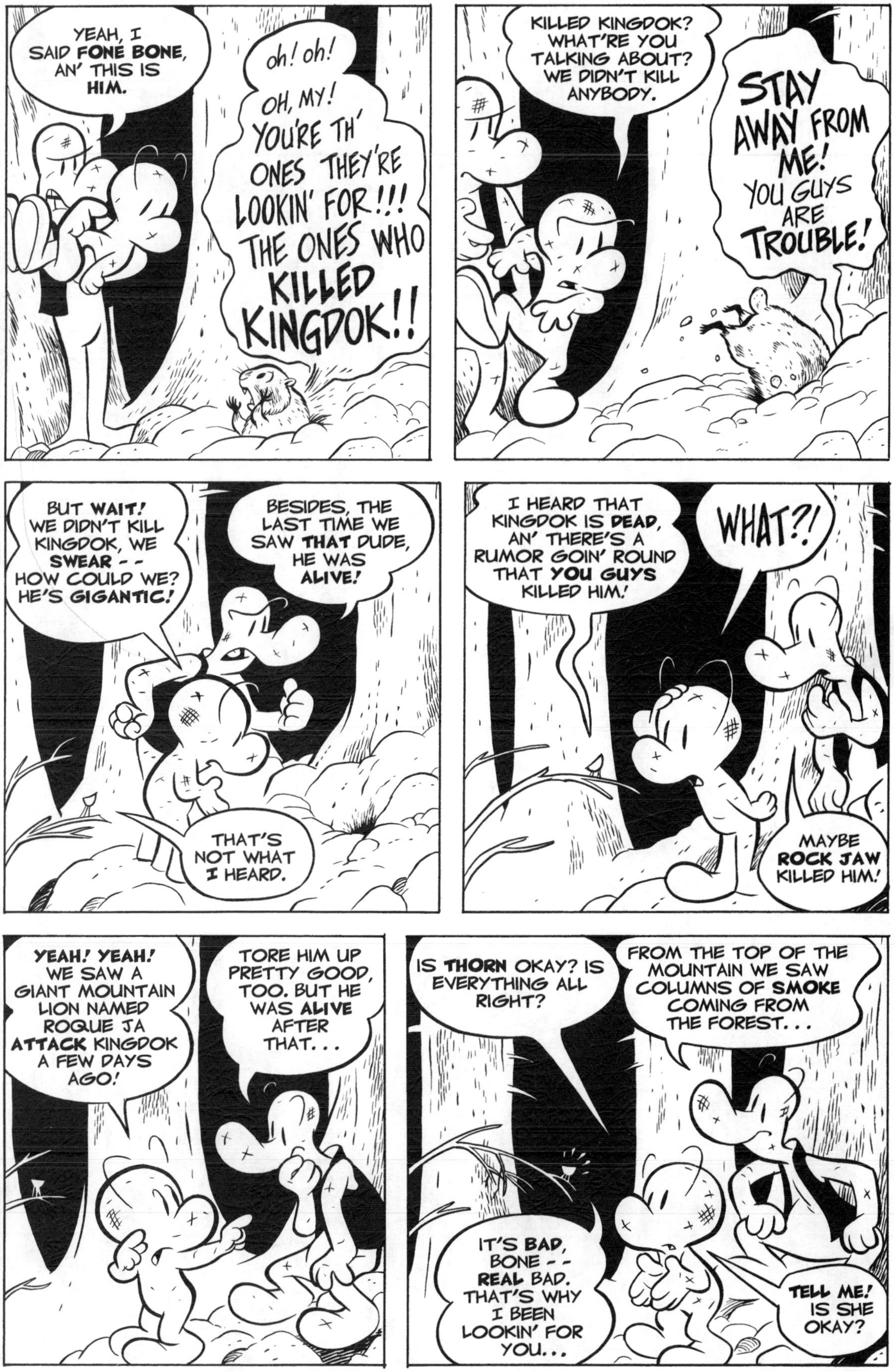
YEAH, I SAID FONE BONE, AN' THIS IS HIM.
oh! oh!
OH, MY! YOU'RE TH' ONES THEY'RE LOOKIN' FOR!!! THE ONES WHO KILLED KINGDOK!!
KILLED KINGDOK? WHAT'RE YOU TALKING ABOUT? WE DIDN'T KILL ANYBODY.
STAY AWAY FROM ME! YOU GUYS ARE TROUBLE!
BUT WAIT! WE DIDN'T KILL KINGDOK, WE SWEAR - - HOW COULD WE? HE'S GIGANTIC!
BESIDES, THE LAST TIME WE SAW THAT DUDE, HE WAS ALIVE!
THAT'S NOT WHAT I HEARD.
I HEARD THAT KINGDOK IS DEAD, AN' THERE'S A RUMOR GOIN' ROUND THAT YOU GUYS KILLED HIM!
WHAT?!
MAYBE ROCK JAW KILLED HIM!
YEAH! YEAH! WE SAW A GIANT MOUNTAIN LION NAMED ROQUE JA ATTACK KINGDOK A FEW DAYS AGO!
TORE HIM UP PRETTY GOOD, TOO. BUT HE WAS ALIVE AFTER THAT...
IS THORN OKAY? IS EVERYTHING ALL RIGHT?
FROM THE TOP OF THE MOUNTAIN WE SAW COLUMNS OF SMOKE COMING FROM THE FOREST...
IT'S BAD, BONE - - REAL BAD. THAT'S WHY I BEEN LOOKIN' FOR YOU...
TELL ME! IS SHE OKAY?

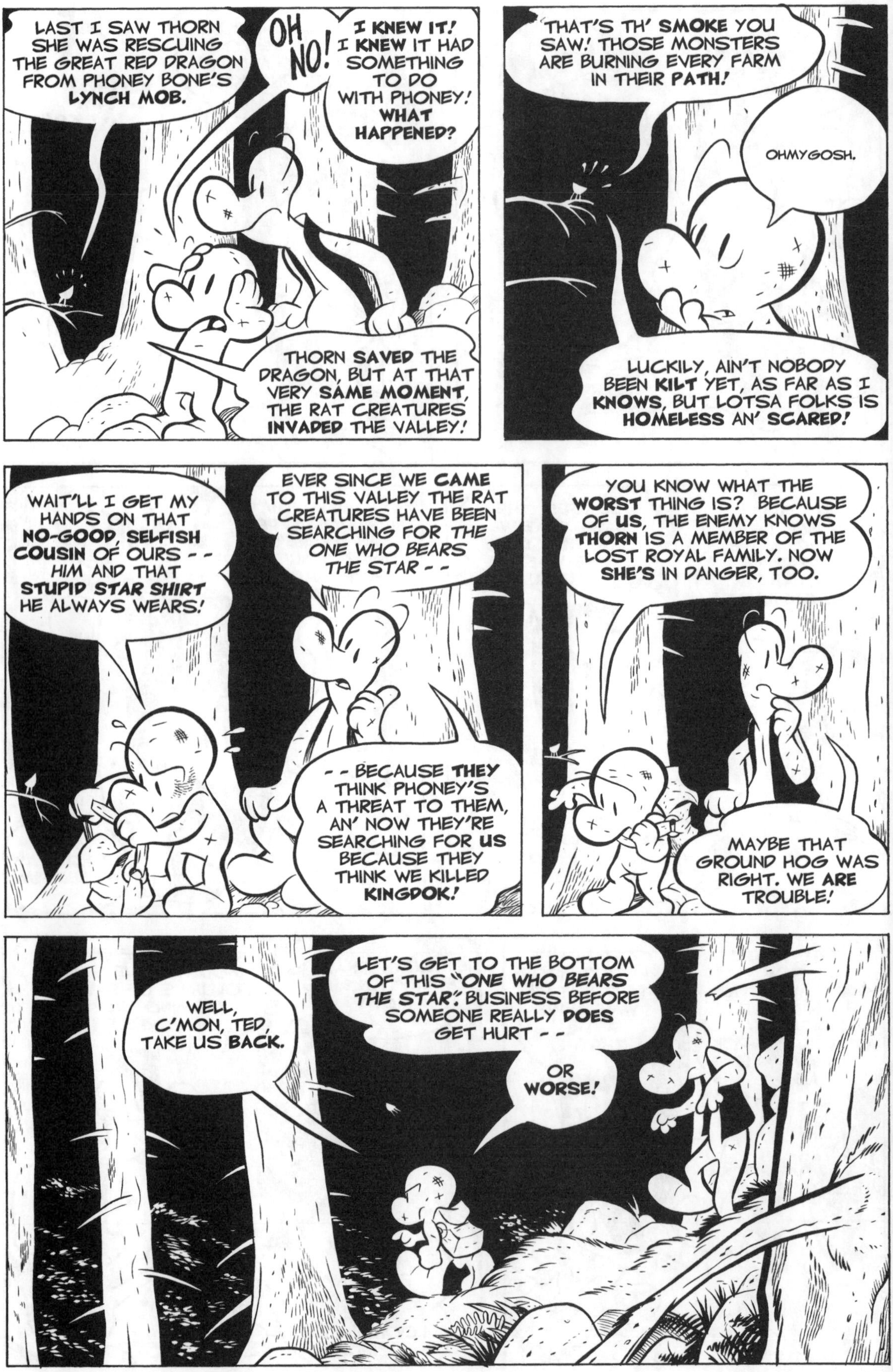
LAST I SAW THORN SHE WAS RESCUING THE GREAT RED DRAGON FROM PHONEY BONE'S LYNCH MOB.
OH NO!
I KNEW IT! I KNEW IT HAD SOMETHING TO DO WITH PHONEY! WHAT HAPPENED?
THORN SAVED THE DRAGON, BUT AT THAT VERY SAME MOMENT, THE RAT CREATURES INVADED THE VALLEY!
THAT'S TH' SMOKE YOU SAW! THOSE MONSTERS ARE BURNING EVERY FARM IN THEIR PATH!
OHMYGOSH.
LUCKILY, AIN'T NOBODY BEEN KILT YET, AS FAR AS I KNOWS, BUT LOTSA FOLKS IS HOMELESS AN' SCARED!
WAIT'LL I GET MY HANDS ON THAT NO-GOOD, SELFISH COUSIN OF OURS -- HIM AND THAT STUPID STAR SHIRT HE ALWAYS WEARS!
EVER SINCE WE CAME TO THIS VALLEY THE RAT CREATURES HAVE BEEN SEARCHING FOR THE ONE WHO BEARS THE STAR --
-- BECAUSE THEY THINK PHONEY'S A THREAT TO THEM, AN' NOW THEY'RE SEARCHING FOR US BECAUSE THEY THINK WE KILLED KINGDOK!
YOU KNOW WHAT THE WORST THING IS? BECAUSE OF US, THE ENEMY KNOWS THORN IS A MEMBER OF THE LOST ROYAL FAMILY. NOW SHE'S IN DANGER, TOO.
MAYBE THAT GROUND HOG WAS RIGHT. WE ARE TROUBLE!
WELL, C'MON, TED, TAKE US BACK.
LET'S GET TO THE BOTTOM OF THIS "ONE WHO BEARS THE STAR" BUSINESS BEFORE SOMEONE REALLY DOES GET HURT --
OR WORSE!

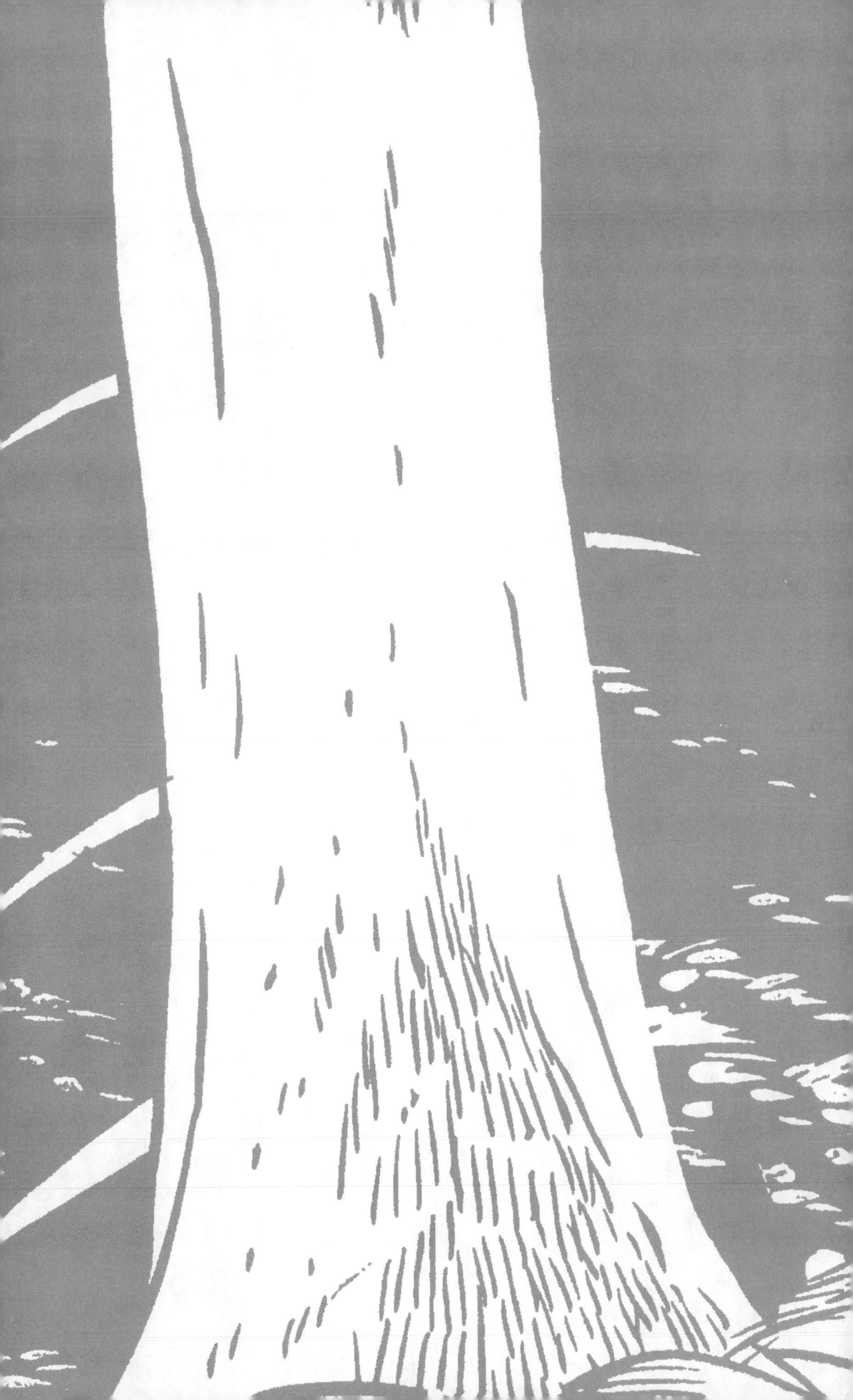

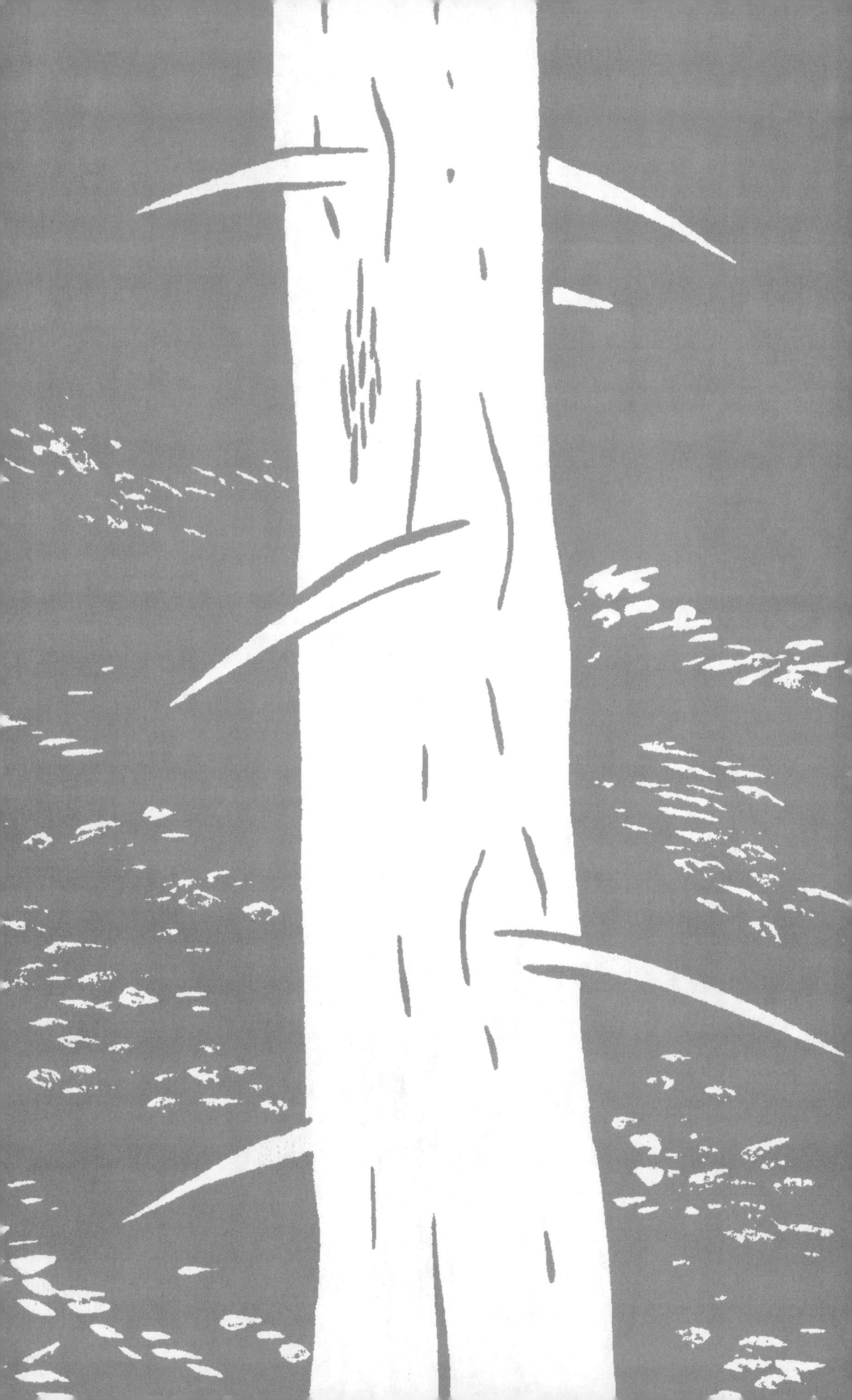

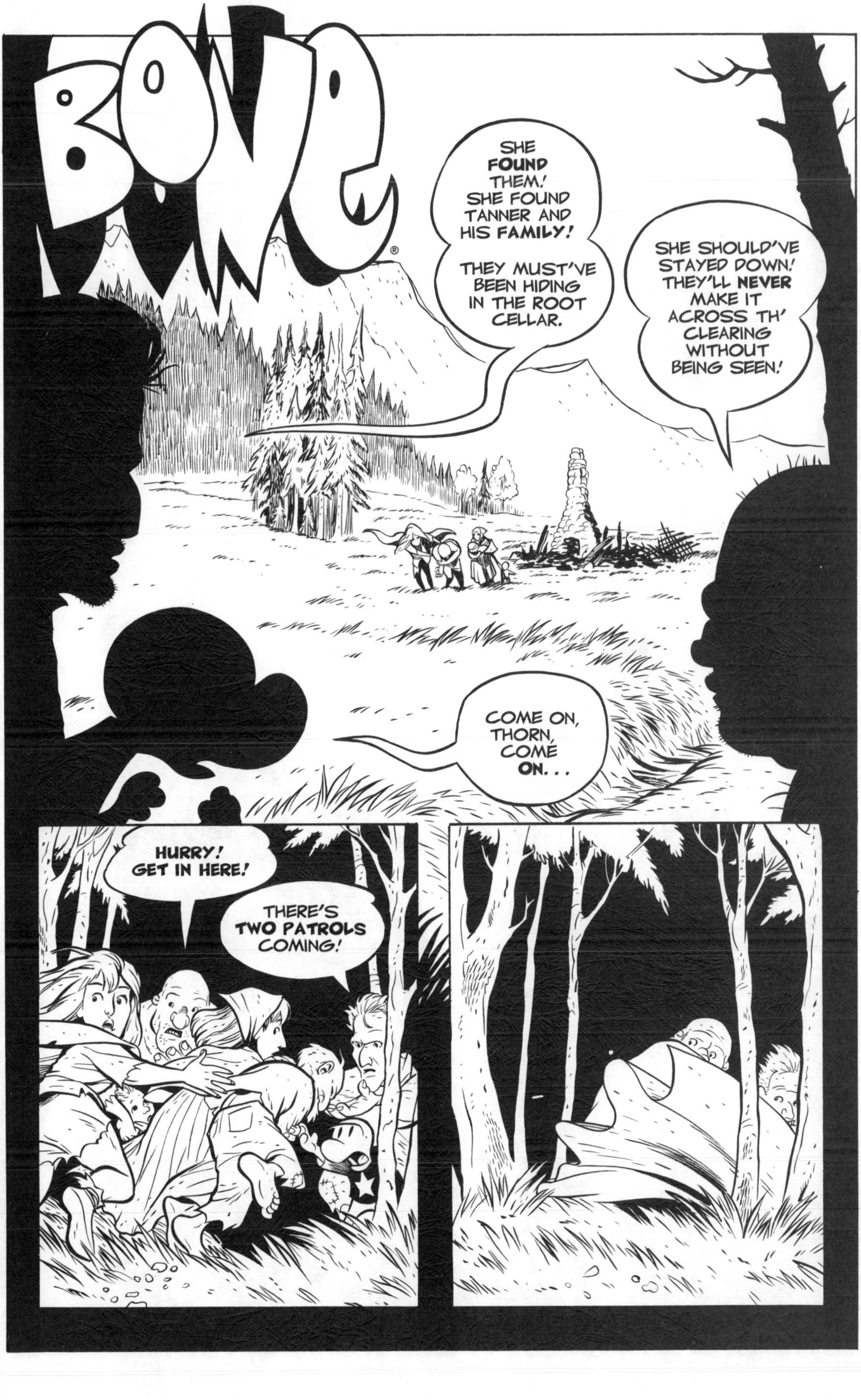
BONE®
SHE FOUND THEM! SHE FOUND TANNER AND HIS FAMILY!
THEY MUST'VE BEEN HIDING IN THE ROOT CELLAR.
SHE SHOULD'VE STAYED DOWN! THEY'LL NEVER MAKE IT ACROSS TH' CLEARING WITHOUT BEING SEEN!
COME ON, THORN, COME ON...
HURRY! GET IN HERE!
THERE'S TWO PATROLS COMING!

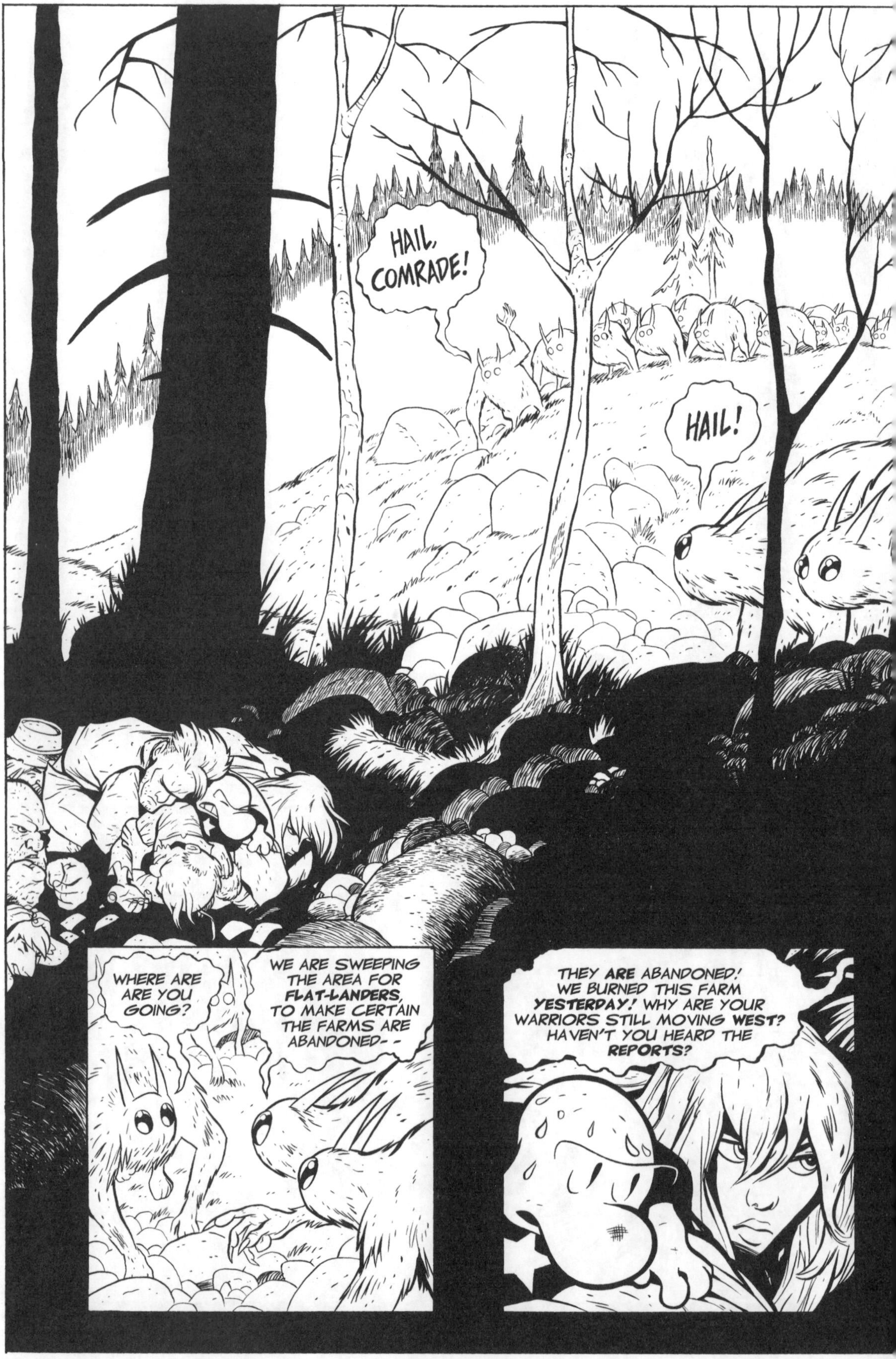
HAIL, COMRADE!
HAIL!
WHERE ARE ARE YOU GOING?
WE ARE SWEEPING THE AREA FOR FLAT-LANDERS, TO MAKE CERTAIN THE FARMS ARE ABANDONED- -
THEY ARE ABANDONED! WE BURNED THIS FARM YESTERDAY! WHY ARE YOUR WARRIORS STILL MOVING WEST? HAVEN'T YOU HEARD THE REPORTS?

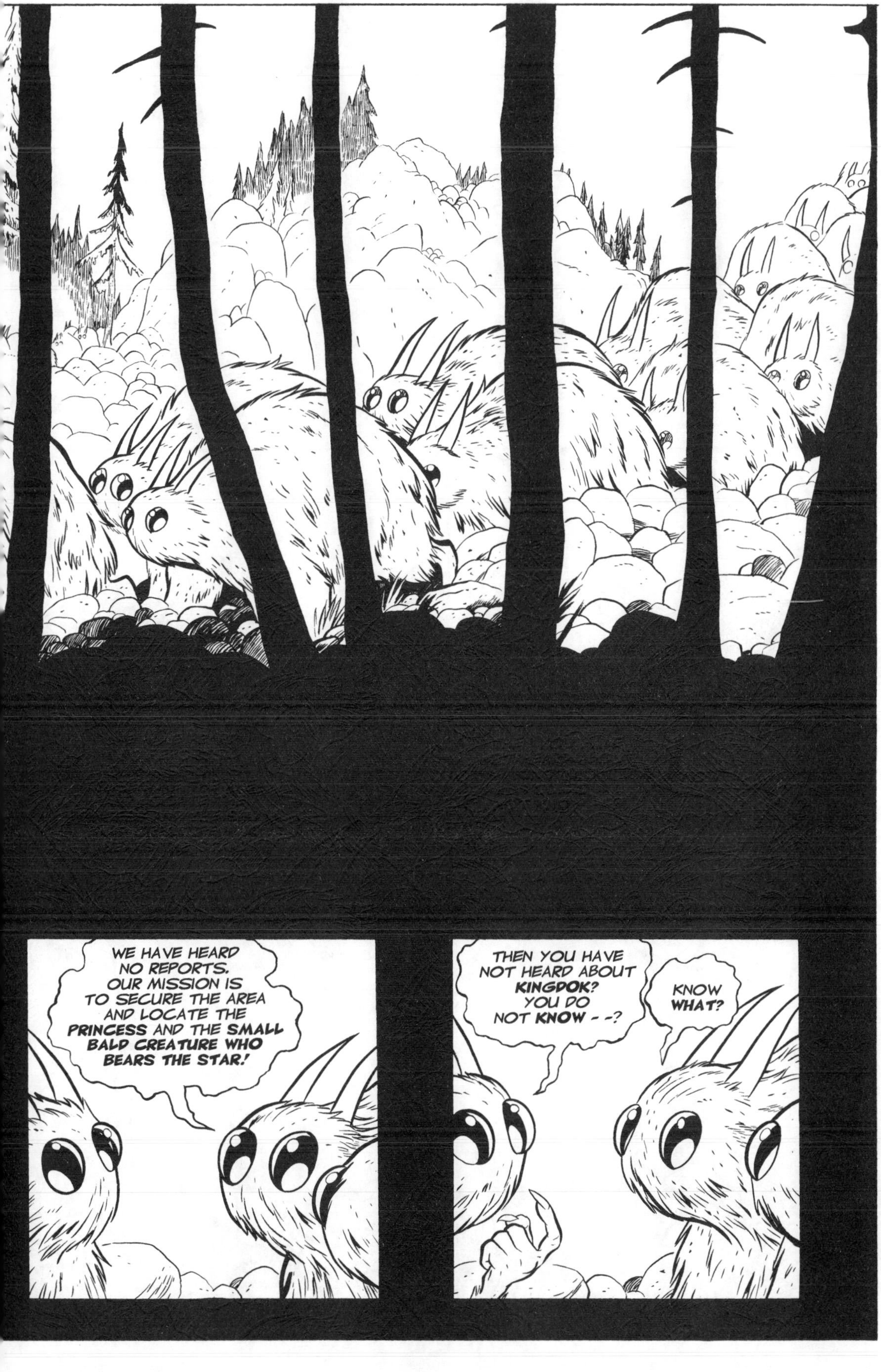
WE HAVE HEARD NO REPORTS. OUR MISSION IS TO SECURE THE AREA AND LOCATE THE **PRINCESS** AND THE **SMALL BALD CREATURE WHO BEARS THE STAR!**
THEN YOU HAVE NOT HEARD ABOUT **KINGDOK**? YOU DO NOT **KNOW** - -?
KNOW **WHAT?**

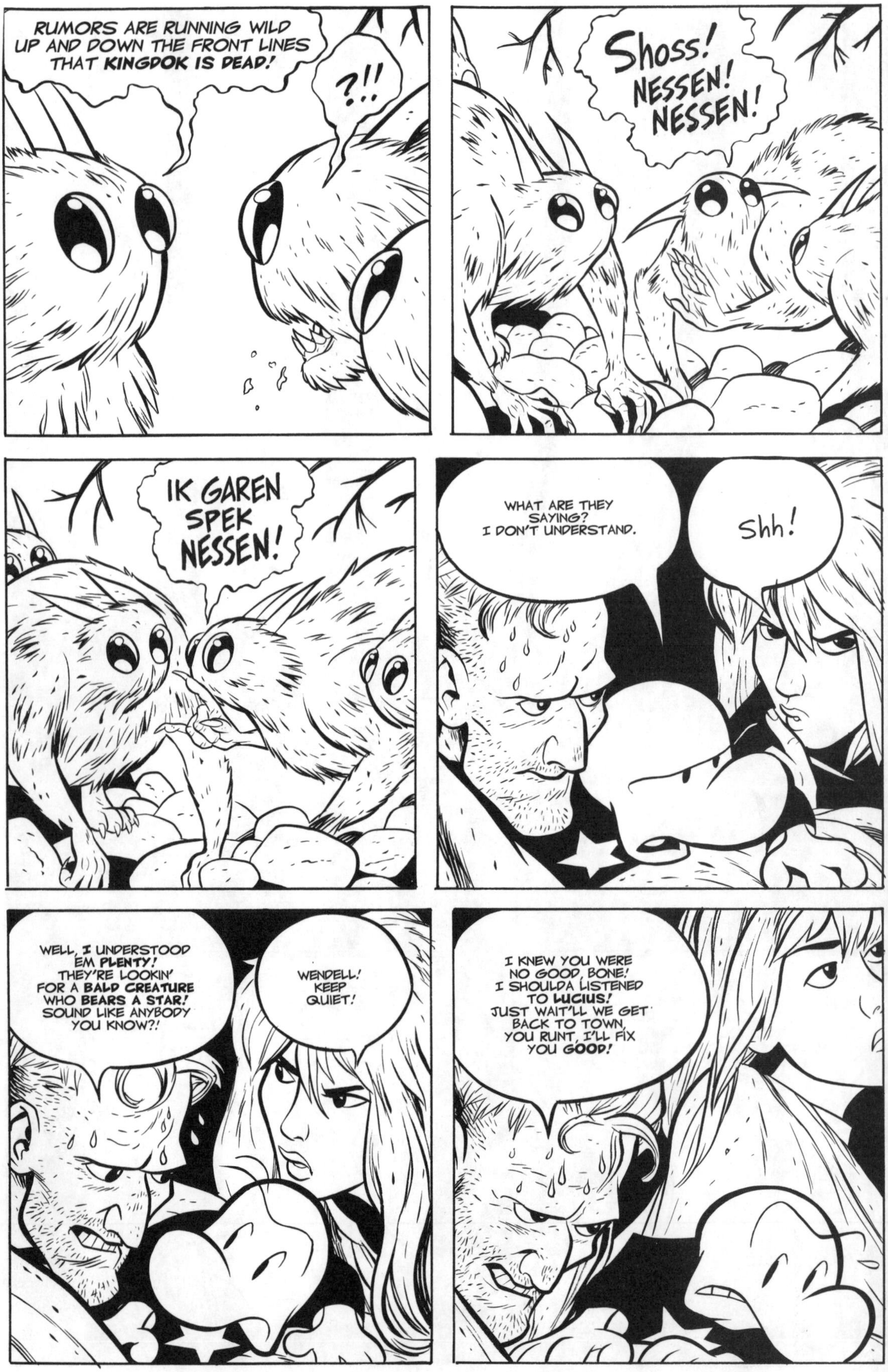

RUMORS ARE RUNNING WILD UP AND DOWN THE FRONT LINES THAT **KINGDOK IS DEAD!**
?!!
Shoss! NESSEN! NESSEN!
IK GAREN SPEK NESSEN!
WHAT ARE THEY SAYING? I DON'T UNDERSTAND.
Shh!
WELL, I UNDERSTOOD EM **PLENTY!** THEY'RE LOOKIN' FOR A **BALD CREATURE** WHO **BEARS A STAR!** SOUND LIKE ANYBODY YOU KNOW?!
WENDELL! KEEP QUIET!
I KNEW YOU WERE NO GOOD, BONE! I SHOULDA LISTENED TO **LUCIUS!** JUST WAIT'LL WE GET BACK TO TOWN, YOU RUNT, I'LL FIX YOU **GOOD!**

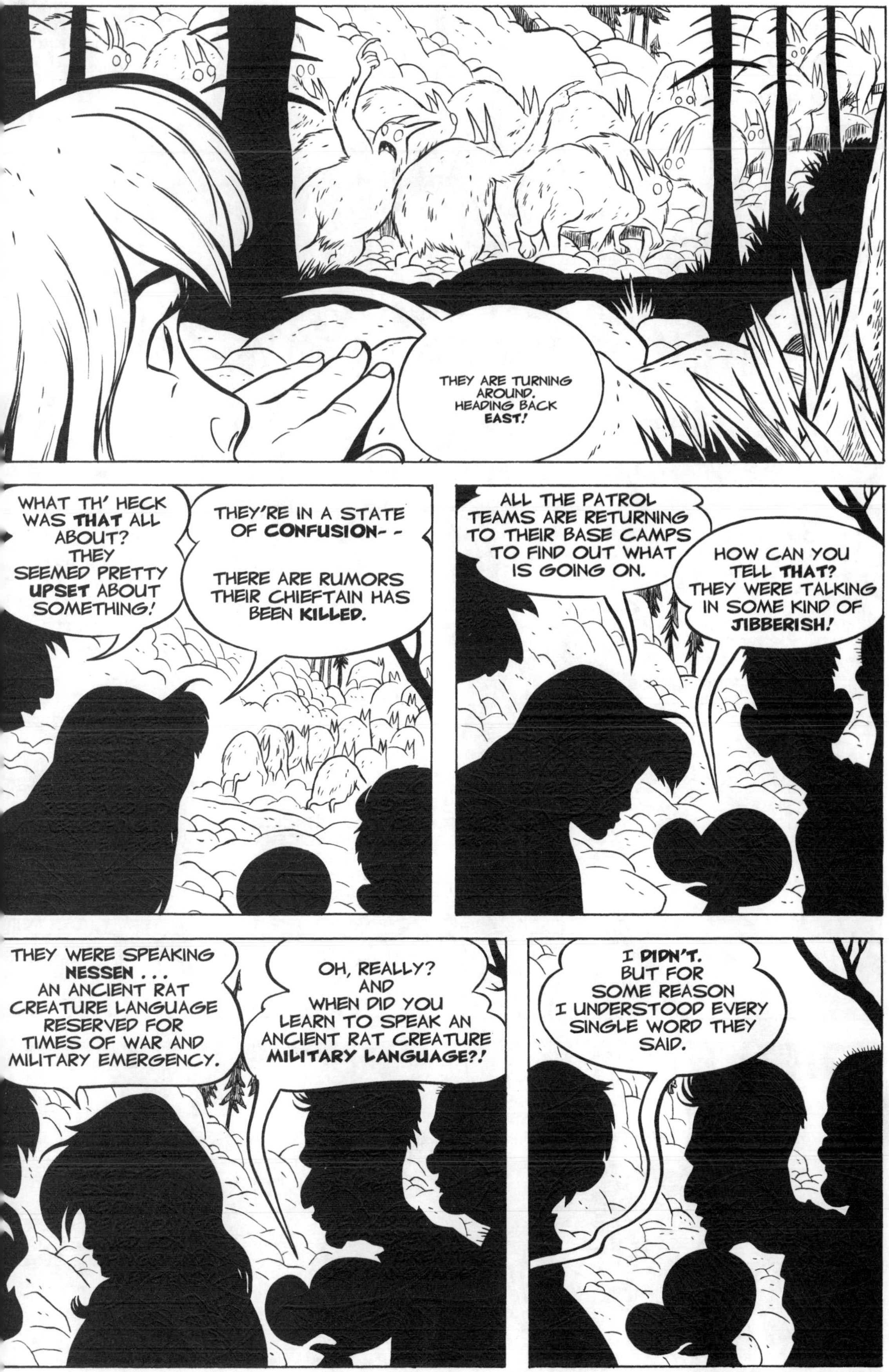

THEY ARE TURNING AROUND. HEADING BACK **EAST!**
WHAT TH' HECK WAS **THAT** ALL ABOUT? THEY SEEMED PRETTY **UPSET** ABOUT SOMETHING!
THEY'RE IN A STATE OF **CONFUSION**- -
THERE ARE RUMORS THEIR CHIEFTAIN HAS BEEN **KILLED.**
ALL THE PATROL TEAMS ARE RETURNING TO THEIR BASE CAMPS TO FIND OUT WHAT IS GOING ON.
HOW CAN YOU TELL **THAT?** THEY WERE TALKING IN SOME KIND OF **JIBBERISH!**
THEY WERE SPEAKING **NESSEN** . . . AN ANCIENT RAT CREATURE LANGUAGE RESERVED FOR TIMES OF WAR AND MILITARY EMERGENCY.
OH, REALLY? AND WHEN DID YOU LEARN TO SPEAK AN ANCIENT RAT CREATURE **MILITARY LANGUAGE?!**
I **DIDN'T.** BUT FOR SOME REASON I UNDERSTOOD EVERY SINGLE WORD THEY SAID.

MRS. TANNER, WE HAVE SOME FOOD AND WATER FOR YOUR FAMILY AT A SMALL CAMP NOT FAR FROM HERE...

...THAT'S WHERE THE REST OF THE VILLAGERS ARE. WE'RE GOING TO SEND YOU BACK THERE UNTIL WE CAN DETERMINE THAT THE TOWN IS SAFE.

WHY IS THIS **HAPPENING**, THORN? WHY ARE THE HAIRY MEN **DOING** THIS?

WE'RE TRYING TO FIND OUT.

I THINK WE KNOW **ENOUGH!** LET'S STRING THE LITTLE RUNT UP **RIGHT NOW!**

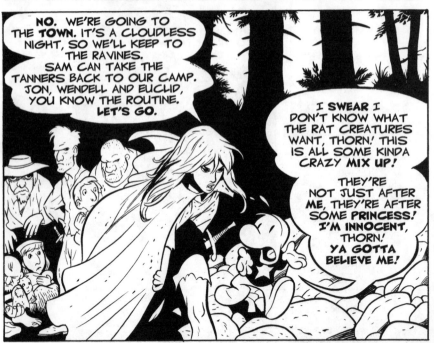

NO. WE'RE GOING TO THE **TOWN.** IT'S A CLOUDLESS NIGHT, SO WE'LL KEEP TO THE RAVINES. SAM CAN TAKE THE TANNERS BACK TO OUR CAMP. JON, WENDELL AND EUCLID, YOU KNOW THE ROUTINE. **LET'S GO.**

I SWEAR I DON'T KNOW WHAT THE RAT CREATURES WANT, THORN! THIS IS ALL SOME KINDA CRAZY **MIX UP!**

THEY'RE NOT JUST AFTER **ME,** THEY'RE AFTER SOME PRINCESS! I'M INNOCENT, THORN! YA GOTTA BELIEVE ME!

I **DO** BELIEVE YOU. THAT'S THE **ONLY** REASON I HAVEN'T LET WENDELL AND EUCLID STRING YOU UP.

YOU-- YOU MEAN IT? YOU BELIEVE ME?

YES, I DO. WOULD YOU BELIEVE **ME** IF I SAID THE PRINCESS WAS INNOCENT, TOO?

!

NOW LET'S GO SEE WHAT'S LEFT OF OUR TOWN.

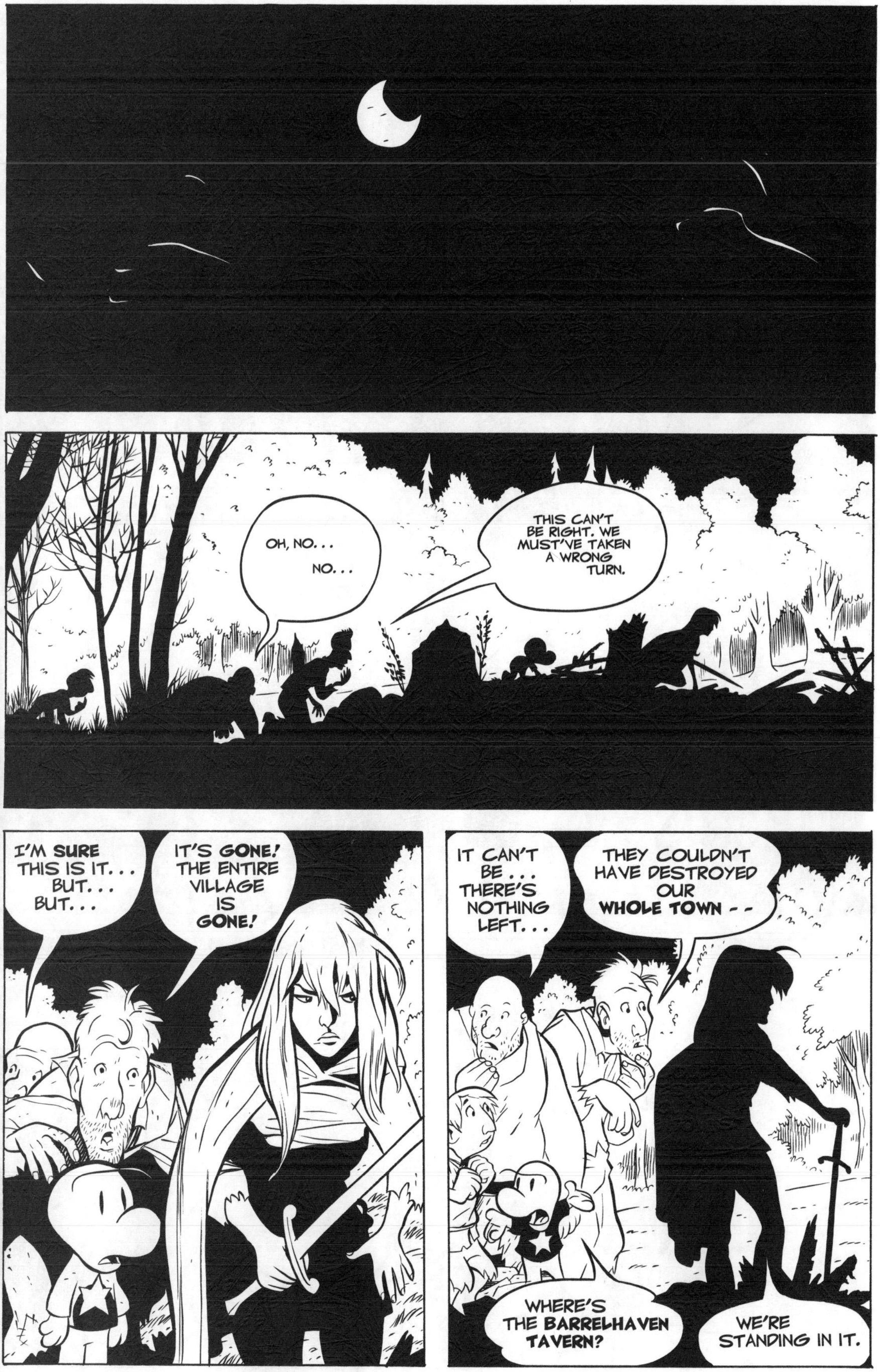

OH, NO...
NO...
THIS CAN'T BE RIGHT. WE MUST'VE TAKEN A WRONG TURN.
I'M SURE THIS IS IT... BUT... BUT...
IT'S GONE! THE ENTIRE VILLAGE IS GONE!
IT CAN'T BE... THERE'S NOTHING LEFT...
THEY COULDN'T HAVE DESTROYED OUR WHOLE TOWN --
WHERE'S THE BARRELHAVEN TAVERN?
WE'RE STANDING IN IT.

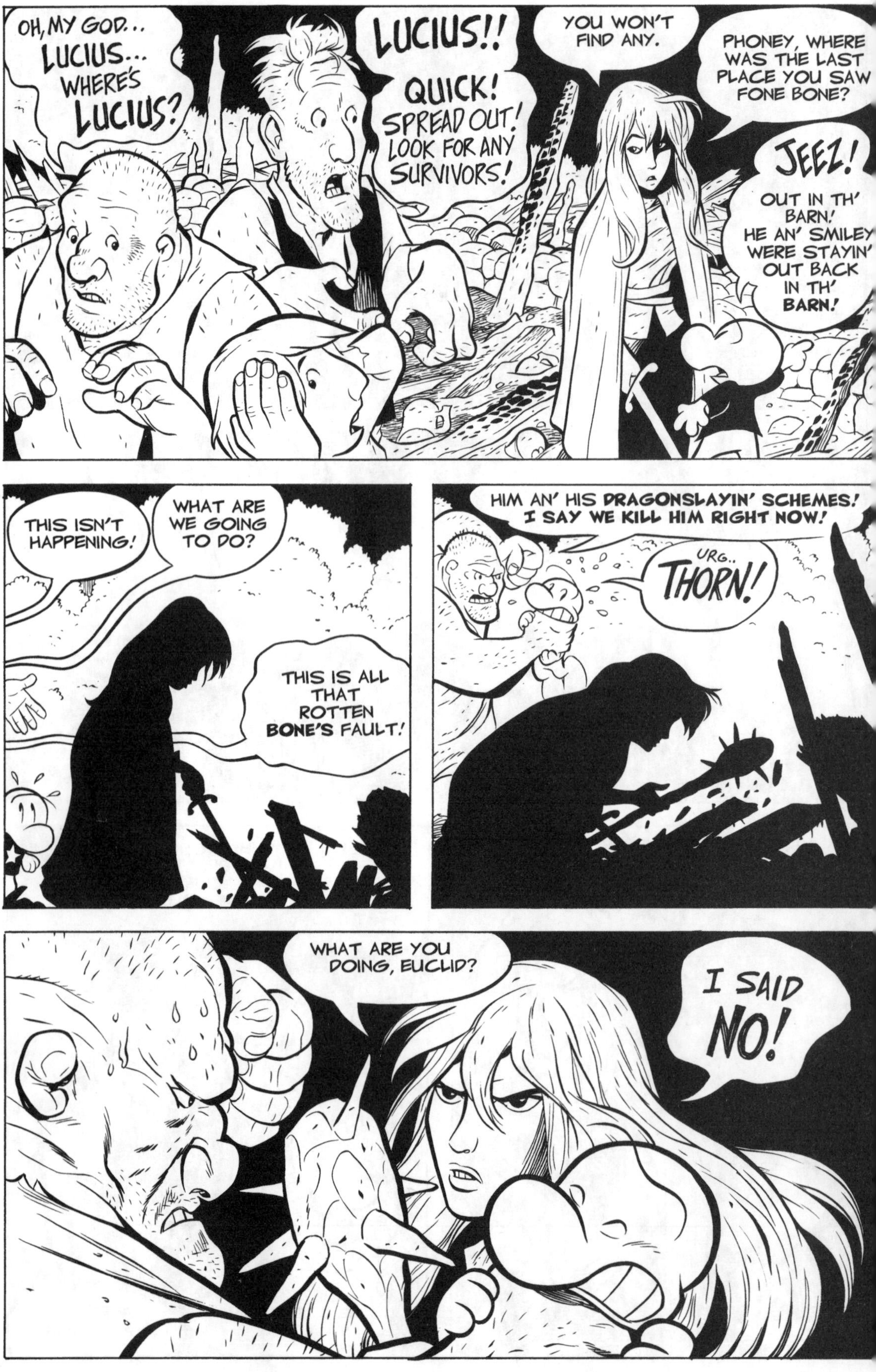
OH, MY GOD... LUCIUS... WHERE'S LUCIUS?
LUCIUS!!
QUICK! SPREAD OUT! LOOK FOR ANY SURVIVORS!
YOU WON'T FIND ANY.
PHONEY, WHERE WAS THE LAST PLACE YOU SAW FONE BONE?
JEEZ!
OUT IN TH' BARN! HE AN' SMILEY WERE STAYIN' OUT BACK IN TH' BARN!
THIS ISN'T HAPPENING!
WHAT ARE WE GOING TO DO?
THIS IS ALL THAT ROTTEN BONE'S FAULT!
HIM AN' HIS DRAGONSLAYIN' SCHEMES! I SAY WE KILL HIM RIGHT NOW!
URG.. THORN!
WHAT ARE YOU DOING, EUCLID?
I SAID NO!

STOP ACTING LIKE AN **ANIMAL.** HASN'T THERE BEEN ENOUGH VIOLENCE? NOW PUT PHONEY BONE **DOWN.**

NO!! HE SWINDLED US AND DESTROYED OUR TOWN!

HE DIDN'T ATTACK THE VILLAGE! THE **RAT CREATURES** DID!

HE TRICKED US INTO CHASIN' AFTER **DRAGONS!** WE WERE AWAY FROM OUR **HOMES** WHEN WE SHOULDA BEEN **HERE** DEFENDING THE **VILLAGE!**

NOBODY **FORCED** YOU TO FOLLOW HIM! YOU WERE A **MOB** LOOKING FOR SCAPEGOATS!

BUT IF WE HAD BEEN **HERE,** THEN LUCIUS MIGHT STILL BE **ALIVE!**

WE DON'T KNOW WHAT HAPPENED TO LUCIUS... BUT WHATEVER IT WAS, IF YOU **HAD** BEEN HERE, YOU WOULD HAVE **SHARED** HIS FATE!

AND SO WOULD ALL THE OTHER VILLAGERS WHO WERE **WITH** YOU HUNTING DRAGONS! THIS BONE PROBABLY SAVED **HALF THE VILLAGE** BY TAKING YOU UP INTO THE MOUNTAINS!

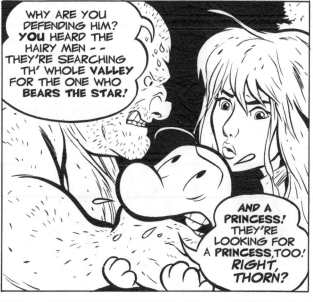

WHY ARE YOU DEFENDING HIM? **YOU** HEARD THE HAIRY MEN -- THEY'RE SEARCHING TH' WHOLE **VALLEY** FOR THE ONE WHO **BEARS THE STAR!**

AND A **PRINCESS!** THEY'RE LOOKING FOR A PRINCESS, TOO! **RIGHT, THORN?**

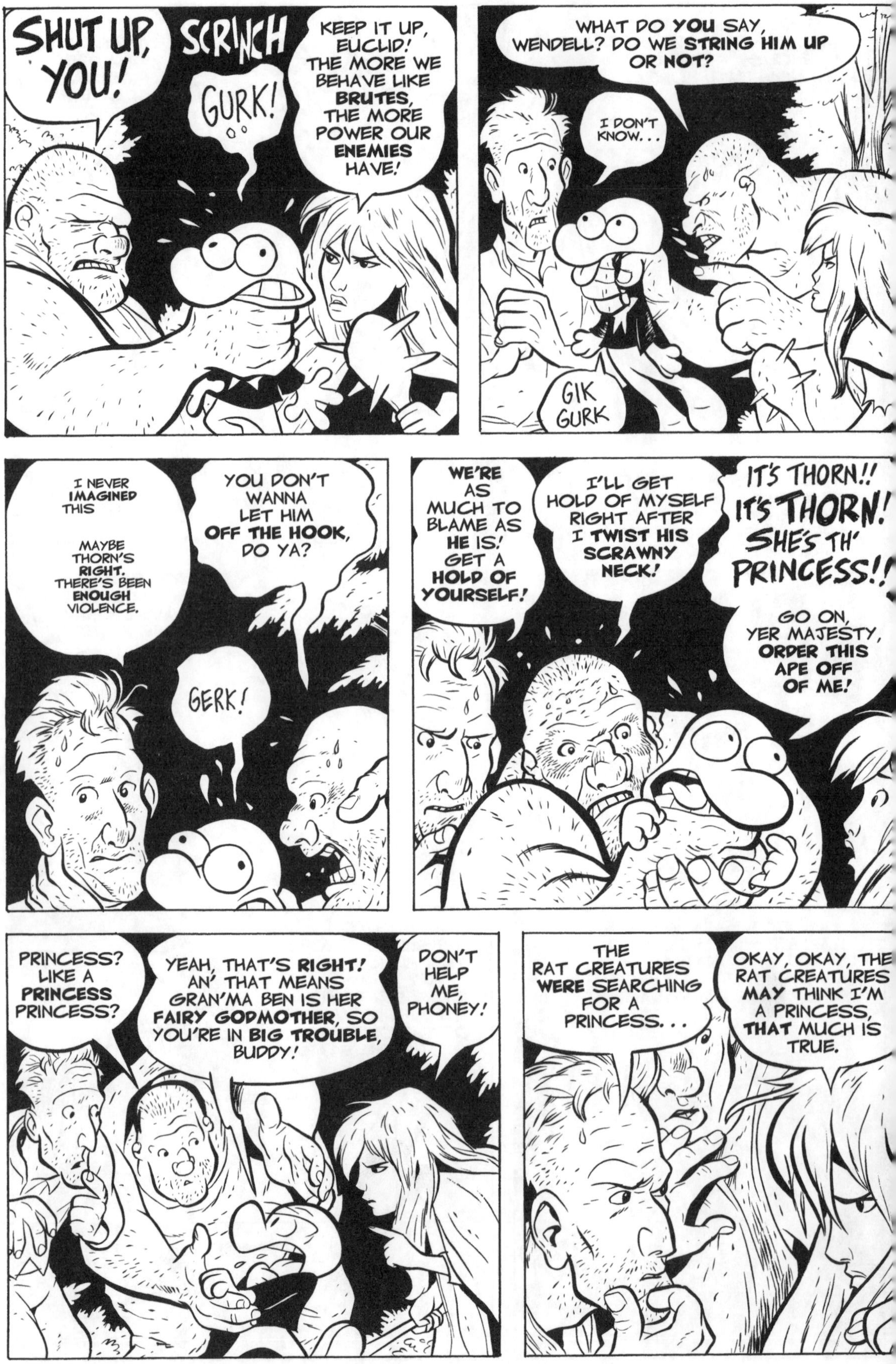

SHUT UP, YOU!
SCRINCH
GURK!
KEEP IT UP, EUCLID! THE MORE WE BEHAVE LIKE BRUTES, THE MORE POWER OUR ENEMIES HAVE!
WHAT DO YOU SAY, WENDELL? DO WE STRING HIM UP OR NOT?
I DON'T KNOW...
GIK GURK
I NEVER IMAGINED THIS
MAYBE THORN'S RIGHT. THERE'S BEEN ENOUGH VIOLENCE.
YOU DON'T WANNA LET HIM OFF THE HOOK, DO YA?
GERK!
WE'RE AS MUCH TO BLAME AS HE IS! GET A HOLD OF YOURSELF!
I'LL GET HOLD OF MYSELF RIGHT AFTER I TWIST HIS SCRAWNY NECK!
IT'S THORN!! IT'S THORN! SHE'S TH' PRINCESS!!
GO ON, YER MAJESTY, ORDER THIS APE OFF OF ME!
PRINCESS? LIKE A PRINCESS PRINCESS?
YEAH, THAT'S RIGHT! AN' THAT MEANS GRAN'MA BEN IS HER FAIRY GODMOTHER, SO YOU'RE IN BIG TROUBLE, BUDDY!
DON'T HELP ME, PHONEY!
THE RAT CREATURES WERE SEARCHING FOR A PRINCESS...
OKAY, OKAY, THE RAT CREATURES MAY THINK I'M A PRINCESS, THAT MUCH IS TRUE.

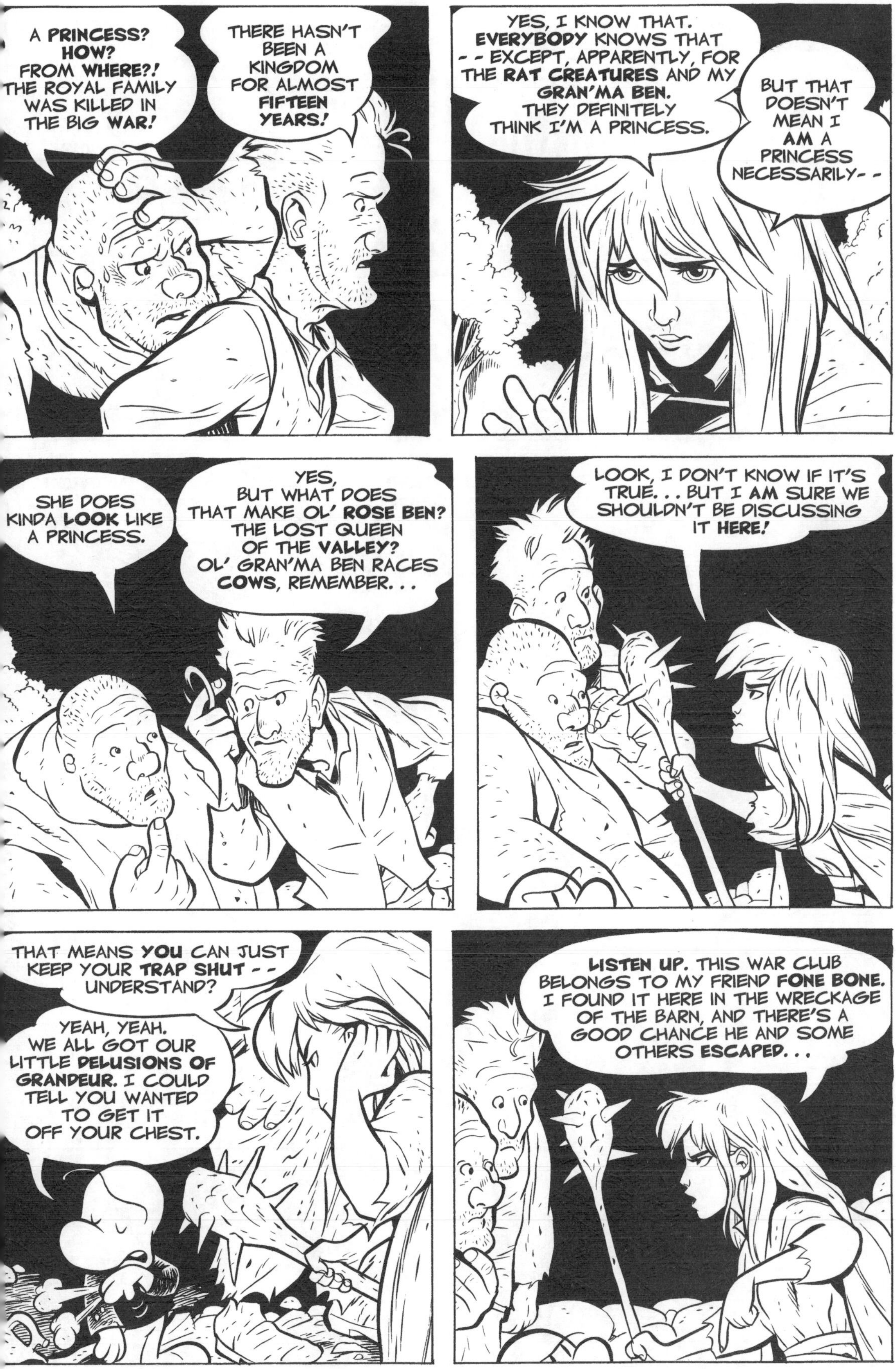
A PRINCESS? HOW? FROM WHERE?! THE ROYAL FAMILY WAS KILLED IN THE BIG WAR!
THERE HASN'T BEEN A KINGDOM FOR ALMOST FIFTEEN YEARS!
YES, I KNOW THAT. EVERYBODY KNOWS THAT - - EXCEPT, APPARENTLY, FOR THE RAT CREATURES AND MY GRAN'MA BEN. THEY DEFINITELY THINK I'M A PRINCESS.
BUT THAT DOESN'T MEAN I AM A PRINCESS NECESSARILY- -
SHE DOES KINDA LOOK LIKE A PRINCESS.
YES, BUT WHAT DOES THAT MAKE OL' ROSE BEN? THE LOST QUEEN OF THE VALLEY? OL' GRAN'MA BEN RACES COWS, REMEMBER...
LOOK, I DON'T KNOW IF IT'S TRUE... BUT I AM SURE WE SHOULDN'T BE DISCUSSING IT HERE!
THAT MEANS YOU CAN JUST KEEP YOUR TRAP SHUT - - UNDERSTAND?
YEAH, YEAH. WE ALL GOT OUR LITTLE DELUSIONS OF GRANDEUR. I COULD TELL YOU WANTED TO GET IT OFF YOUR CHEST.
LISTEN UP. THIS WAR CLUB BELONGS TO MY FRIEND FONE BONE. I FOUND IT HERE IN THE WRECKAGE OF THE BARN, AND THERE'S A GOOD CHANCE HE AND SOME OTHERS ESCAPED...

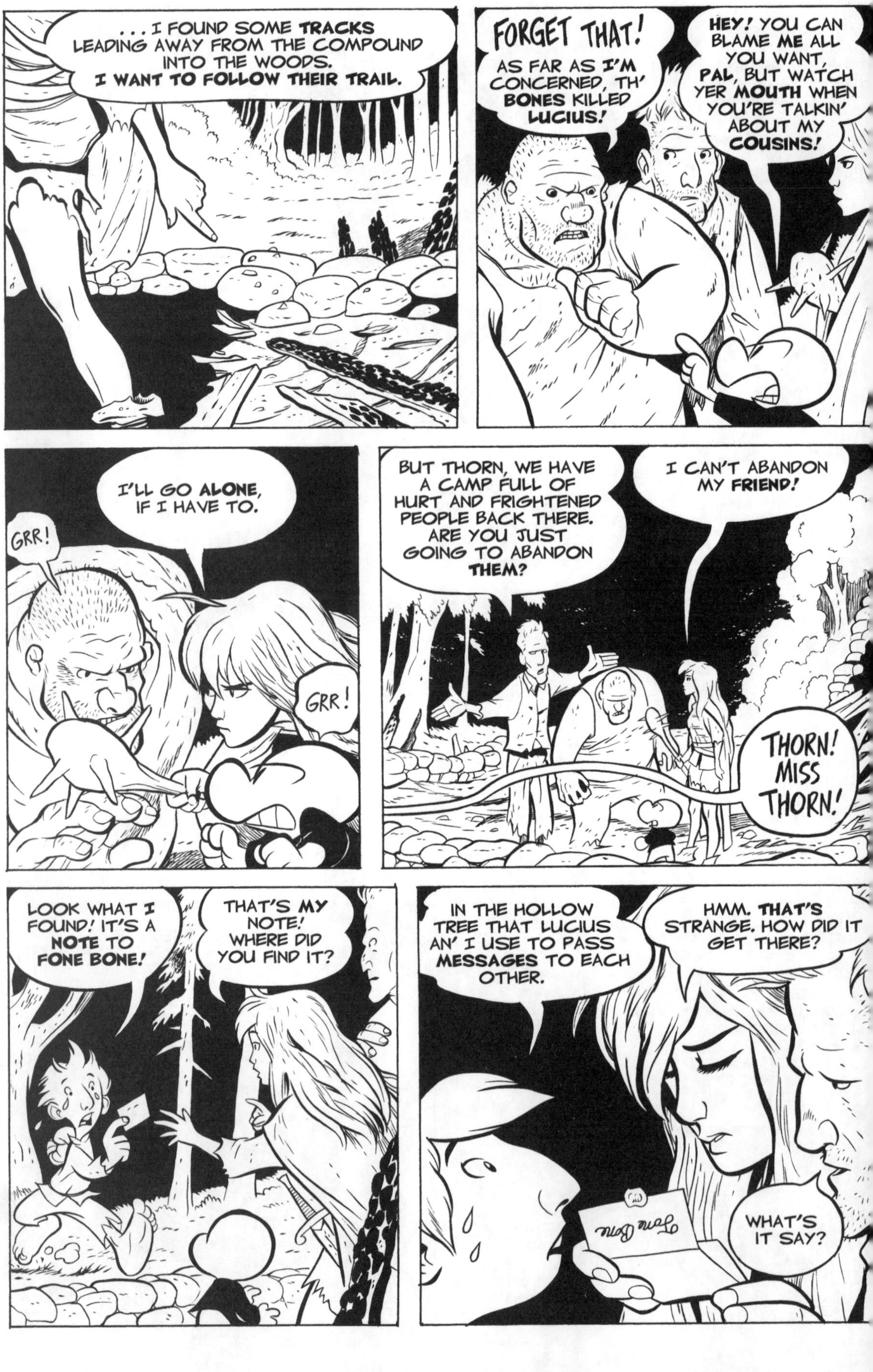

. . . I FOUND SOME TRACKS LEADING AWAY FROM THE COMPOUND INTO THE WOODS. I WANT TO FOLLOW THEIR TRAIL.
FORGET THAT!
AS FAR AS I'M CONCERNED, TH' BONES KILLED LUCIUS!
HEY! YOU CAN BLAME ME ALL YOU WANT, PAL, BUT WATCH YER MOUTH WHEN YOU'RE TALKIN' ABOUT MY COUSINS!
I'LL GO ALONE, IF I HAVE TO.
GRR!
GRR!
BUT THORN, WE HAVE A CAMP FULL OF HURT AND FRIGHTENED PEOPLE BACK THERE. ARE YOU JUST GOING TO ABANDON THEM?
I CAN'T ABANDON MY FRIEND!
THORN! MISS THORN!
LOOK WHAT I FOUND! IT'S A NOTE TO FONE BONE!
THAT'S MY NOTE! WHERE DID YOU FIND IT?
IN THE HOLLOW TREE THAT LUCIUS AN' I USE TO PASS MESSAGES TO EACH OTHER.
HMM. THAT'S STRANGE. HOW DID IT GET THERE?
WHAT'S IT SAY?

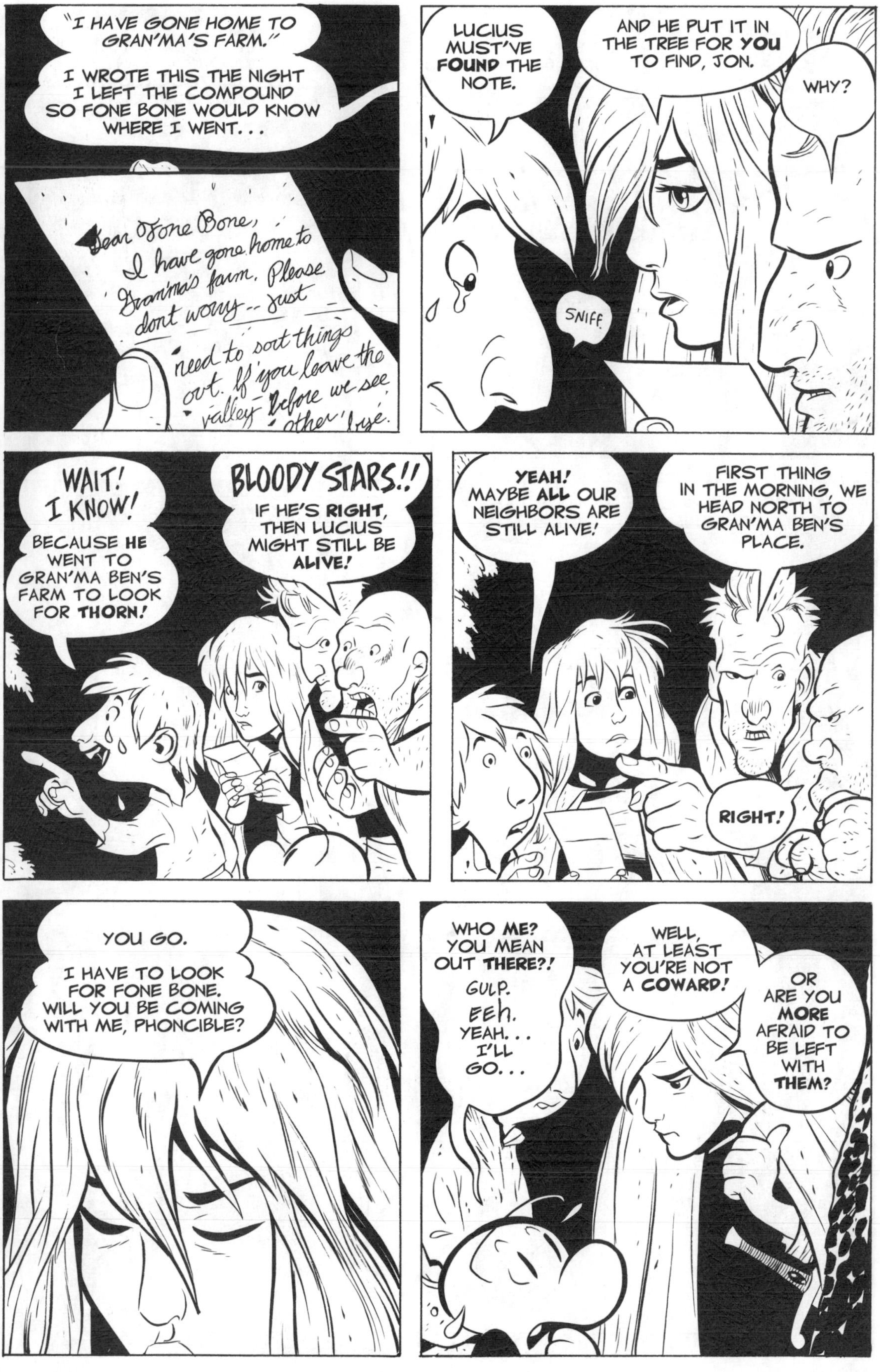
"I HAVE GONE HOME TO GRAN'MA'S FARM."
I WROTE THIS THE NIGHT I LEFT THE COMPOUND SO FONE BONE WOULD KNOW WHERE I WENT...
Dear Fone Bone,
I have gone home to Gran'ma's farm. Please dont worry -- just
need to sort things out. If you leave the valley before we see
other bye.
LUCIUS MUST'VE FOUND THE NOTE.
AND HE PUT IT IN THE TREE FOR YOU TO FIND, JON.
WHY?
SNIFF.
WAIT! I KNOW!
BECAUSE HE WENT TO GRAN'MA BEN'S FARM TO LOOK FOR THORN!
BLOODY STARS!!
IF HE'S RIGHT, THEN LUCIUS MIGHT STILL BE ALIVE!
YEAH! MAYBE ALL OUR NEIGHBORS ARE STILL ALIVE!
FIRST THING IN THE MORNING, WE HEAD NORTH TO GRAN'MA BEN'S PLACE.
RIGHT!
YOU GO.
I HAVE TO LOOK FOR FONE BONE. WILL YOU BE COMING WITH ME, PHONCIBLE?
WHO ME? YOU MEAN OUT THERE?!
GULP.
EEH.
YEAH... I'LL GO...
WELL, AT LEAST YOU'RE NOT A COWARD!
OR ARE YOU MORE AFRAID TO BE LEFT WITH THEM?

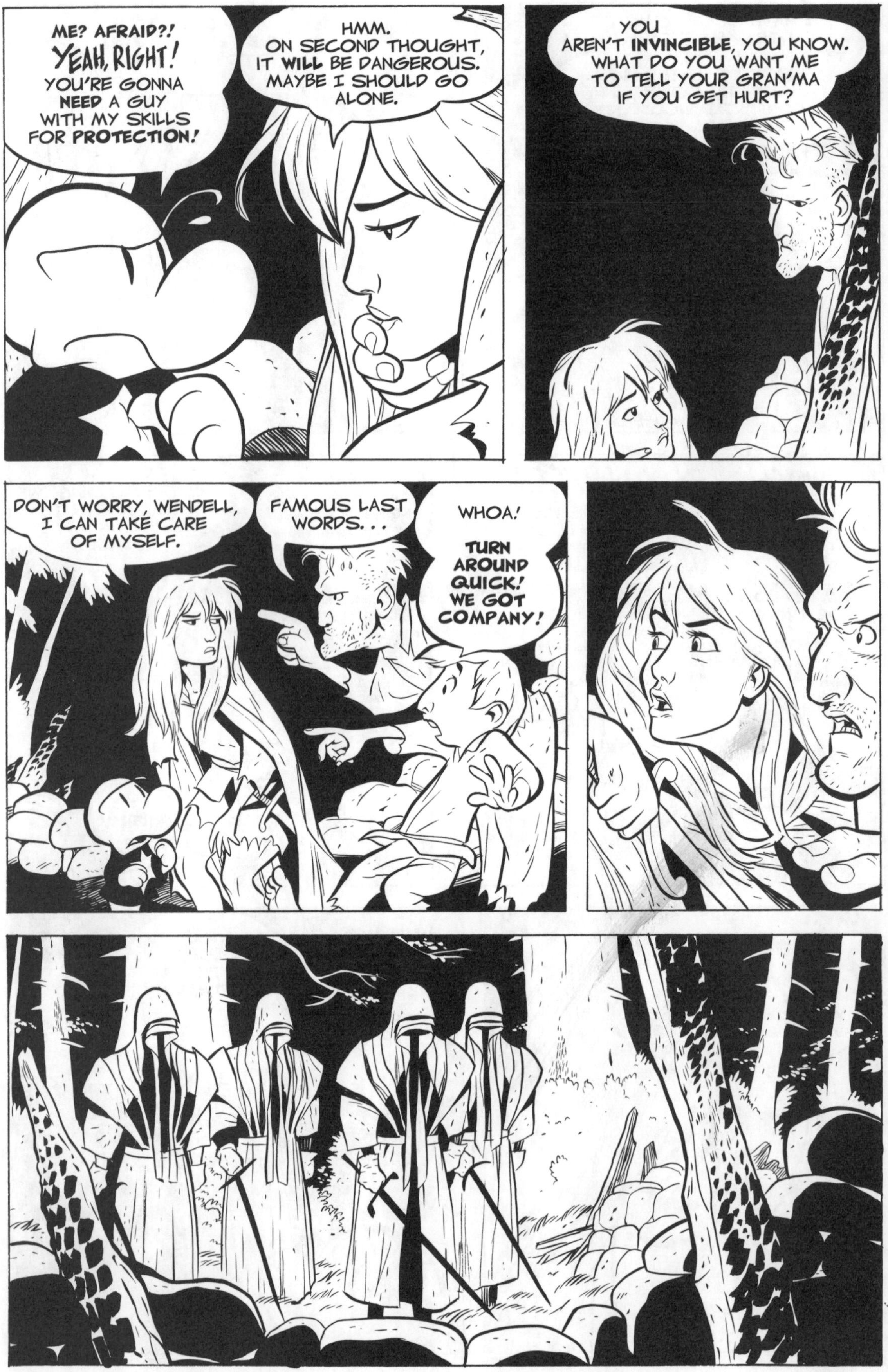
ME? AFRAID?! YEAH, RIGHT! YOU'RE GONNA NEED A GUY WITH MY SKILLS FOR PROTECTION!
HMM. ON SECOND THOUGHT, IT WILL BE DANGEROUS. MAYBE I SHOULD GO ALONE.
YOU AREN'T INVINCIBLE, YOU KNOW. WHAT DO YOU WANT ME TO TELL YOUR GRAN'MA IF YOU GET HURT?
DON'T WORRY, WENDELL, I CAN TAKE CARE OF MYSELF.
FAMOUS LAST WORDS...
WHOA!
TURN AROUND QUICK! WE GOT COMPANY!

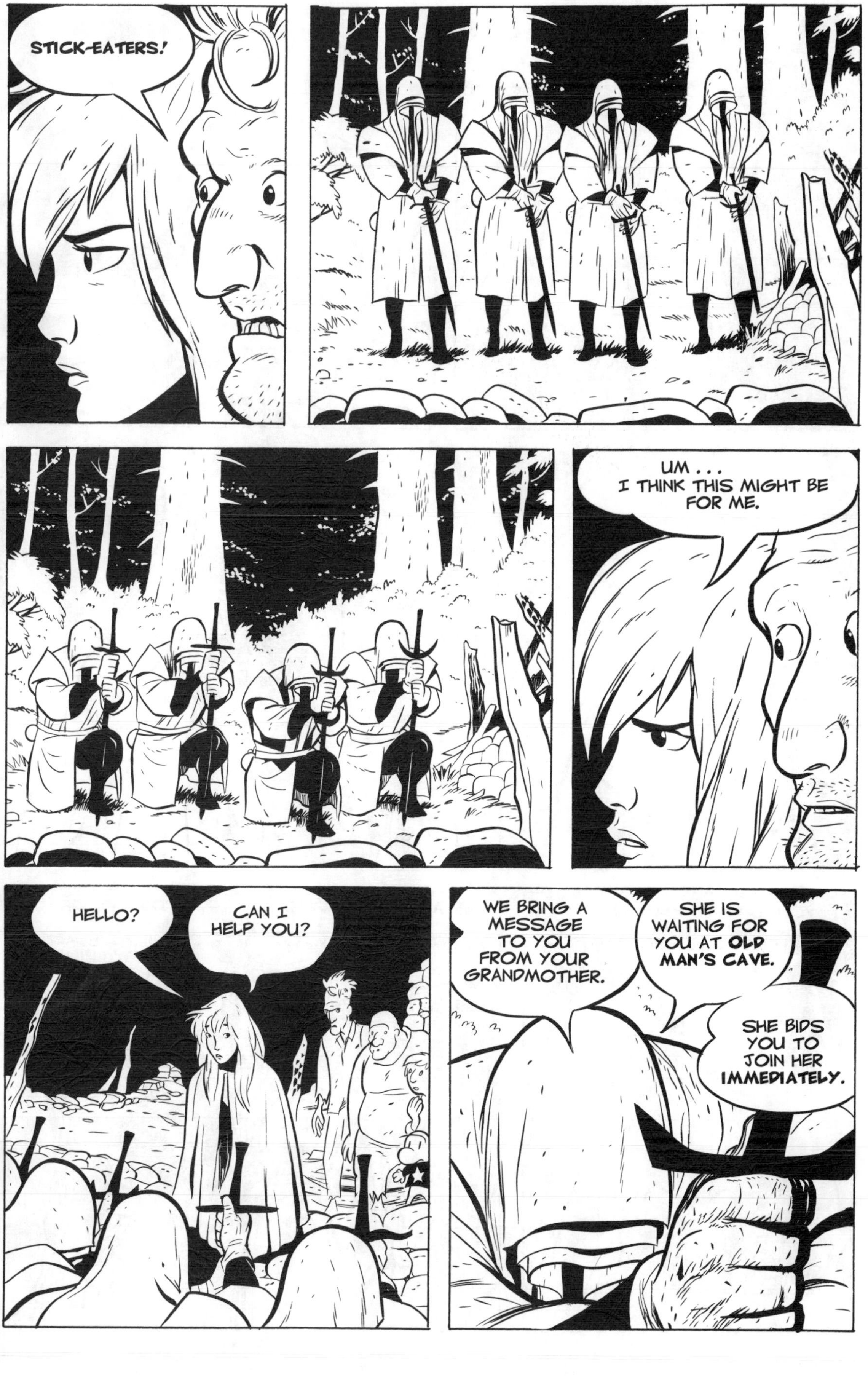
STICK-EATERS!
UM . . . I THINK THIS MIGHT BE FOR ME.
HELLO?
CAN I HELP YOU?
WE BRING A MESSAGE TO YOU FROM YOUR GRANDMOTHER.
SHE IS WAITING FOR YOU AT **OLD MAN'S CAVE**.
SHE BIDS YOU TO JOIN HER **IMMEDIATELY**.

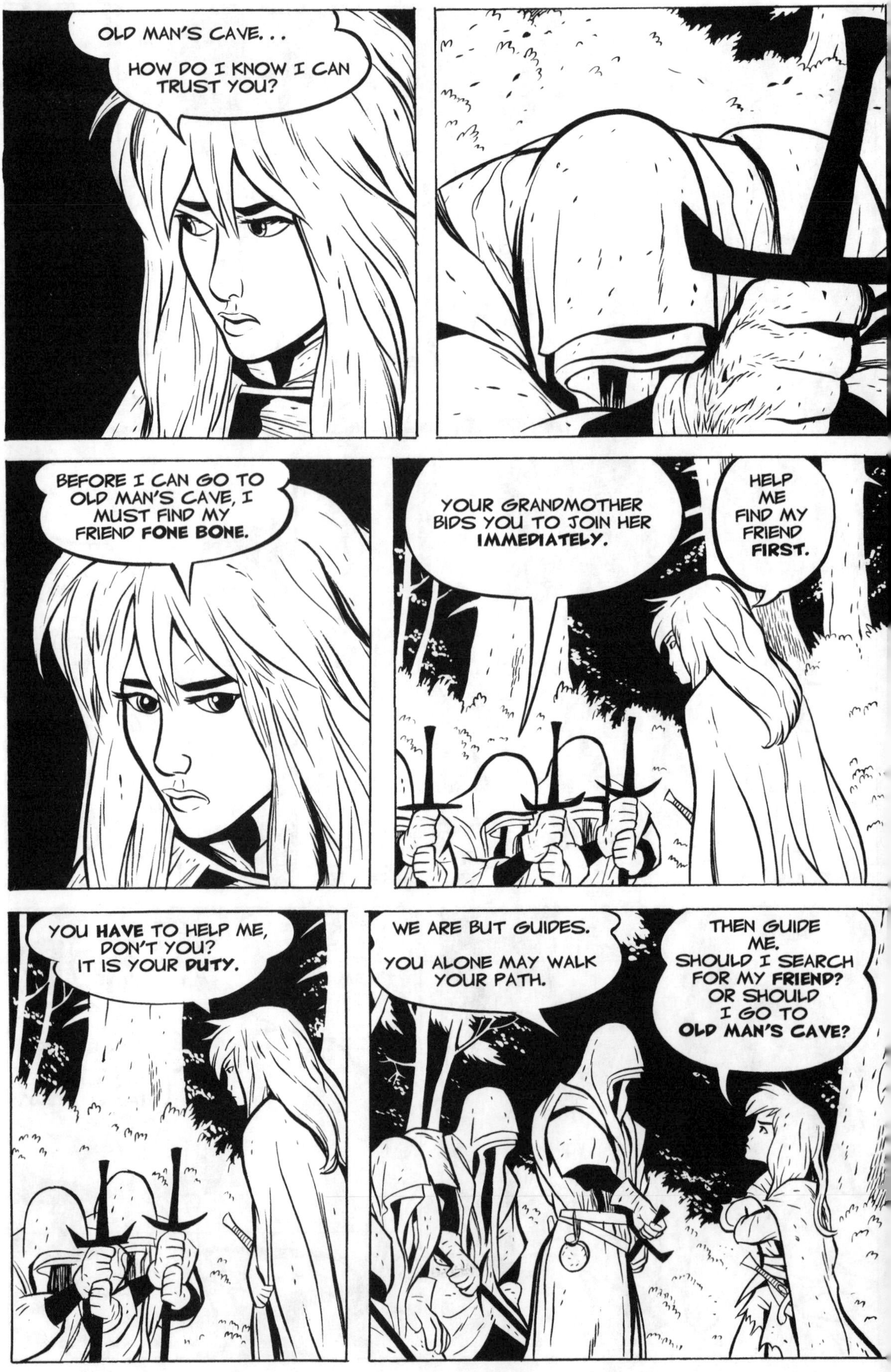
OLD MAN'S CAVE. . .
HOW DO I KNOW I CAN TRUST YOU?
BEFORE I CAN GO TO OLD MAN'S CAVE, I MUST FIND MY FRIEND **FONE BONE.**
YOUR GRANDMOTHER BIDS YOU TO JOIN HER **IMMEDIATELY.**
HELP ME FIND MY FRIEND **FIRST.**
YOU **HAVE** TO HELP ME, DON'T YOU? IT IS YOUR **DUTY.**
WE ARE BUT GUIDES.
YOU ALONE MAY WALK YOUR PATH.
THEN GUIDE ME. SHOULD I SEARCH FOR MY **FRIEND?** OR SHOULD I GO TO **OLD MAN'S CAVE?**

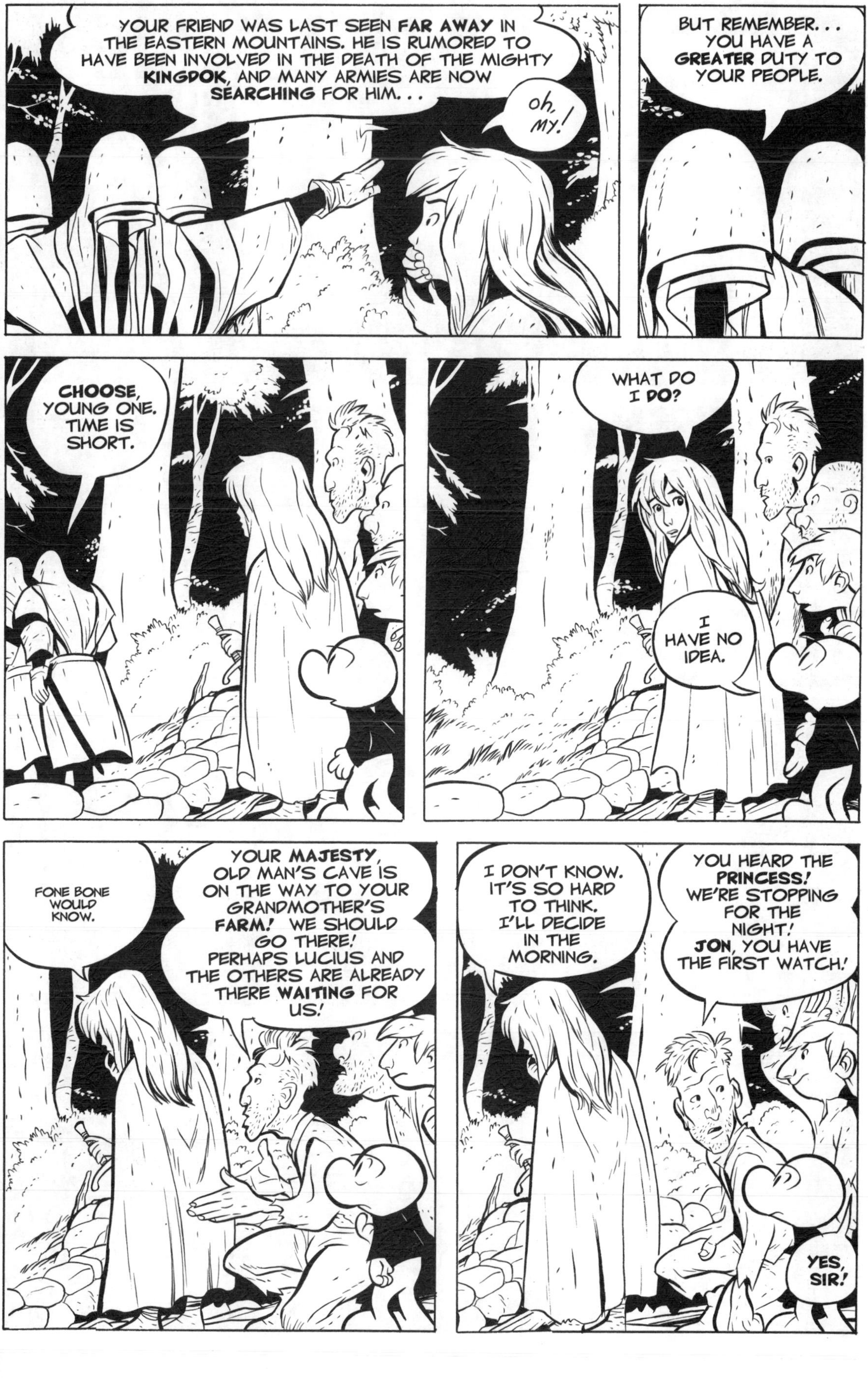
YOUR FRIEND WAS LAST SEEN FAR AWAY IN THE EASTERN MOUNTAINS. HE IS RUMORED TO HAVE BEEN INVOLVED IN THE DEATH OF THE MIGHTY KINGDOK, AND MANY ARMIES ARE NOW SEARCHING FOR HIM...
oh, MY!
BUT REMEMBER... YOU HAVE A GREATER DUTY TO YOUR PEOPLE.
CHOOSE, YOUNG ONE. TIME IS SHORT.
WHAT DO I DO?
I HAVE NO IDEA.
FONE BONE WOULD KNOW.
YOUR MAJESTY, OLD MAN'S CAVE IS ON THE WAY TO YOUR GRANDMOTHER'S FARM! WE SHOULD GO THERE! PERHAPS LUCIUS AND THE OTHERS ARE ALREADY THERE WAITING FOR US!
I DON'T KNOW. IT'S SO HARD TO THINK. I'LL DECIDE IN THE MORNING.
YOU HEARD THE PRINCESS! WE'RE STOPPING FOR THE NIGHT! JON, YOU HAVE THE FIRST WATCH!
YES, SIR!

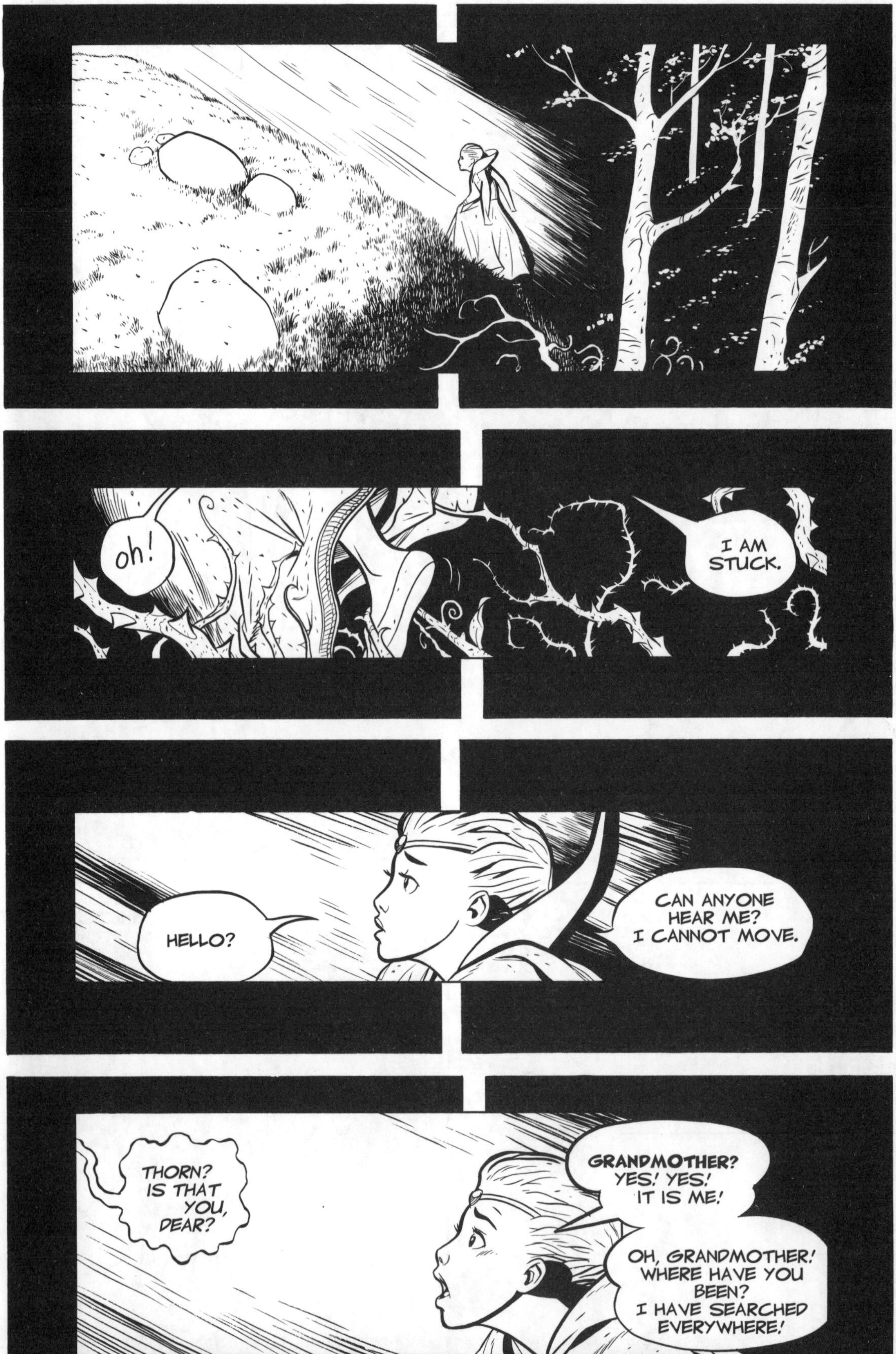
oh!
I AM STUCK.
HELLO?
CAN ANYONE HEAR ME? I CANNOT MOVE.
THORN? IS THAT YOU, DEAR?
GRANDMOTHER? YES! YES! IT IS ME!
OH, GRANDMOTHER! WHERE HAVE YOU BEEN? I HAVE SEARCHED EVERYWHERE!

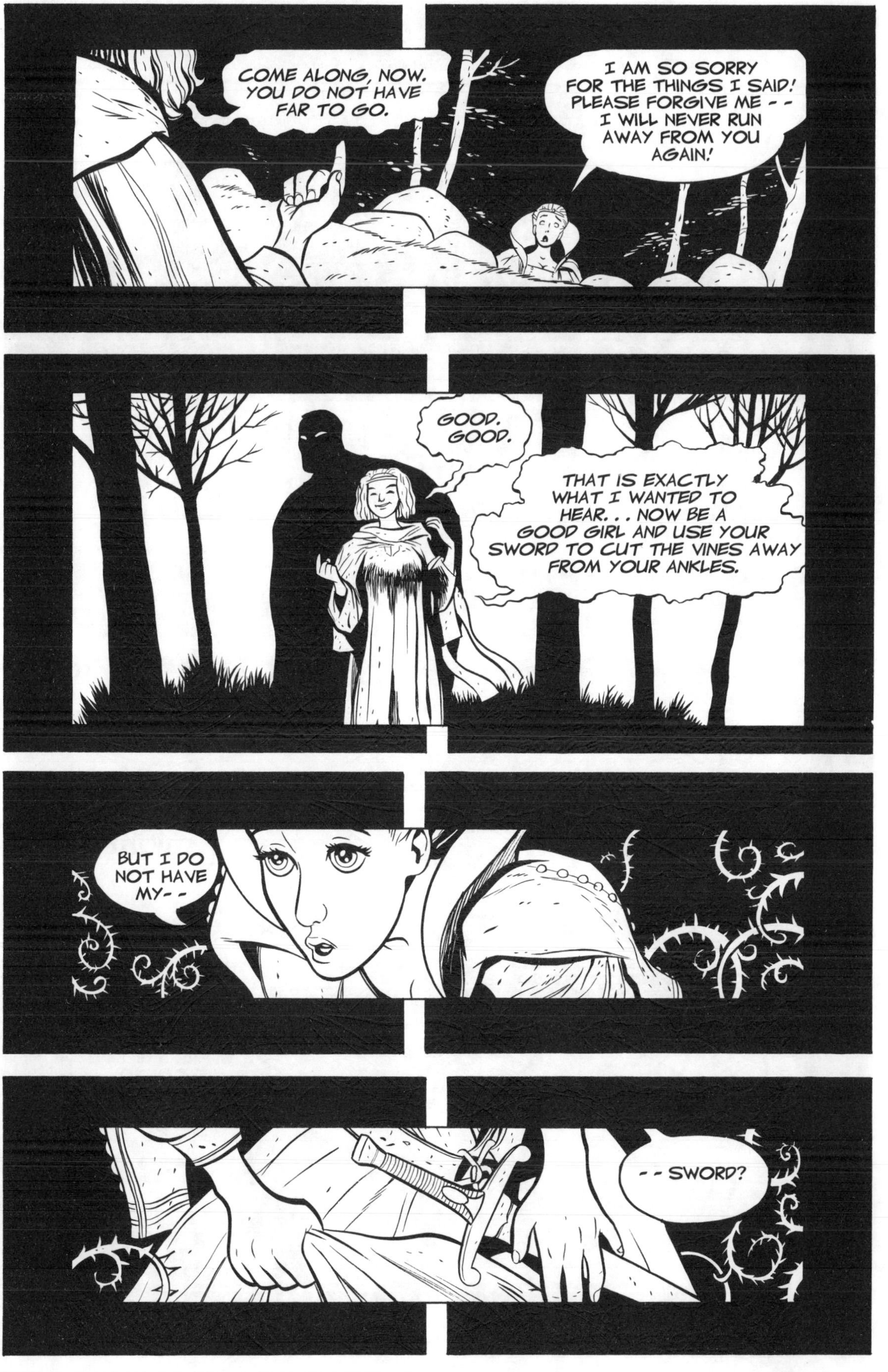
COME ALONG, NOW. YOU DO NOT HAVE FAR TO GO.
I AM SO SORRY FOR THE THINGS I SAID! PLEASE FORGIVE ME - - I WILL NEVER RUN AWAY FROM YOU AGAIN!
GOOD. GOOD.
THAT IS EXACTLY WHAT I WANTED TO HEAR. . . NOW BE A GOOD GIRL AND USE YOUR SWORD TO CUT THE VINES AWAY FROM YOUR ANKLES.
BUT I DO NOT HAVE MY- -
- - SWORD?

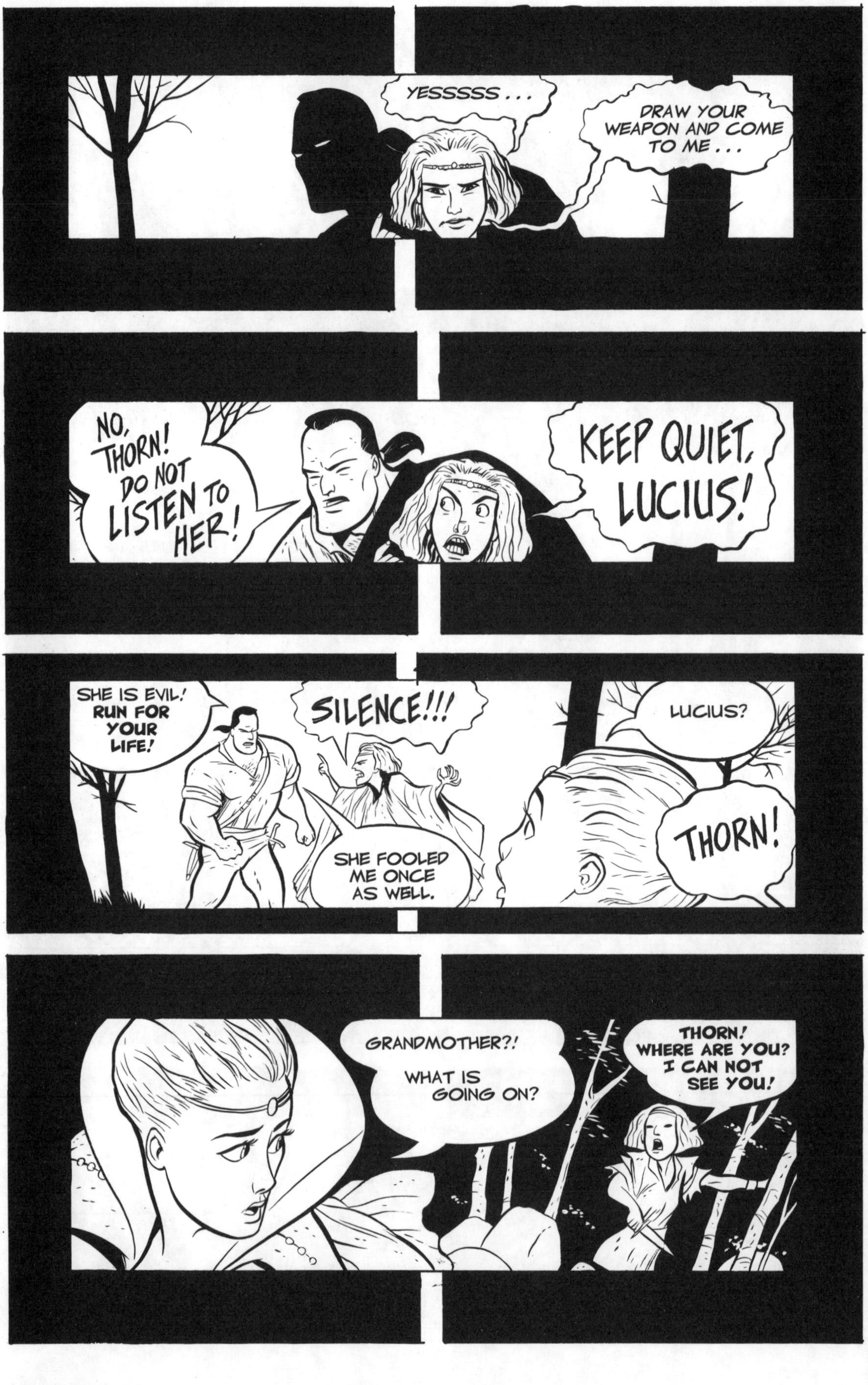
YESSSSS . . .
DRAW YOUR WEAPON AND COME TO ME . . .
NO, THORN! DO NOT LISTEN TO HER!
KEEP QUIET, LUCIUS!
SHE IS EVIL! RUN FOR YOUR LIFE!
SILENCE!!!
SHE FOOLED ME ONCE AS WELL.
LUCIUS?
THORN!
GRANDMOTHER?!
WHAT IS GOING ON?
THORN! WHERE ARE YOU? I CAN NOT SEE YOU!

GIVE ME THE SWORD!
HOLD TIGHT! DO NOT LET GO!!
AAAAAAAAHHH
UUH--
AAUH.
HUH.
HUH.

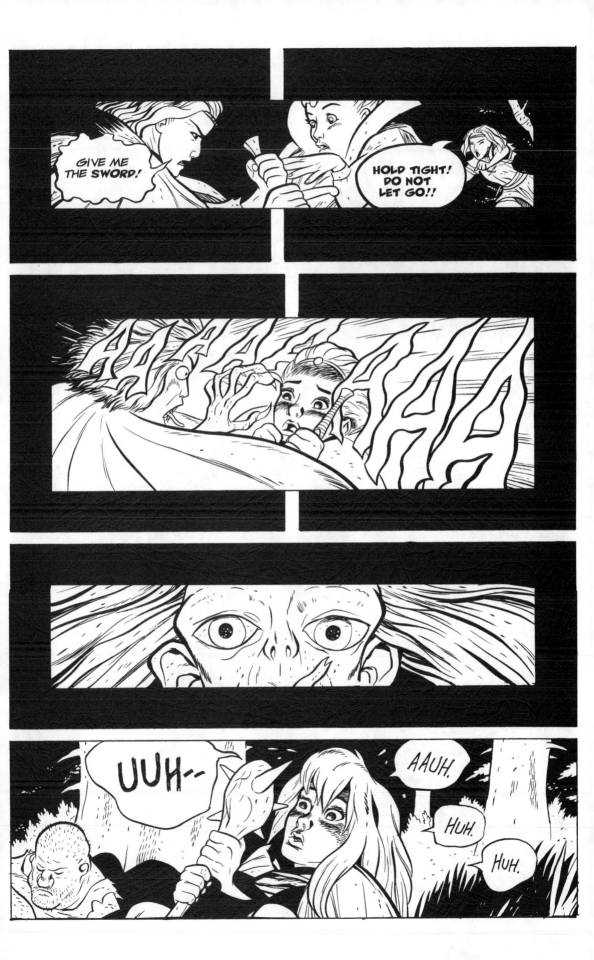

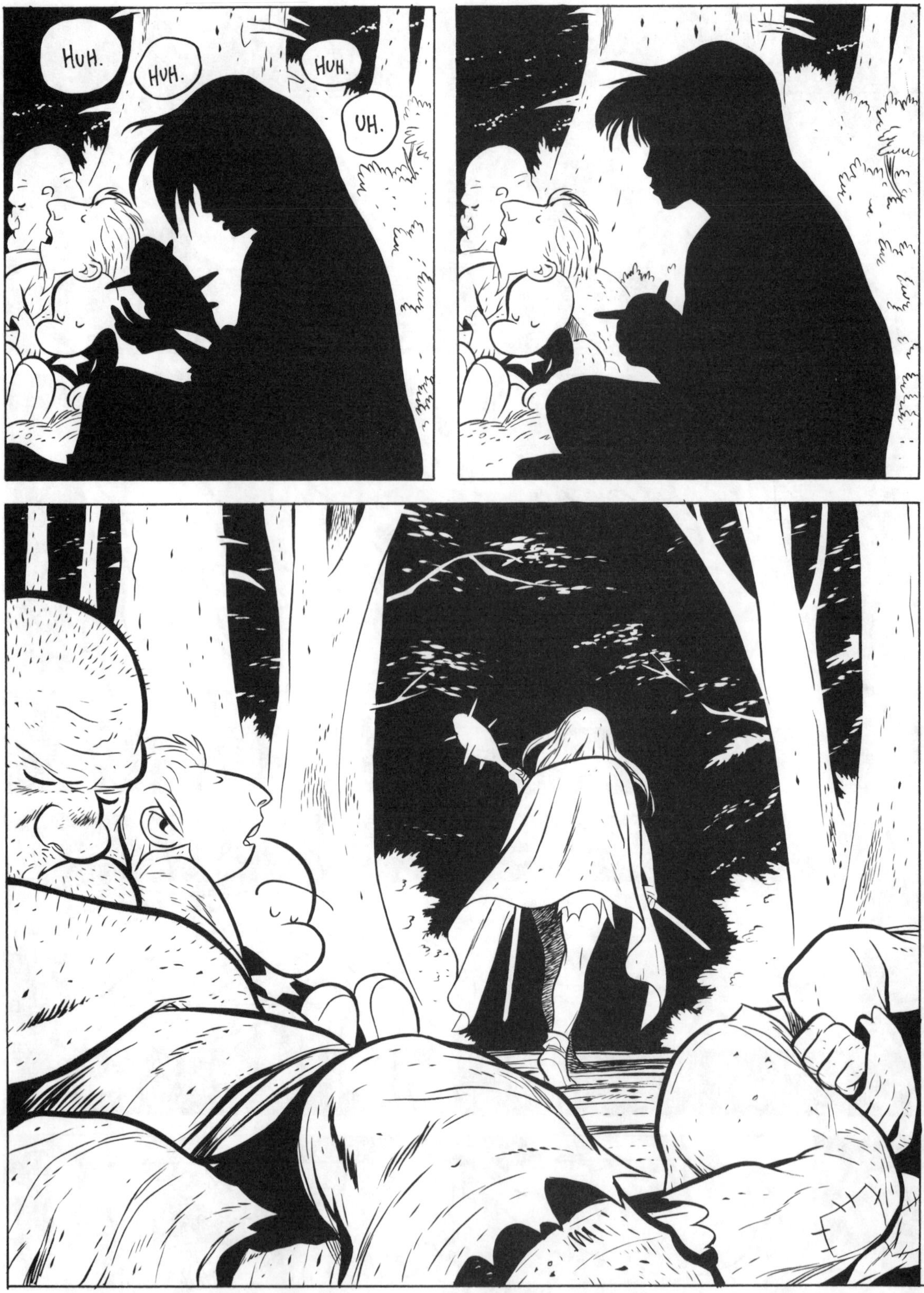
HUH.
HUH.
HUH.
UH.

NEXT: SOUP FOR THE SOUL

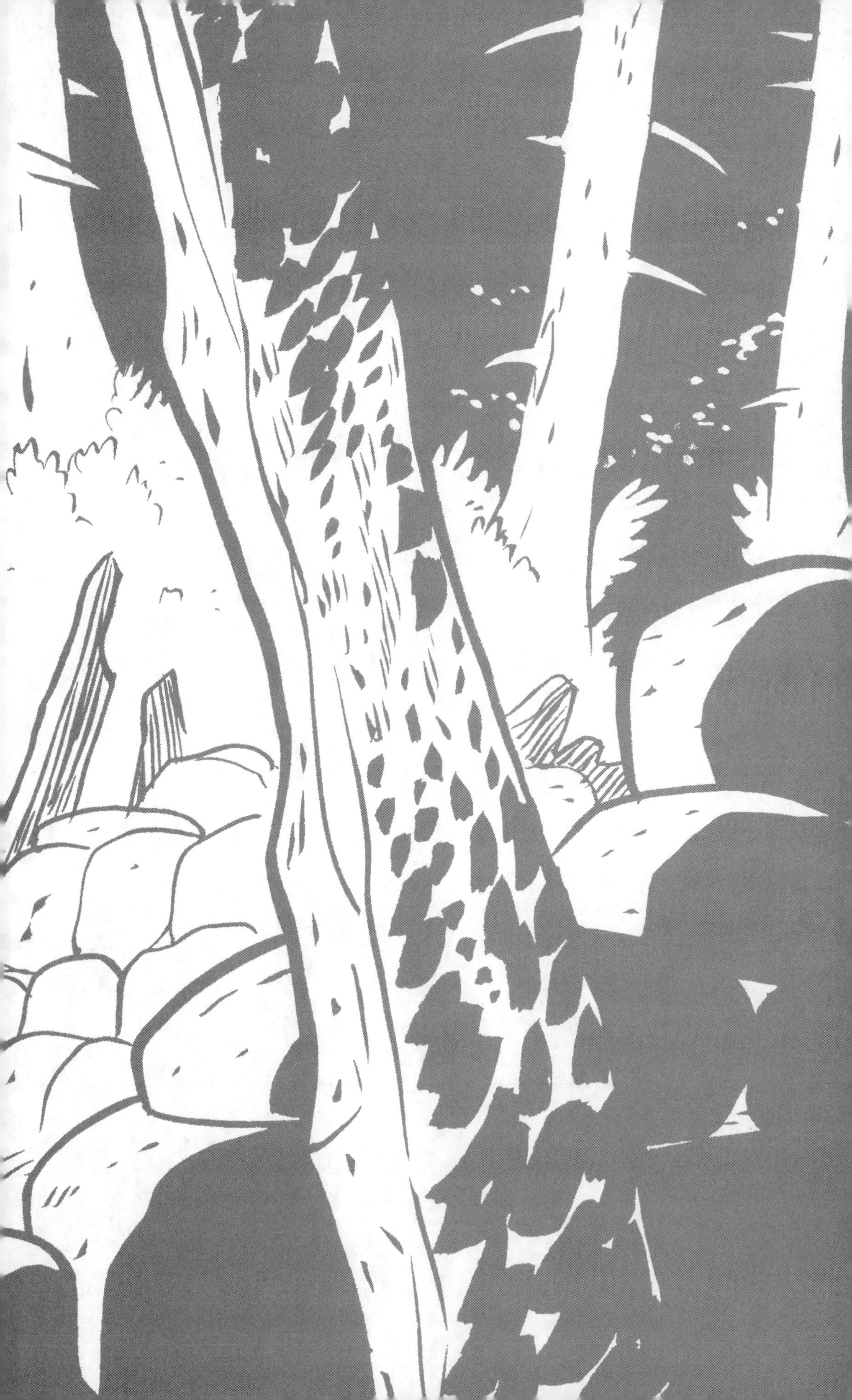

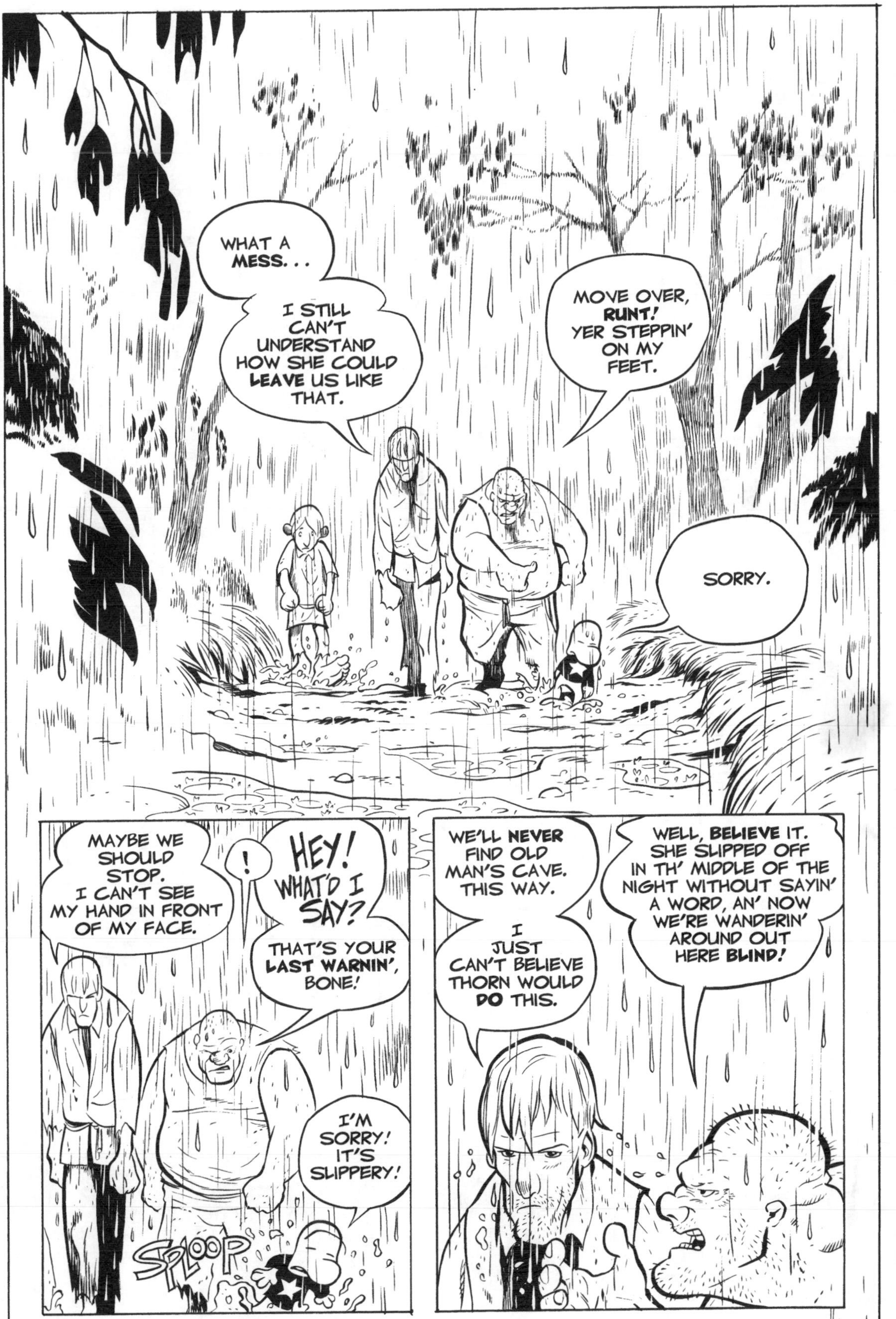
WHAT A MESS. . .
I STILL CAN'T UNDERSTAND HOW SHE COULD LEAVE US LIKE THAT.
MOVE OVER, RUNT! YER STEPPIN' ON MY FEET.
SORRY.
MAYBE WE SHOULD STOP. I CAN'T SEE MY HAND IN FRONT OF MY FACE.
!
HEY! WHAT'D I SAY?
THAT'S YOUR LAST WARNIN', BONE!
I'M SORRY! IT'S SLIPPERY!
SPLOOP
WE'LL NEVER FIND OLD MAN'S CAVE. THIS WAY.
I JUST CAN'T BELIEVE THORN WOULD DO THIS.
WELL, BELIEVE IT. SHE SLIPPED OFF IN TH' MIDDLE OF THE NIGHT WITHOUT SAYIN' A WORD, AN' NOW WE'RE WANDERIN' AROUND OUT HERE BLIND!

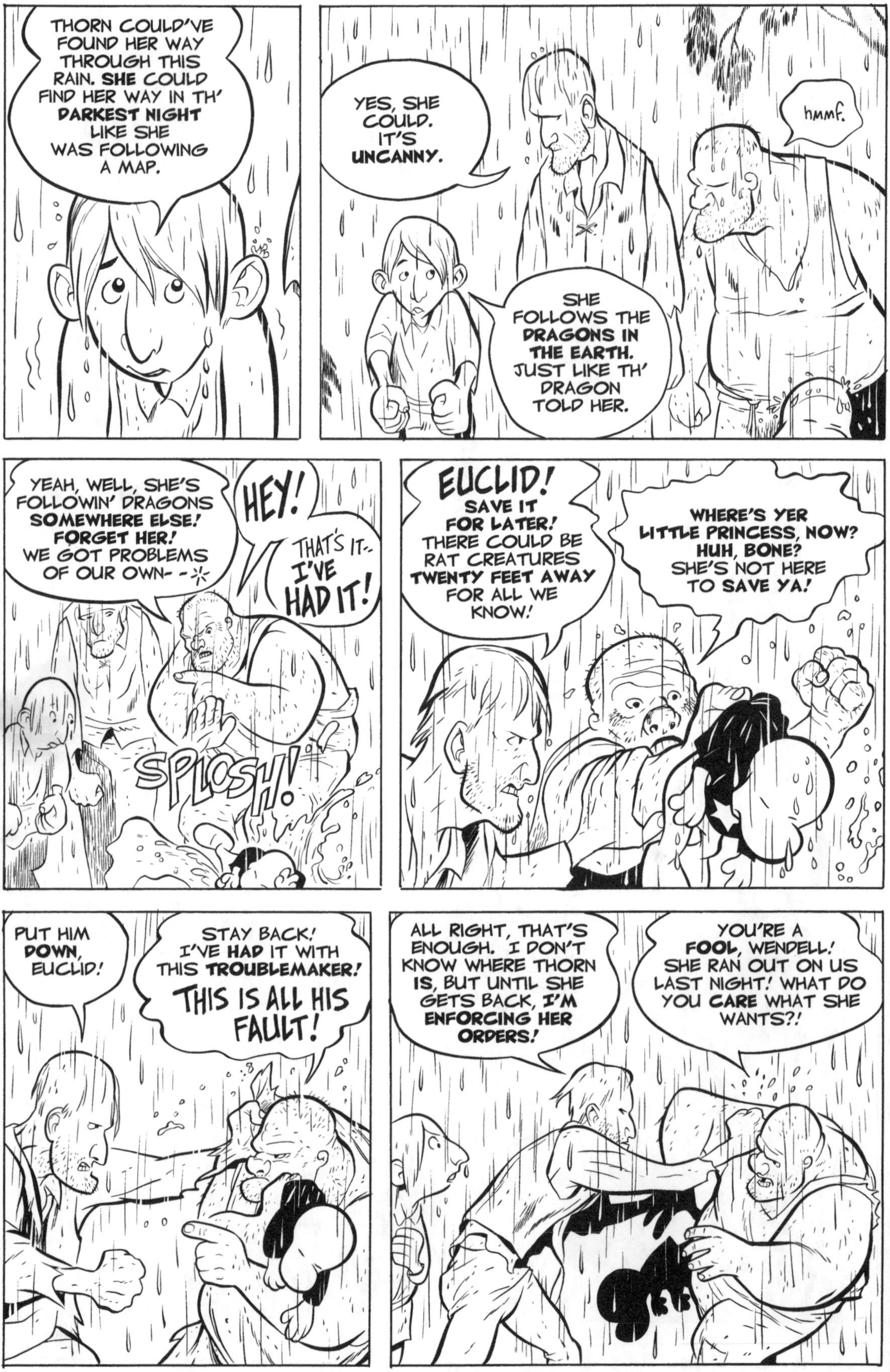
THORN COULD'VE FOUND HER WAY THROUGH THIS RAIN. SHE COULD FIND HER WAY IN TH' DARKEST NIGHT LIKE SHE WAS FOLLOWING A MAP.
YES, SHE COULD. IT'S UNCANNY.
hmmf.
SHE FOLLOWS THE DRAGONS IN THE EARTH. JUST LIKE TH' DRAGON TOLD HER.
YEAH, WELL, SHE'S FOLLOWIN' DRAGONS SOMEWHERE ELSE! FORGET HER! WE GOT PROBLEMS OF OUR OWN- -
HEY!
THAT'S IT- I'VE HAD IT!
SPLOSH!
EUCLID! SAVE IT FOR LATER! THERE COULD BE RAT CREATURES TWENTY FEET AWAY FOR ALL WE KNOW!
WHERE'S YER LITTLE PRINCESS, NOW? HUH, BONE? SHE'S NOT HERE TO SAVE YA!
PUT HIM DOWN, EUCLID!
STAY BACK! I'VE HAD IT WITH THIS TROUBLEMAKER! THIS IS ALL HIS FAULT!
ALL RIGHT, THAT'S ENOUGH. I DON'T KNOW WHERE THORN IS, BUT UNTIL SHE GETS BACK, I'M ENFORCING HER ORDERS!
YOU'RE A FOOL, WENDELL! SHE RAN OUT ON US LAST NIGHT! WHAT DO YOU CARE WHAT SHE WANTS?!

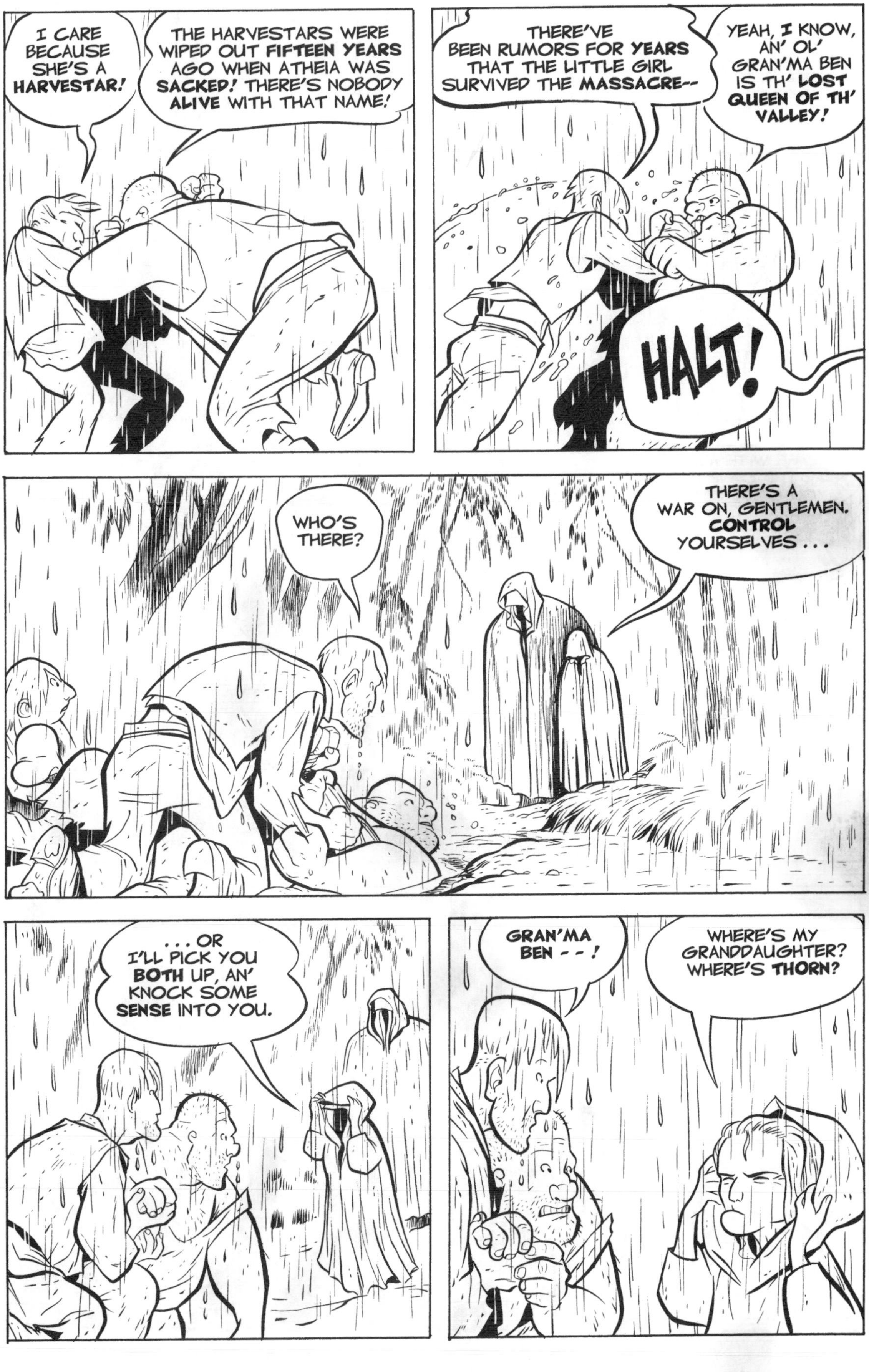

I CARE BECAUSE SHE'S A **HARVESTAR!**
THE HARVESTARS WERE WIPED OUT **FIFTEEN YEARS** AGO WHEN ATHEIA WAS **SACKED!** THERE'S NOBODY **ALIVE** WITH THAT NAME!
THERE'VE BEEN RUMORS FOR **YEARS** THAT THE LITTLE GIRL SURVIVED THE **MASSACRE--**
YEAH, **I** KNOW, AN' OL' GRAN'MA BEN IS TH' **LOST QUEEN OF TH' VALLEY!**
HALT!
WHO'S THERE?
THERE'S A WAR ON, GENTLEMEN. **CONTROL** YOURSELVES . . .
. . . OR I'LL PICK YOU **BOTH** UP, AN' KNOCK SOME **SENSE** INTO YOU.
GRAN'MA BEN --!
WHERE'S MY GRANDDAUGHTER? WHERE'S **THORN?**

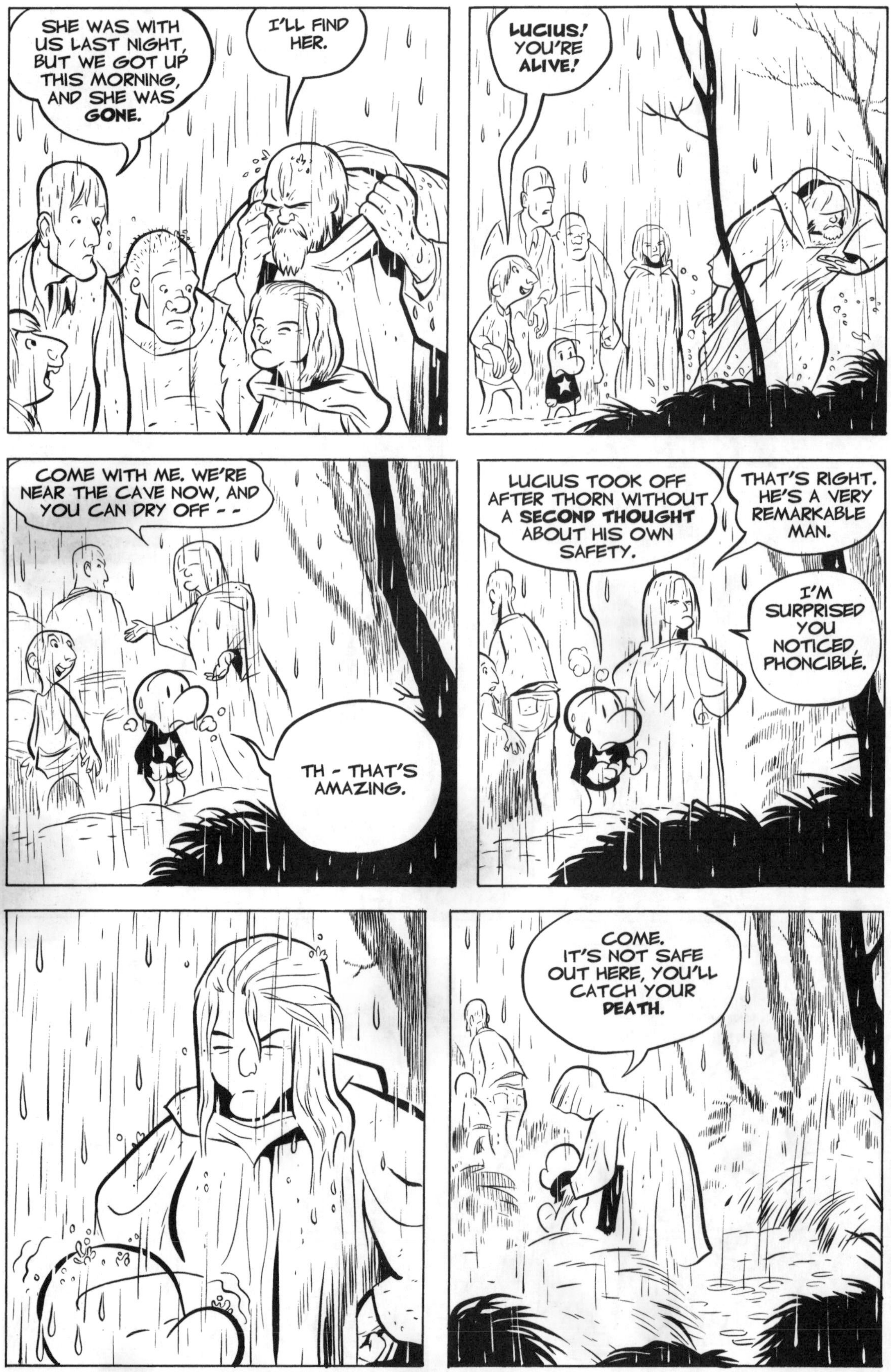
SHE WAS WITH US LAST NIGHT, BUT WE GOT UP THIS MORNING, AND SHE WAS **GONE.**
I'LL FIND HER.
LUCIUS! YOU'RE **ALIVE!**
COME WITH ME. WE'RE NEAR THE CAVE NOW, AND YOU CAN DRY OFF - -
TH - THAT'S AMAZING.
LUCIUS TOOK OFF AFTER THORN WITHOUT A **SECOND THOUGHT** ABOUT HIS OWN SAFETY.
THAT'S RIGHT. HE'S A VERY REMARKABLE MAN.
I'M SURPRISED YOU NOTICED, PHONCIBLE.
COME. IT'S NOT SAFE OUT HERE, YOU'LL CATCH YOUR **DEATH.**

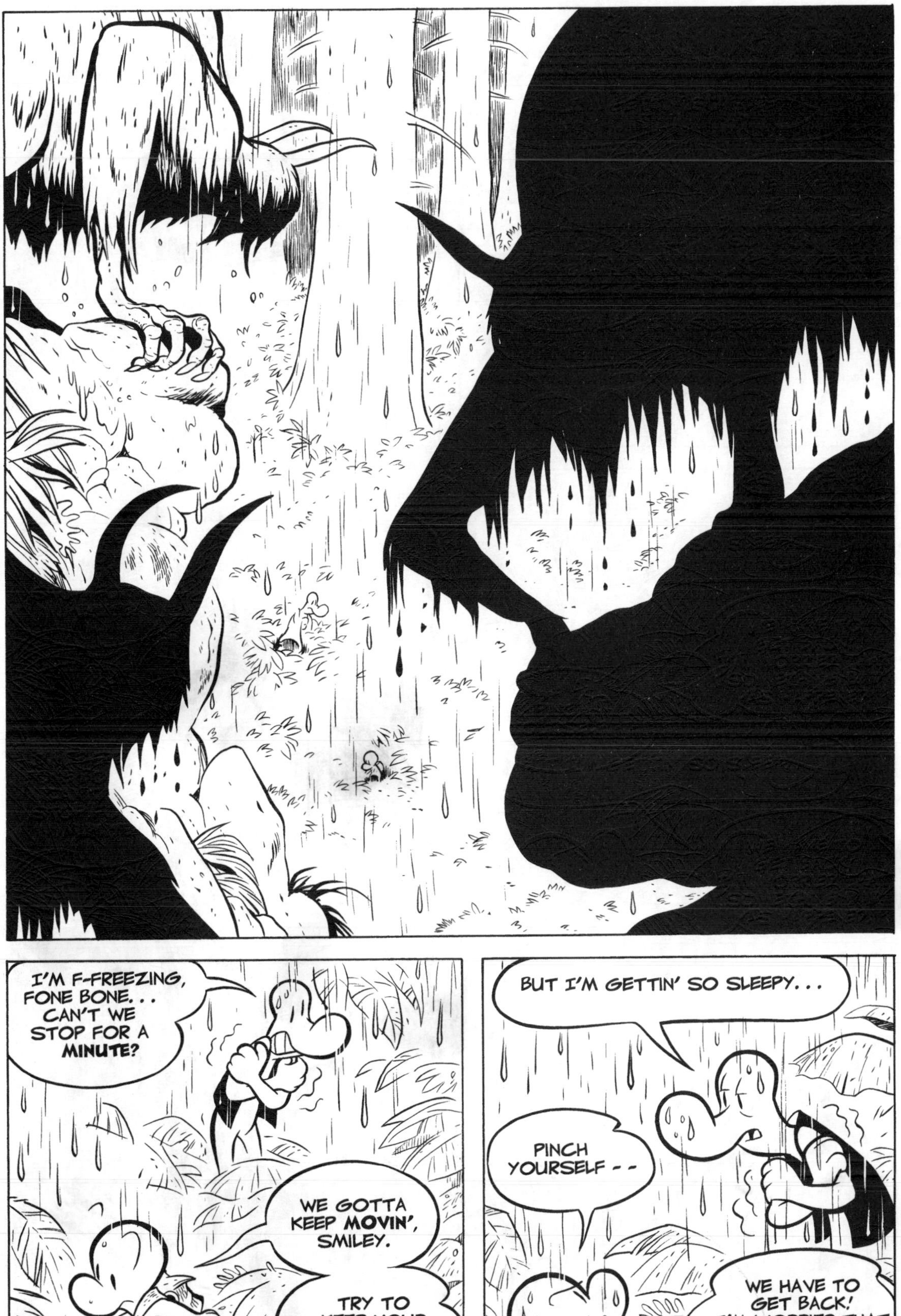
I'M F-FREEZING, FONE BONE... CAN'T WE STOP FOR A **MINUTE**?
WE GOTTA KEEP **MOVIN'**, SMILEY.
TRY TO KEEP YOUR MIND ON OTHER THINGS!
BUT I'M GETTIN' SO SLEEPY...
PINCH YOURSELF - -
WE HAVE TO GET BACK! I'M WORRIED THAT SOMETHING **BAD** HAS HAPPENED!

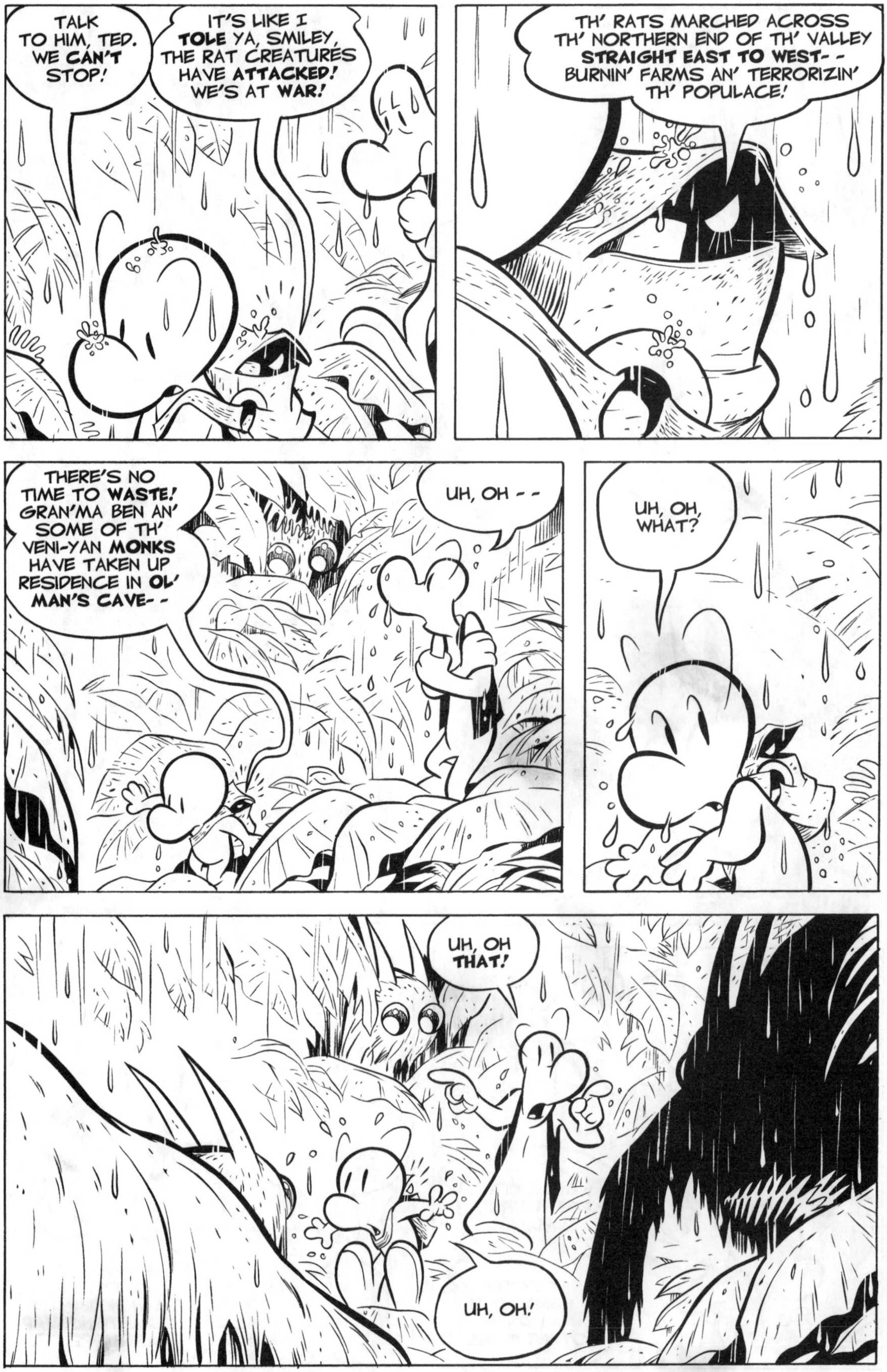
TALK TO HIM, TED. WE CAN'T STOP!
IT'S LIKE I TOLE YA, SMILEY, THE RAT CREATURES HAVE ATTACKED! WE'S AT WAR!
TH' RATS MARCHED ACROSS TH' NORTHERN END OF TH' VALLEY STRAIGHT EAST TO WEST- - BURNIN' FARMS AN' TERRORIZIN' TH' POPULACE!
THERE'S NO TIME TO WASTE! GRAN'MA BEN AN' SOME OF TH' VENI-YAN MONKS HAVE TAKEN UP RESIDENCE IN OL' MAN'S CAVE- -
UH, OH - -
UH, OH, WHAT?
UH, OH THAT!
UH, OH!

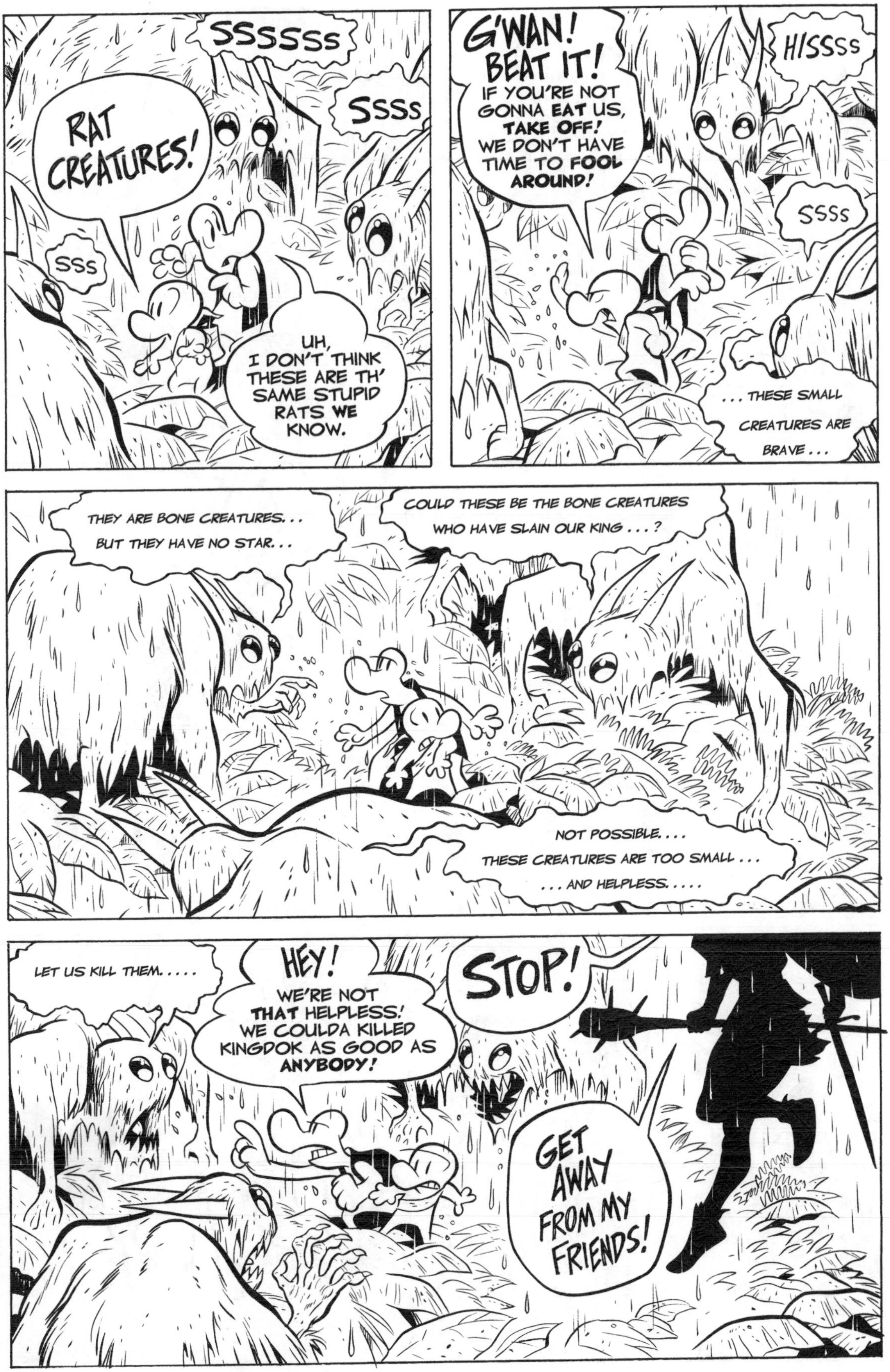
SSSSSS
RAT CREATURES!
SSSS
SSS
UH, I DON'T THINK THESE ARE TH' SAME STUPID RATS WE KNOW.
G'WAN! BEAT IT!
IF YOU'RE NOT GONNA EAT US, TAKE OFF! WE DON'T HAVE TIME TO FOOL AROUND!
HISSSS
SSSS
. . . THESE SMALL CREATURES ARE BRAVE . . .
THEY ARE BONE CREATURES. . . BUT THEY HAVE NO STAR. . .
COULD THESE BE THE BONE CREATURES WHO HAVE SLAIN OUR KING . . . ?
NOT POSSIBLE. . . . THESE CREATURES ARE TOO SMALL . . . . . . AND HELPLESS. . . . .
LET US KILL THEM. . . . .
HEY!
WE'RE NOT THAT HELPLESS! WE COULDA KILLED KINGDOK AS GOOD AS ANYBODY!
STOP!
GET AWAY FROM MY FRIENDS!

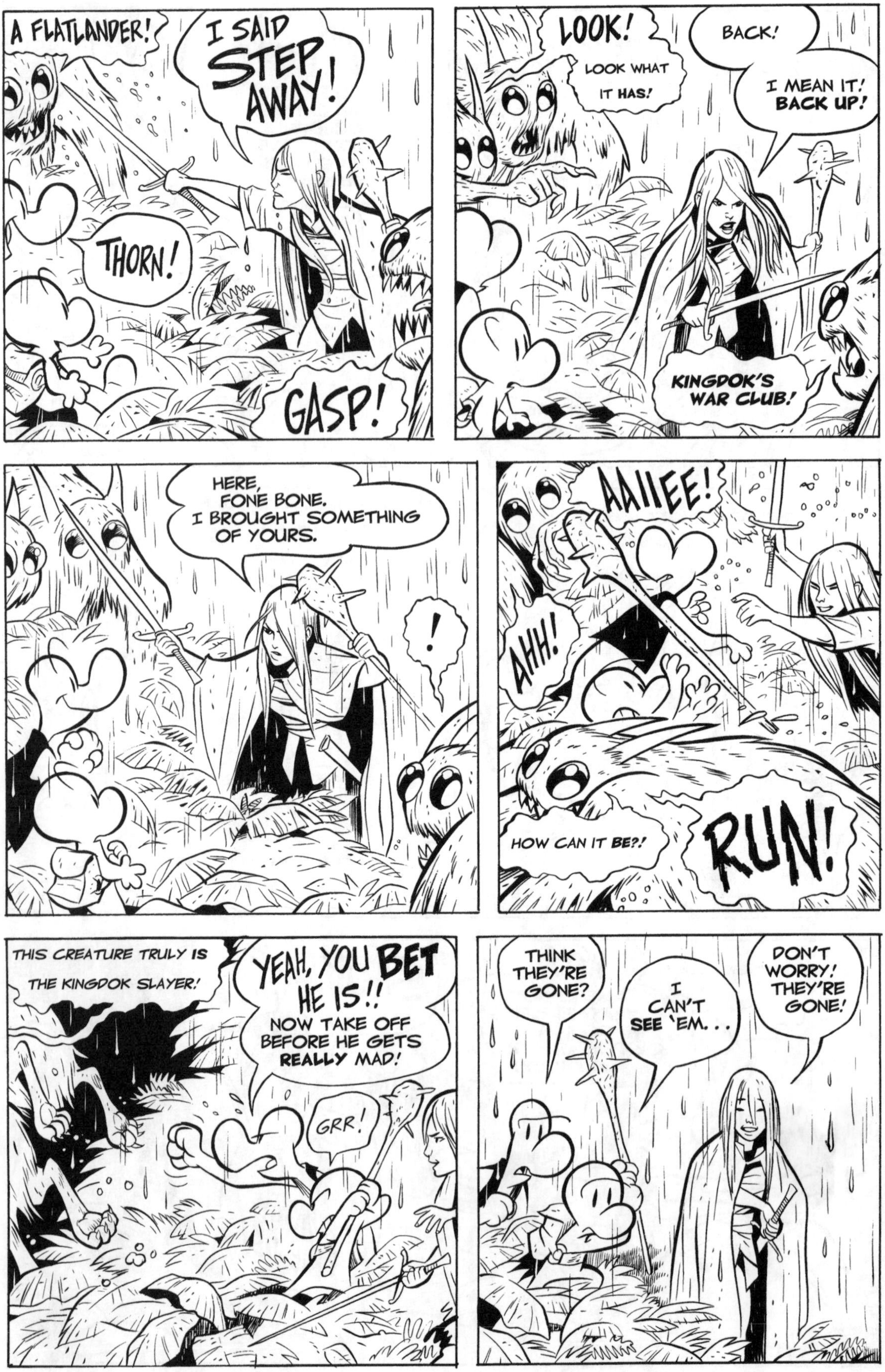
A FLATLANDER!
I SAID STEP AWAY!
THORN!
GASP!
LOOK! LOOK WHAT IT HAS!
BACK! I MEAN IT! BACK UP!
KINGDOK'S WAR CLUB!
HERE, FONE BONE. I BROUGHT SOMETHING OF YOURS.
!
AAIIEE!
AHH!
HOW CAN IT BE?!
RUN!
THIS CREATURE TRULY IS THE KINGDOK SLAYER!
YEAH, YOU BET HE IS!! NOW TAKE OFF BEFORE HE GETS REALLY MAD!
GRR!
THINK THEY'RE GONE?
I CAN'T SEE 'EM...
DON'T WORRY! THEY'RE GONE!

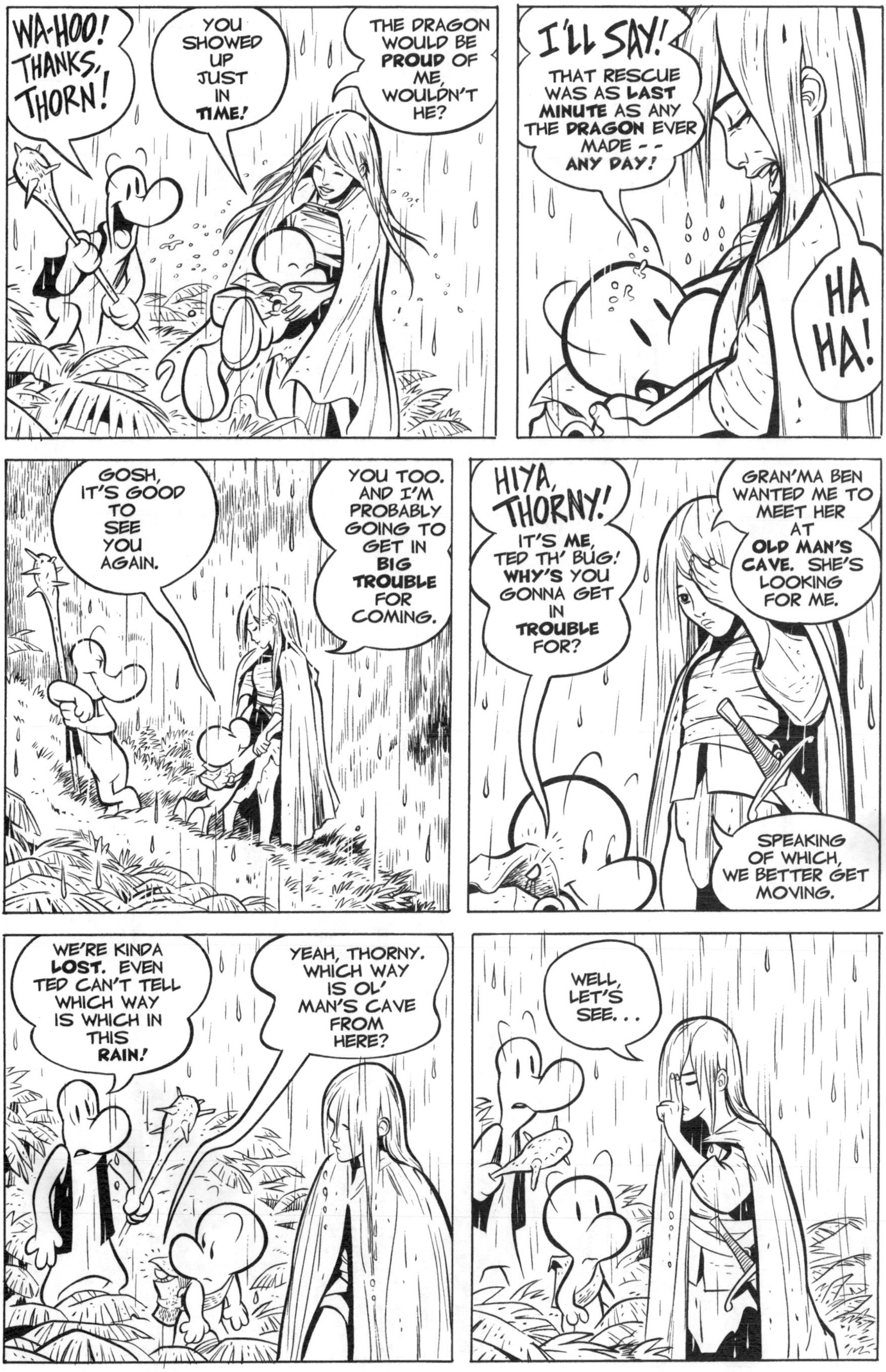

WA-HOO! THANKS, THORN!
YOU SHOWED UP JUST IN TIME!
THE DRAGON WOULD BE PROUD OF ME, WOULDN'T HE?
I'LL SAY!
THAT RESCUE WAS AS LAST MINUTE AS ANY THE DRAGON EVER MADE - - ANY DAY!
HA HA!
GOSH, IT'S GOOD TO SEE YOU AGAIN.
YOU TOO. AND I'M PROBABLY GOING TO GET IN BIG TROUBLE FOR COMING.
HIYA, THORNY!
IT'S ME, TED TH' BUG! WHY'S YOU GONNA GET IN TROUBLE FOR?
GRAN'MA BEN WANTED ME TO MEET HER AT OLD MAN'S CAVE. SHE'S LOOKING FOR ME.
SPEAKING OF WHICH, WE BETTER GET MOVING.
WE'RE KINDA LOST. EVEN TED CAN'T TELL WHICH WAY IS WHICH IN THIS RAIN!
YEAH, THORNY. WHICH WAY IS OL' MAN'S CAVE FROM HERE?
WELL, LET'S SEE...

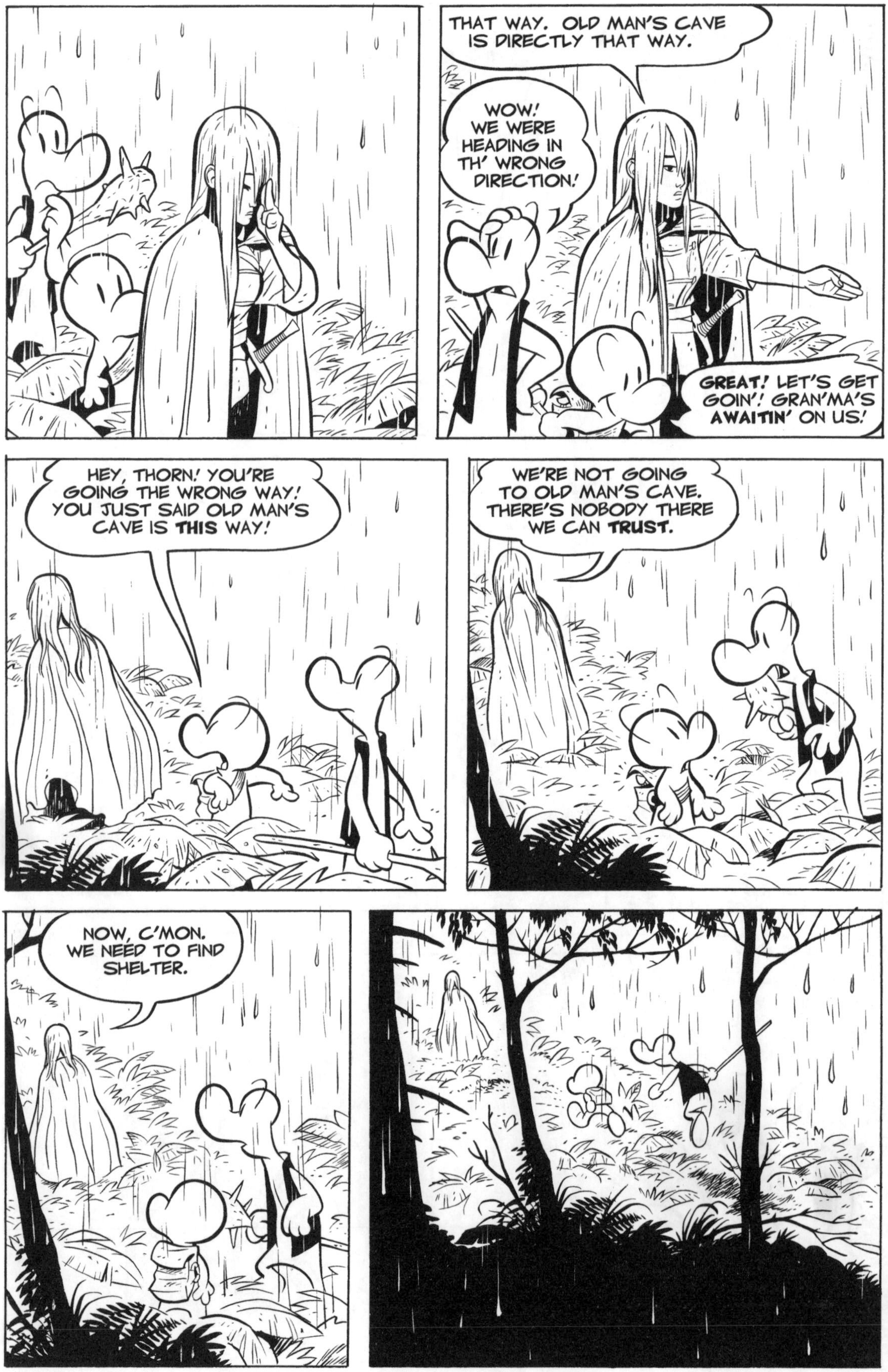
THAT WAY. OLD MAN'S CAVE IS DIRECTLY THAT WAY.
WOW! WE WERE HEADING IN TH' WRONG DIRECTION!
GREAT! LET'S GET GOIN'! GRAN'MA'S AWAITIN' ON US!
HEY, THORN! YOU'RE GOING THE WRONG WAY! YOU JUST SAID OLD MAN'S CAVE IS THIS WAY!
WE'RE NOT GOING TO OLD MAN'S CAVE. THERE'S NOBODY THERE WE CAN TRUST.
NOW, C'MON. WE NEED TO FIND SHELTER.

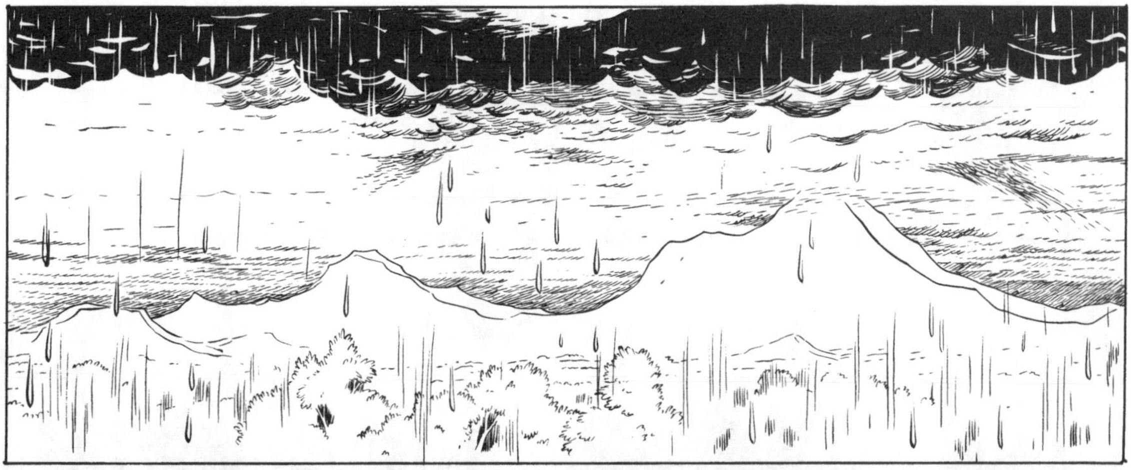

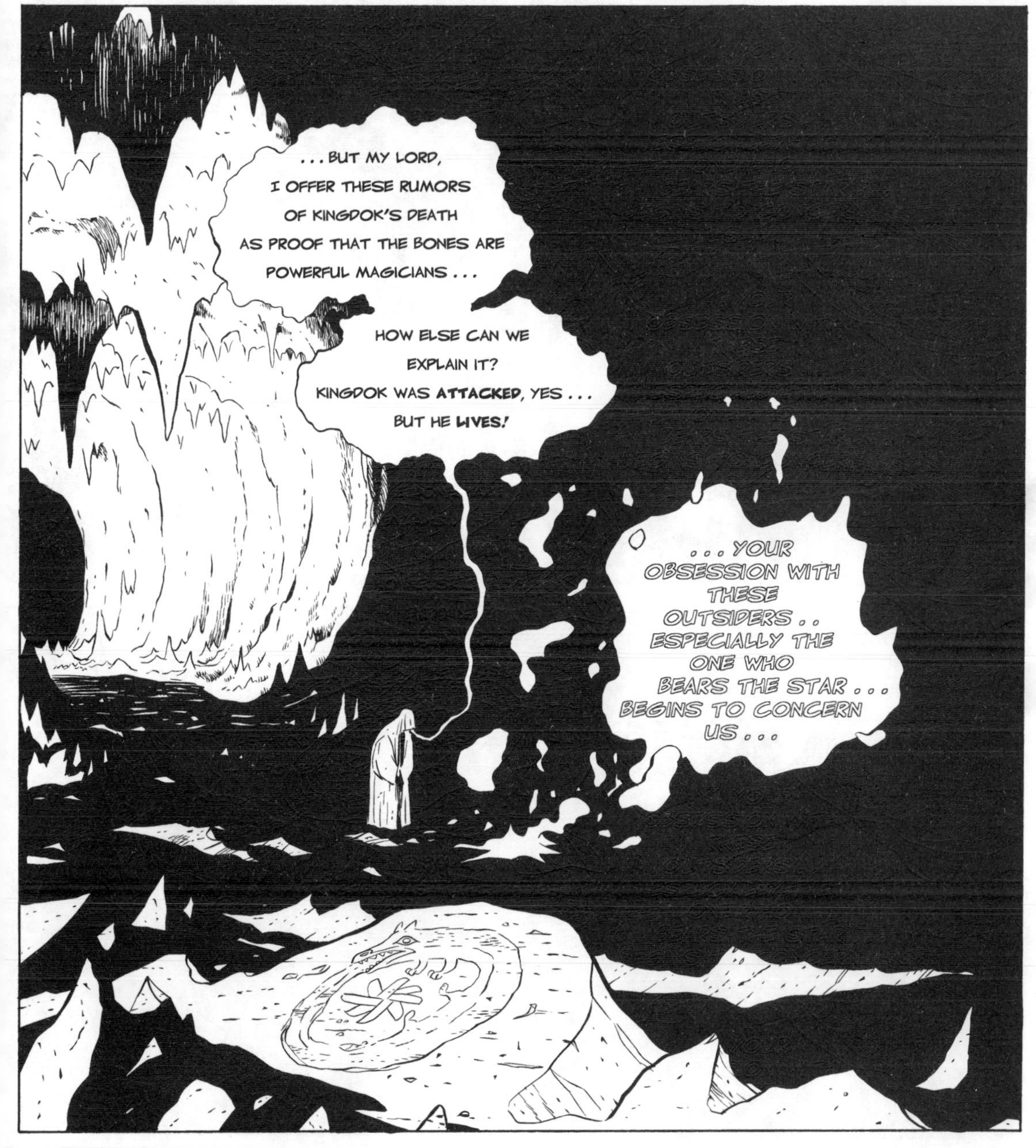

. . . BUT MY LORD, I OFFER THESE RUMORS OF KINGDOK'S DEATH AS PROOF THAT THE BONES ARE POWERFUL MAGICIANS . . .
HOW ELSE CAN WE EXPLAIN IT? KINGDOK WAS **ATTACKED**, YES . . . BUT HE **LIVES!**
. . . YOUR OBSESSION WITH THESE OUTSIDERS . . ESPECIALLY THE ONE WHO BEARS THE STAR . . . BEGINS TO CONCERN US . . .

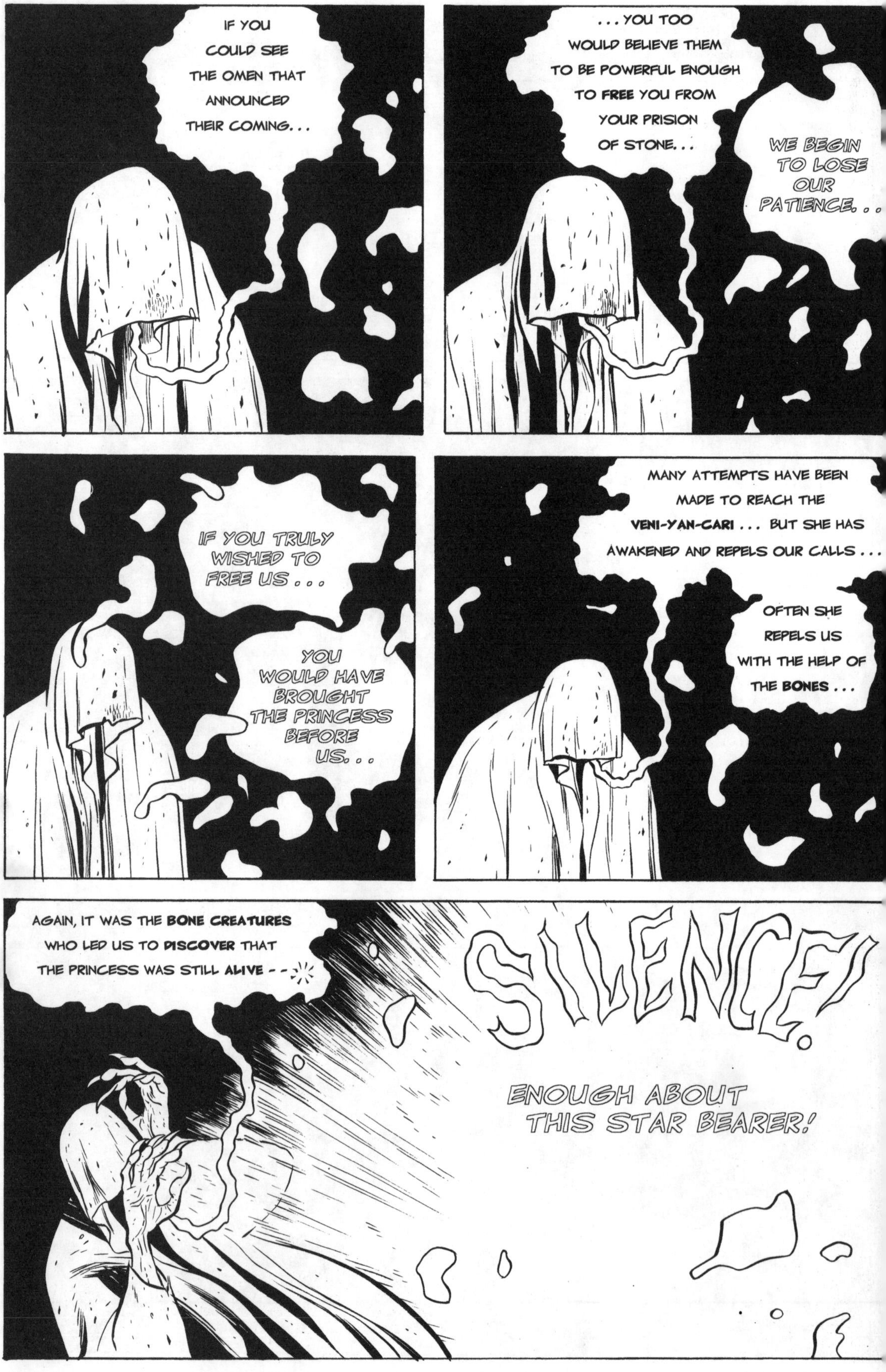
IF YOU COULD SEE THE OMEN THAT ANNOUNCED THEIR COMING...
...YOU TOO WOULD BELIEVE THEM TO BE POWERFUL ENOUGH TO FREE YOU FROM YOUR PRISION OF STONE...
WE BEGIN TO LOSE OUR PATIENCE...
IF YOU TRULY WISHED TO FREE US...
YOU WOULD HAVE BROUGHT THE PRINCESS BEFORE US...
MANY ATTEMPTS HAVE BEEN MADE TO REACH THE VENI-YAN-CARI... BUT SHE HAS AWAKENED AND REPELS OUR CALLS...
OFTEN SHE REPELS US WITH THE HELP OF THE BONES...
AGAIN, IT WAS THE BONE CREATURES WHO LED US TO DISCOVER THAT THE PRINCESS WAS STILL ALIVE --
SILENCE!
ENOUGH ABOUT THIS STAR BEARER!

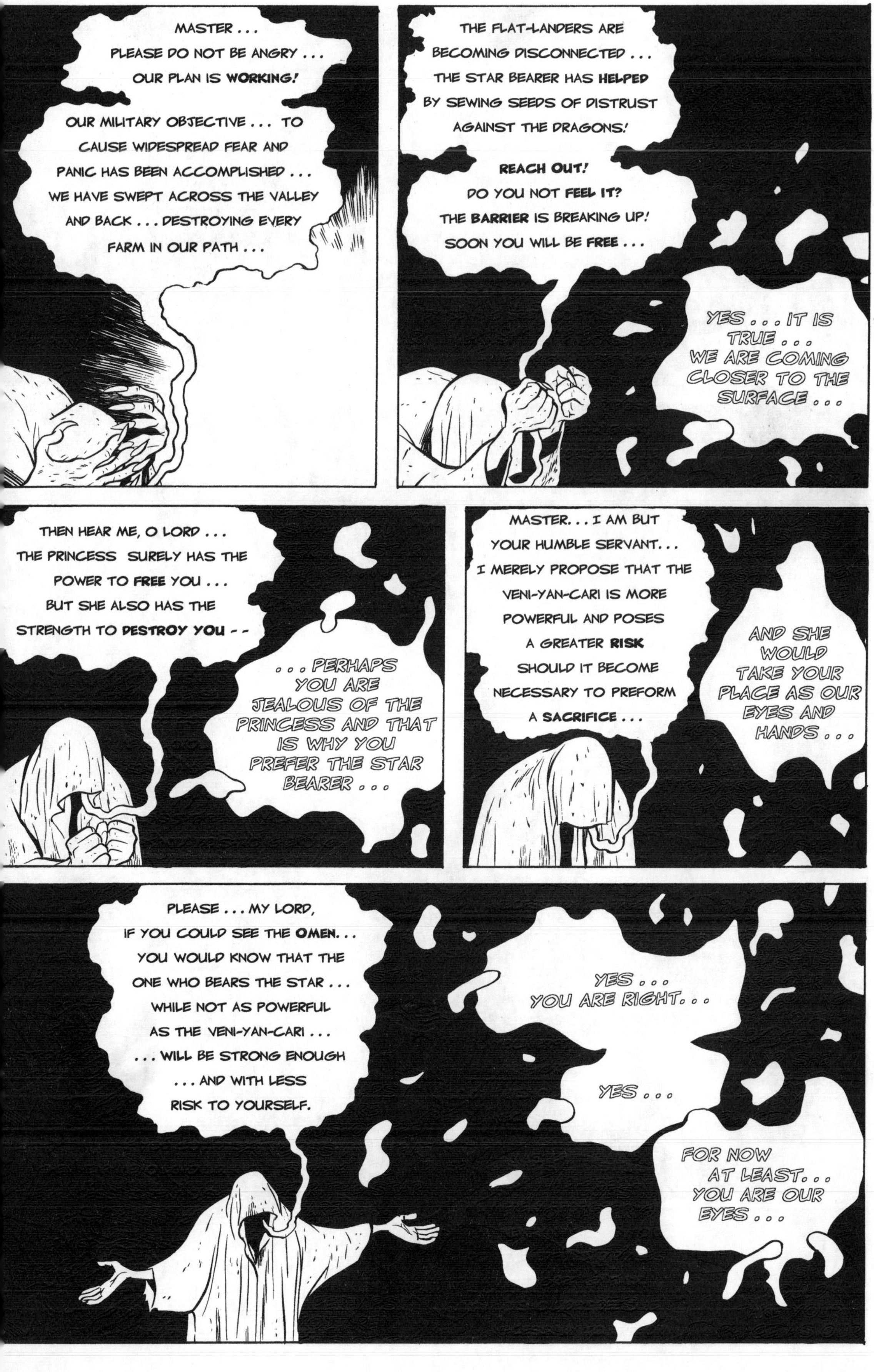

MASTER . . . PLEASE DO NOT BE ANGRY . . . OUR PLAN IS WORKING! OUR MILITARY OBJECTIVE . . . TO CAUSE WIDESPREAD FEAR AND PANIC HAS BEEN ACCOMPLISHED . . . WE HAVE SWEPT ACROSS THE VALLEY AND BACK . . . DESTROYING EVERY FARM IN OUR PATH . . .
THE FLAT-LANDERS ARE BECOMING DISCONNECTED . . . THE STAR BEARER HAS HELPED BY SEWING SEEDS OF DISTRUST AGAINST THE DRAGONS! REACH OUT! DO YOU NOT FEEL IT? THE BARRIER IS BREAKING UP! SOON YOU WILL BE FREE . . .
YES . . . IT IS TRUE . . . WE ARE COMING CLOSER TO THE SURFACE . . .
THEN HEAR ME, O LORD . . . THE PRINCESS SURELY HAS THE POWER TO FREE YOU . . . BUT SHE ALSO HAS THE STRENGTH TO DESTROY YOU - -
. . . PERHAPS YOU ARE JEALOUS OF THE PRINCESS AND THAT IS WHY YOU PREFER THE STAR BEARER . . .
MASTER. . . I AM BUT YOUR HUMBLE SERVANT. . . I MERELY PROPOSE THAT THE VENI-YAN-CARI IS MORE POWERFUL AND POSES A GREATER RISK SHOULD IT BECOME NECESSARY TO PREFORM A SACRIFICE . . .
AND SHE WOULD TAKE YOUR PLACE AS OUR EYES AND HANDS . . .
PLEASE . . . MY LORD, IF YOU COULD SEE THE OMEN. . . YOU WOULD KNOW THAT THE ONE WHO BEARS THE STAR . . . WHILE NOT AS POWERFUL AS THE VENI-YAN-CARI . . . . . . WILL BE STRONG ENOUGH . . . AND WITH LESS RISK TO YOURSELF.
YES . . . YOU ARE RIGHT. . .
YES . . .
FOR NOW AT LEAST. . . YOU ARE OUR EYES . . .

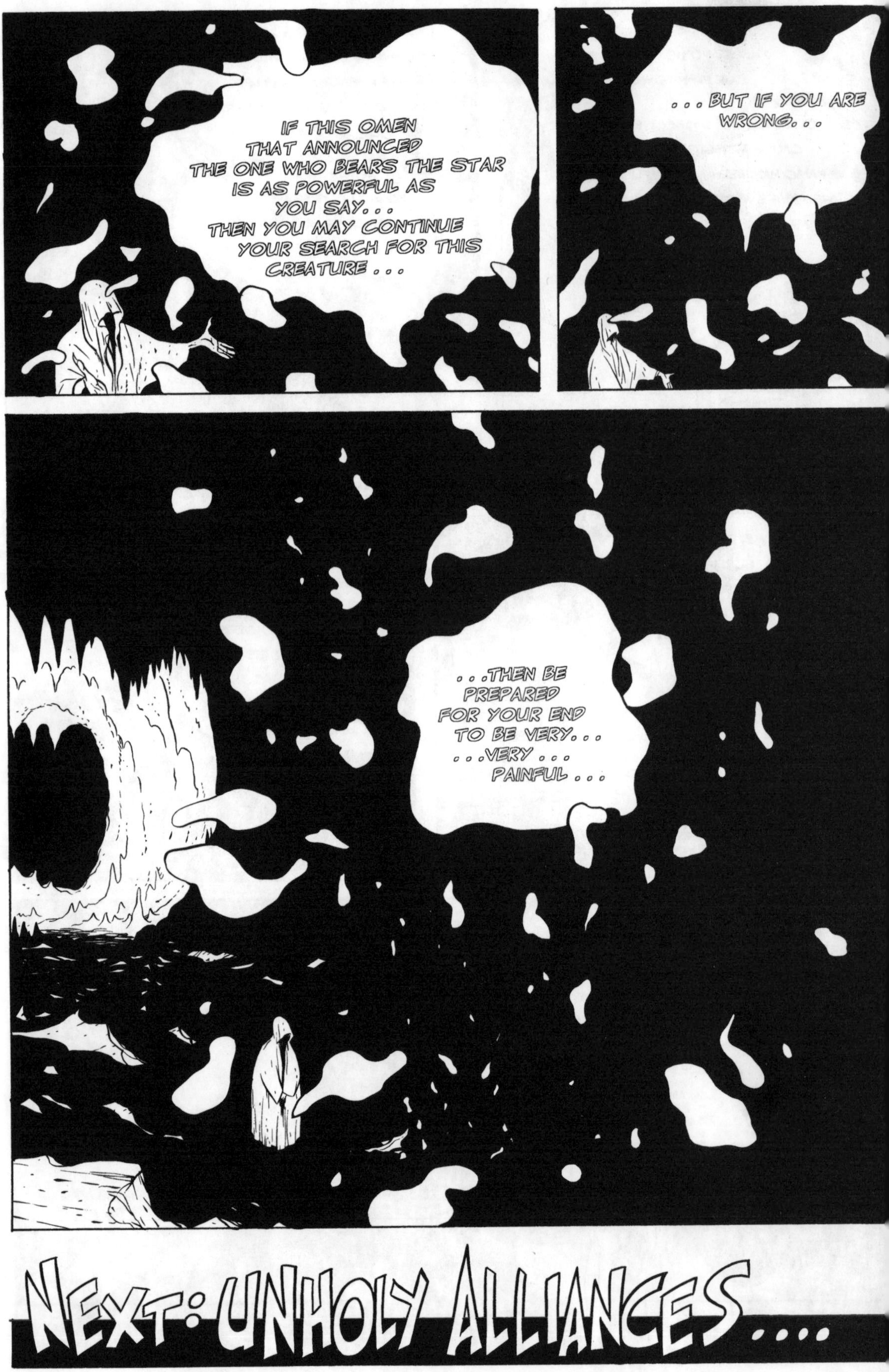
IF THIS OMEN THAT ANNOUNCED THE ONE WHO BEARS THE STAR IS AS POWERFUL AS YOU SAY... THEN YOU MAY CONTINUE YOUR SEARCH FOR THIS CREATURE...
...BUT IF YOU ARE WRONG...
...THEN BE PREPARED FOR YOUR END TO BE VERY... ...VERY... PAINFUL...
NEXT: UNHOLY ALLIANCES....

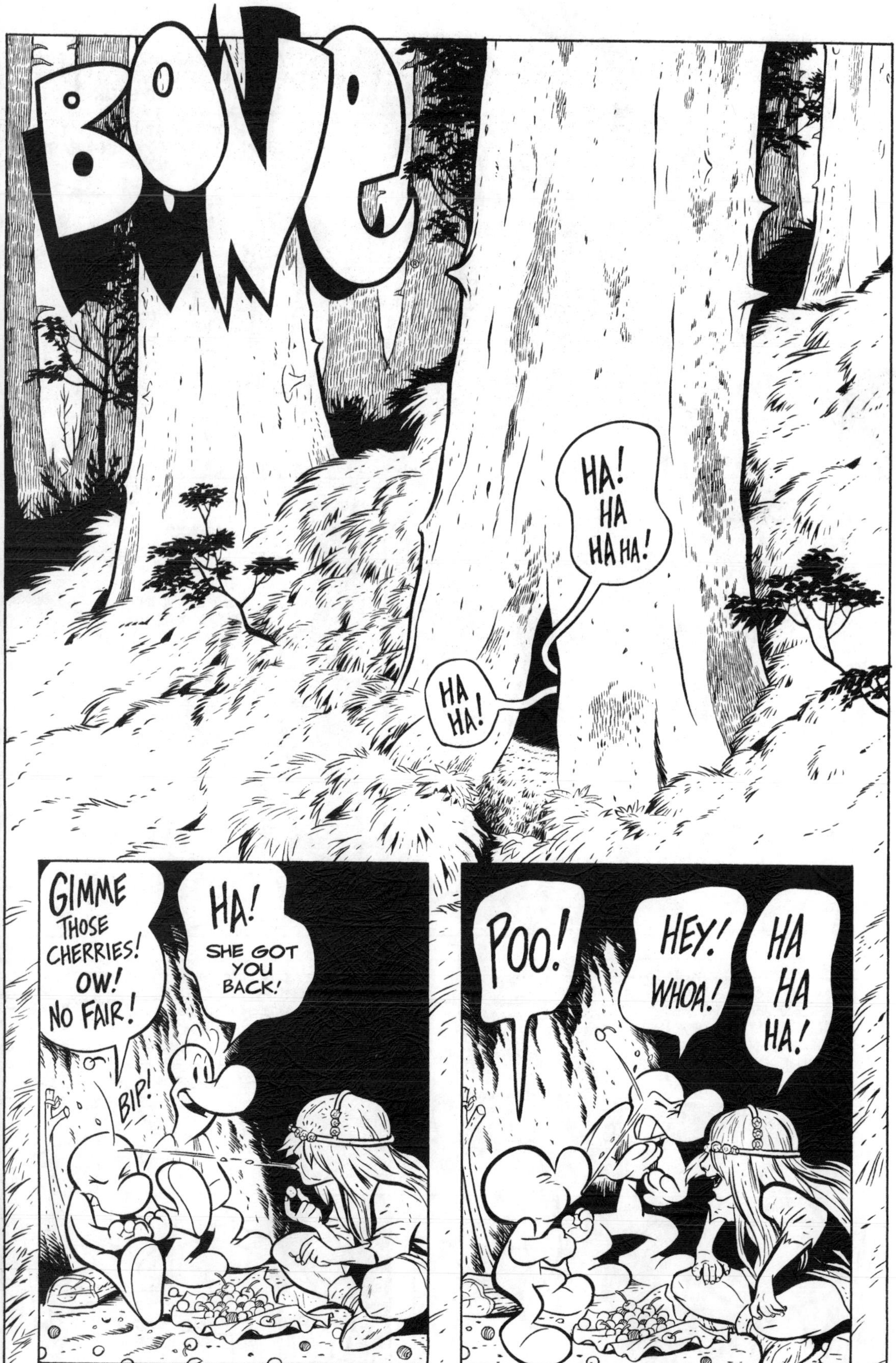
BONE®
HA! HA HA HA!
HA HA!
GIMME THOSE CHERRIES! OW! NO FAIR!
HA! SHE GOT YOU BACK!
BIP!
POO!
HEY! WHOA!
HA HA HA!

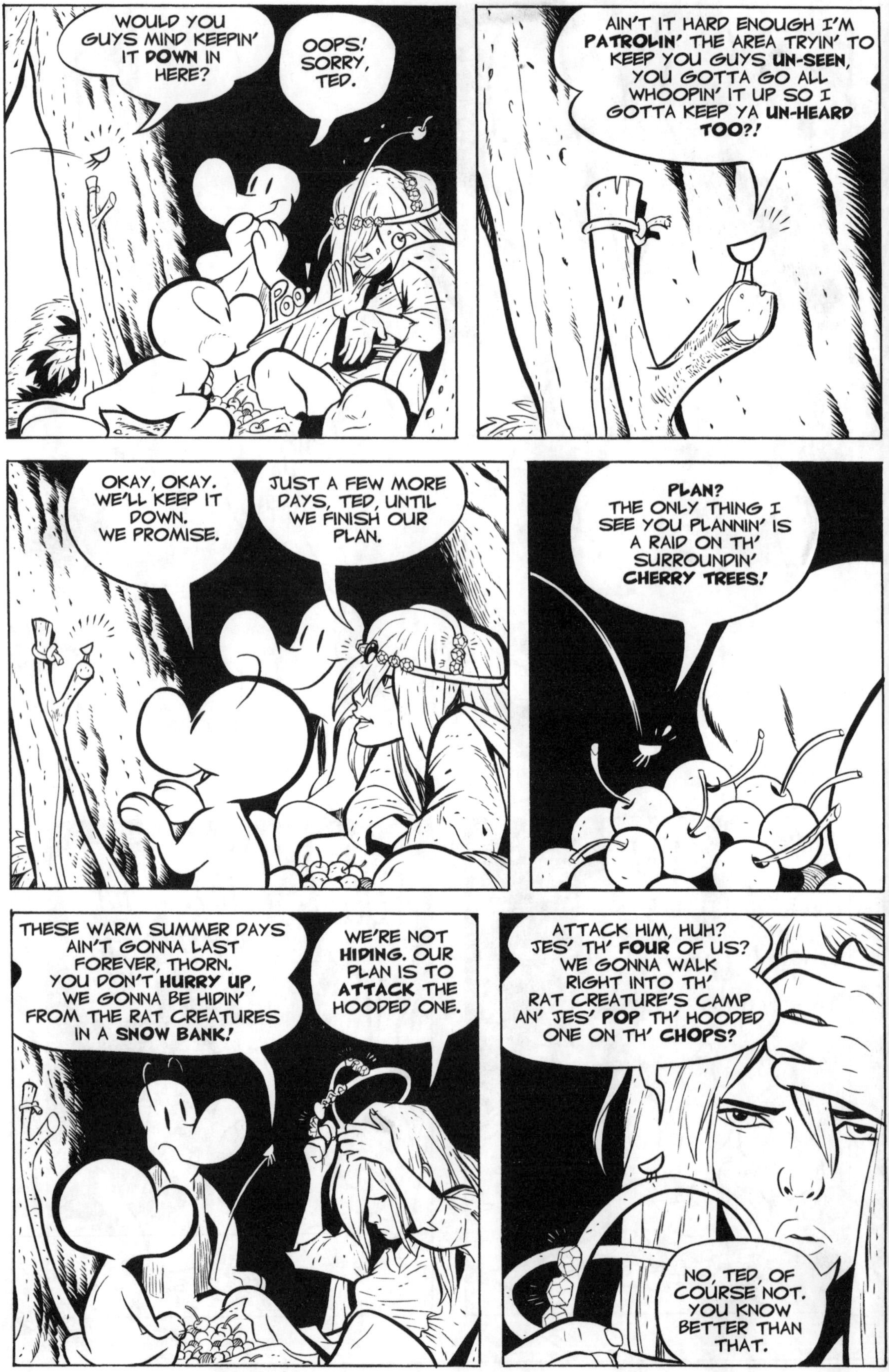
WOULD YOU GUYS MIND KEEPIN' IT **DOWN** IN HERE?
OOPS! SORRY, TED.
POOF!
AIN'T IT HARD ENOUGH I'M **PATROLIN'** THE AREA TRYIN' TO KEEP YOU GUYS **UN-SEEN**, YOU GOTTA GO ALL WHOOPIN' IT UP SO I GOTTA KEEP YA **UN-HEARD TOO?!**
OKAY, OKAY. WE'LL KEEP IT DOWN. WE PROMISE.
JUST A FEW MORE DAYS, TED, UNTIL WE FINISH OUR PLAN.
PLAN? THE ONLY THING I SEE YOU PLANNIN' IS A RAID ON TH' SURROUNDIN' **CHERRY TREES!**
THESE WARM SUMMER DAYS AIN'T GONNA LAST FOREVER, THORN. YOU DON'T **HURRY UP**, WE GONNA BE HIDIN' FROM THE RAT CREATURES IN A **SNOW BANK!**
WE'RE NOT **HIDING.** OUR PLAN IS TO **ATTACK** THE HOODED ONE.
ATTACK HIM, HUH? JES' TH' **FOUR** OF US? WE GONNA WALK RIGHT INTO TH' RAT CREATURE'S CAMP AN' JES' **POP** TH' HOODED ONE ON TH' **CHOPS?**
NO, TED, OF COURSE NOT. YOU KNOW BETTER THAN THAT.

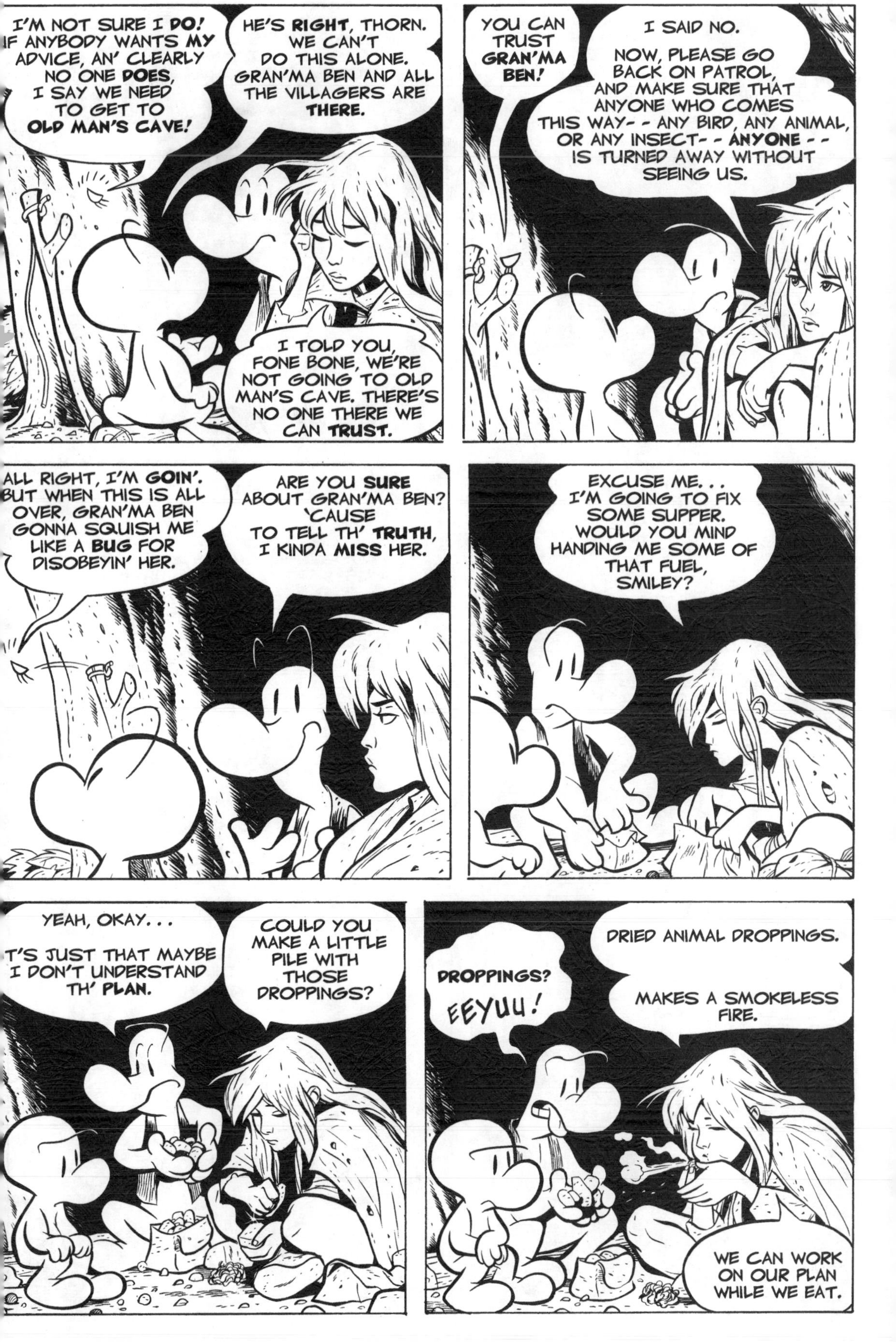
I'M NOT SURE I DO! IF ANYBODY WANTS MY ADVICE, AN' CLEARLY NO ONE DOES, I SAY WE NEED TO GET TO OLD MAN'S CAVE!
HE'S RIGHT, THORN. WE CAN'T DO THIS ALONE. GRAN'MA BEN AND ALL THE VILLAGERS ARE THERE.
I TOLD YOU, FONE BONE, WE'RE NOT GOING TO OLD MAN'S CAVE. THERE'S NO ONE THERE WE CAN TRUST.
YOU CAN TRUST GRAN'MA BEN!
I SAID NO.
NOW, PLEASE GO BACK ON PATROL, AND MAKE SURE THAT ANYONE WHO COMES THIS WAY- - ANY BIRD, ANY ANIMAL, OR ANY INSECT- - ANYONE - - IS TURNED AWAY WITHOUT SEEING US.
ALL RIGHT, I'M GOIN'. BUT WHEN THIS IS ALL OVER, GRAN'MA BEN GONNA SQUISH ME LIKE A BUG FOR DISOBEYIN' HER.
ARE YOU SURE ABOUT GRAN'MA BEN? 'CAUSE TO TELL TH' TRUTH, I KINDA MISS HER.
EXCUSE ME. . . I'M GOING TO FIX SOME SUPPER. WOULD YOU MIND HANDING ME SOME OF THAT FUEL, SMILEY?
YEAH, OKAY. . .
T'S JUST THAT MAYBE I DON'T UNDERSTAND TH' PLAN.
COULD YOU MAKE A LITTLE PILE WITH THOSE DROPPINGS?
DROPPINGS?
EEYUU!
DRIED ANIMAL DROPPINGS.
MAKES A SMOKELESS FIRE.
WE CAN WORK ON OUR PLAN WHILE WE EAT.

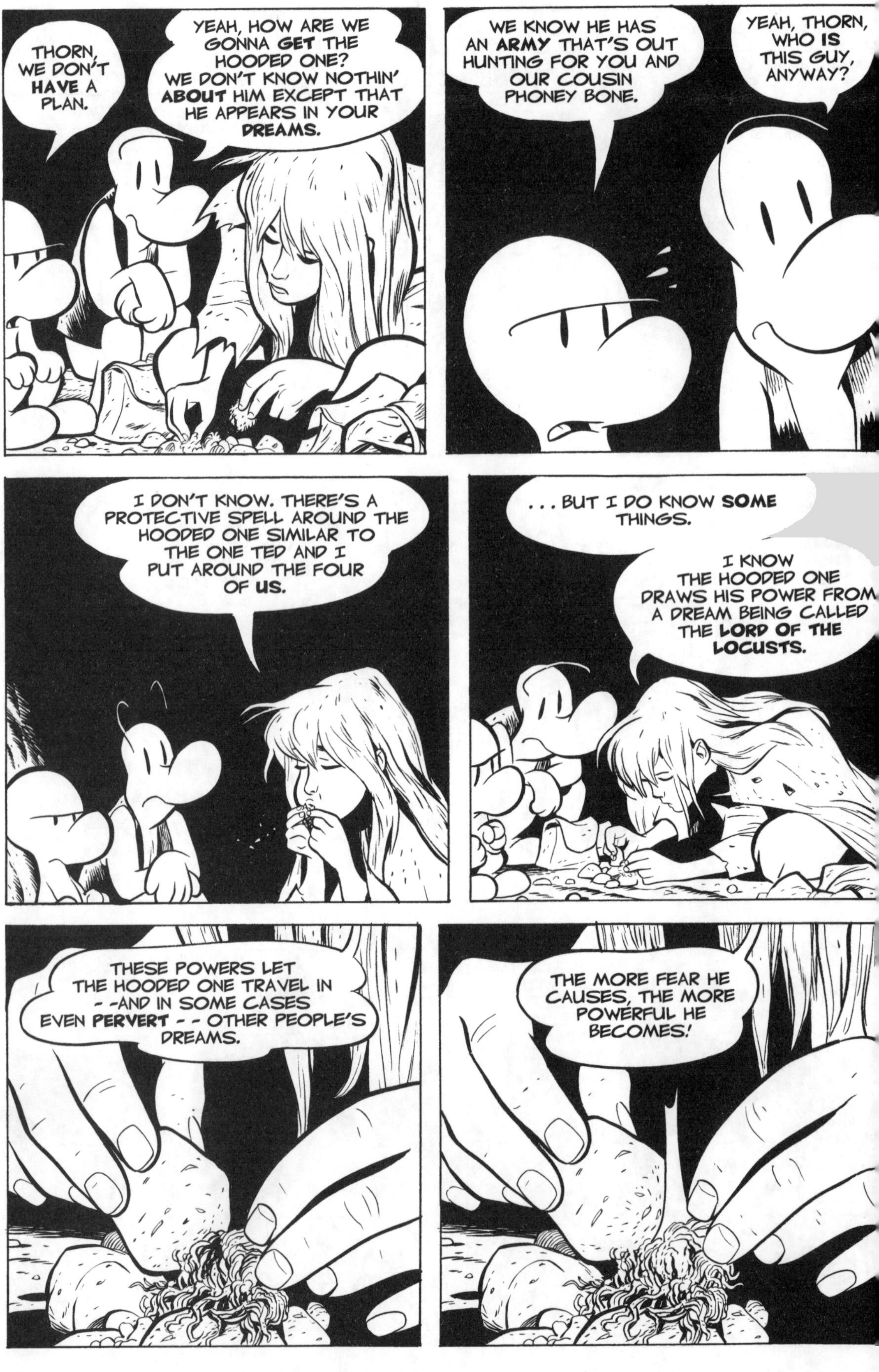
THORN, WE DON'T **HAVE** A PLAN.
YEAH, HOW ARE WE GONNA **GET** THE HOODED ONE? WE DON'T KNOW NOTHIN' **ABOUT** HIM EXCEPT THAT HE APPEARS IN YOUR **DREAMS.**
WE KNOW HE HAS AN **ARMY** THAT'S OUT HUNTING FOR YOU AND OUR COUSIN PHONEY BONE.
YEAH, THORN, WHO **IS** THIS GUY, ANYWAY?
I DON'T KNOW. THERE'S A PROTECTIVE SPELL AROUND THE HOODED ONE SIMILAR TO THE ONE TED AND I PUT AROUND THE FOUR OF **US.**
. . . BUT I DO KNOW **SOME** THINGS.
I KNOW THE HOODED ONE DRAWS HIS POWER FROM A DREAM BEING CALLED THE **LORD OF THE LOCUSTS.**
THESE POWERS LET THE HOODED ONE TRAVEL IN - -AND IN SOME CASES EVEN **PERVERT** - - OTHER PEOPLE'S DREAMS.
THE MORE FEAR HE CAUSES, THE MORE POWERFUL HE BECOMES!

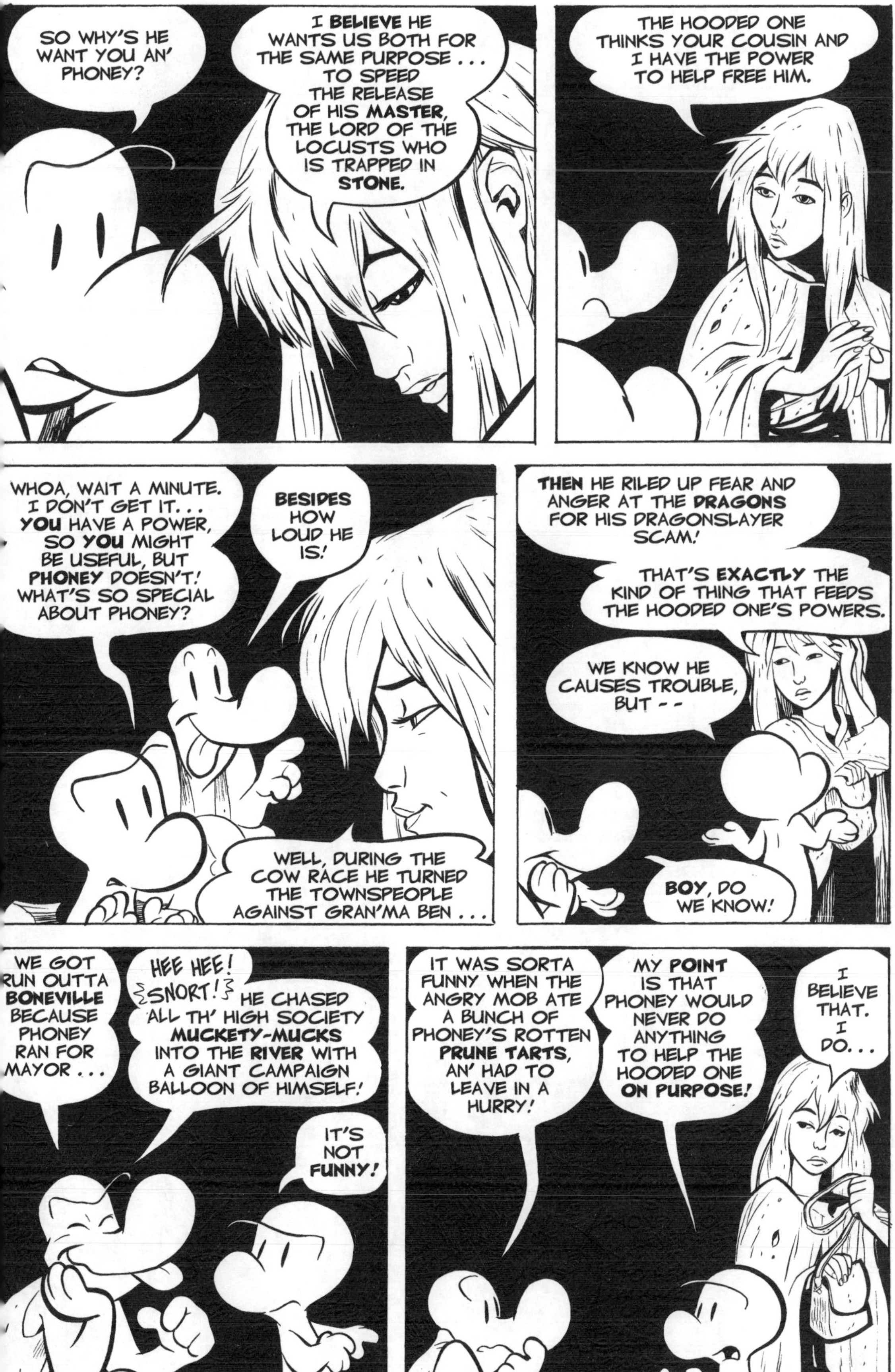
SO WHY'S HE WANT YOU AN' PHONEY?
I **BELIEVE** HE WANTS US BOTH FOR THE SAME PURPOSE . . . TO SPEED THE RELEASE OF HIS **MASTER**, THE LORD OF THE LOCUSTS WHO IS TRAPPED IN **STONE**.
THE HOODED ONE THINKS YOUR COUSIN AND I HAVE THE POWER TO HELP FREE HIM.
WHOA, WAIT A MINUTE. I DON'T GET IT. . . **YOU** HAVE A POWER, SO **YOU** MIGHT BE USEFUL, BUT **PHONEY** DOESN'T! WHAT'S SO SPECIAL ABOUT PHONEY?
BESIDES HOW LOUD HE IS!
WELL, DURING THE COW RACE HE TURNED THE TOWNSPEOPLE AGAINST GRAN'MA BEN . . .
THEN HE RILED UP FEAR AND ANGER AT THE **DRAGONS** FOR HIS DRAGONSLAYER SCAM!
THAT'S **EXACTLY** THE KIND OF THING THAT FEEDS THE HOODED ONE'S POWERS.
WE KNOW HE CAUSES TROUBLE, BUT - -
BOY, DO WE KNOW!
WE GOT RUN OUTTA **BONEVILLE** BECAUSE PHONEY RAN FOR MAYOR . . .
HEE HEE! SNORT!
HE CHASED ALL TH' HIGH SOCIETY **MUCKETY-MUCKS** INTO THE **RIVER** WITH A GIANT CAMPAIGN BALLOON OF HIMSELF!
IT'S NOT **FUNNY**!
IT WAS SORTA FUNNY WHEN THE ANGRY MOB ATE A BUNCH OF PHONEY'S ROTTEN **PRUNE TARTS**, AN' HAD TO LEAVE IN A HURRY!
MY **POINT** IS THAT PHONEY WOULD NEVER DO ANYTHING TO HELP THE HOODED ONE **ON PURPOSE**!
I BELIEVE THAT. I DO. . .

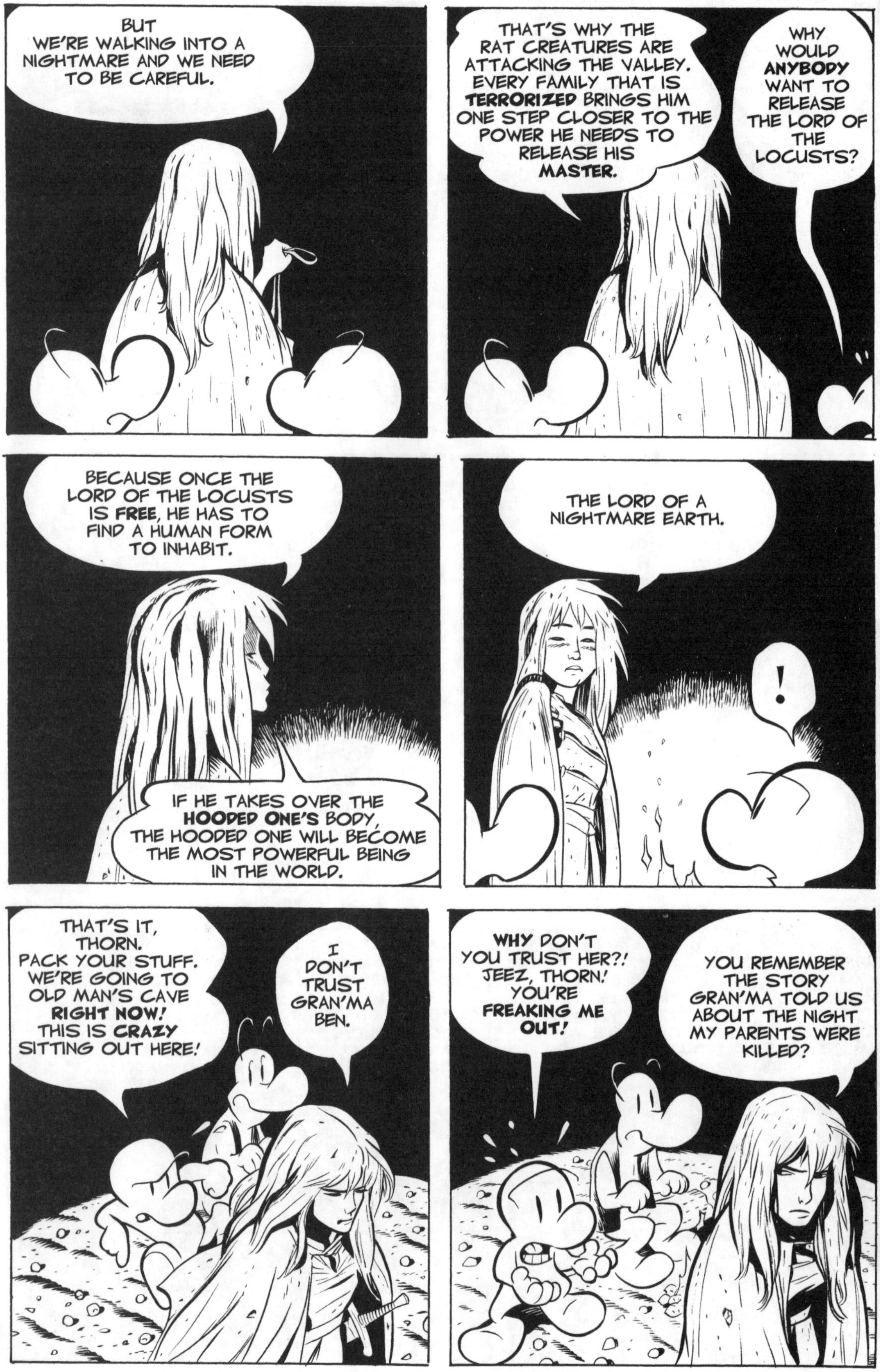
BUT WE'RE WALKING INTO A NIGHTMARE AND WE NEED TO BE CAREFUL.
THAT'S WHY THE RAT CREATURES ARE ATTACKING THE VALLEY. EVERY FAMILY THAT IS TERRORIZED BRINGS HIM ONE STEP CLOSER TO THE POWER HE NEEDS TO RELEASE HIS MASTER.
WHY WOULD ANYBODY WANT TO RELEASE THE LORD OF THE LOCUSTS?
BECAUSE ONCE THE LORD OF THE LOCUSTS IS FREE, HE HAS TO FIND A HUMAN FORM TO INHABIT.
IF HE TAKES OVER THE HOODED ONE'S BODY, THE HOODED ONE WILL BECOME THE MOST POWERFUL BEING IN THE WORLD.
THE LORD OF A NIGHTMARE EARTH.
!
THAT'S IT, THORN. PACK YOUR STUFF. WE'RE GOING TO OLD MAN'S CAVE RIGHT NOW! THIS IS CRAZY SITTING OUT HERE!
I DON'T TRUST GRAN'MA BEN.
WHY DON'T YOU TRUST HER?! JEEZ, THORN! YOU'RE FREAKING ME OUT!
YOU REMEMBER THE STORY GRAN'MA TOLD US ABOUT THE NIGHT MY PARENTS WERE KILLED?

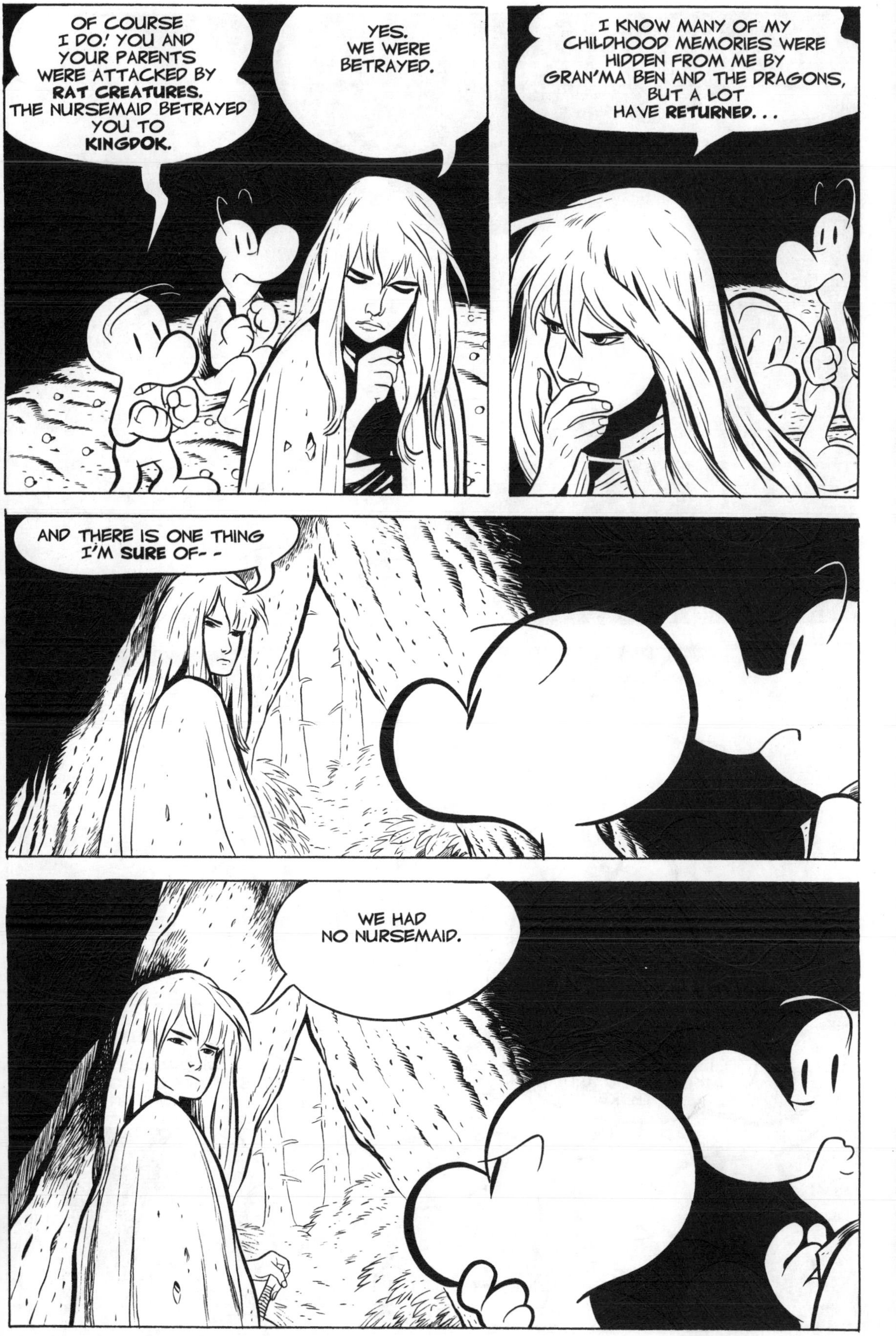
OF COURSE I DO! YOU AND YOUR PARENTS WERE ATTACKED BY **RAT CREATURES.** THE NURSEMAID BETRAYED YOU TO **KINGDOK.**
YES. WE WERE BETRAYED.
I KNOW MANY OF MY CHILDHOOD MEMORIES WERE HIDDEN FROM ME BY GRAN'MA BEN AND THE DRAGONS, BUT A LOT HAVE **RETURNED**. . .
AND THERE IS ONE THING I'M **SURE** OF- -
WE HAD NO NURSEMAID.

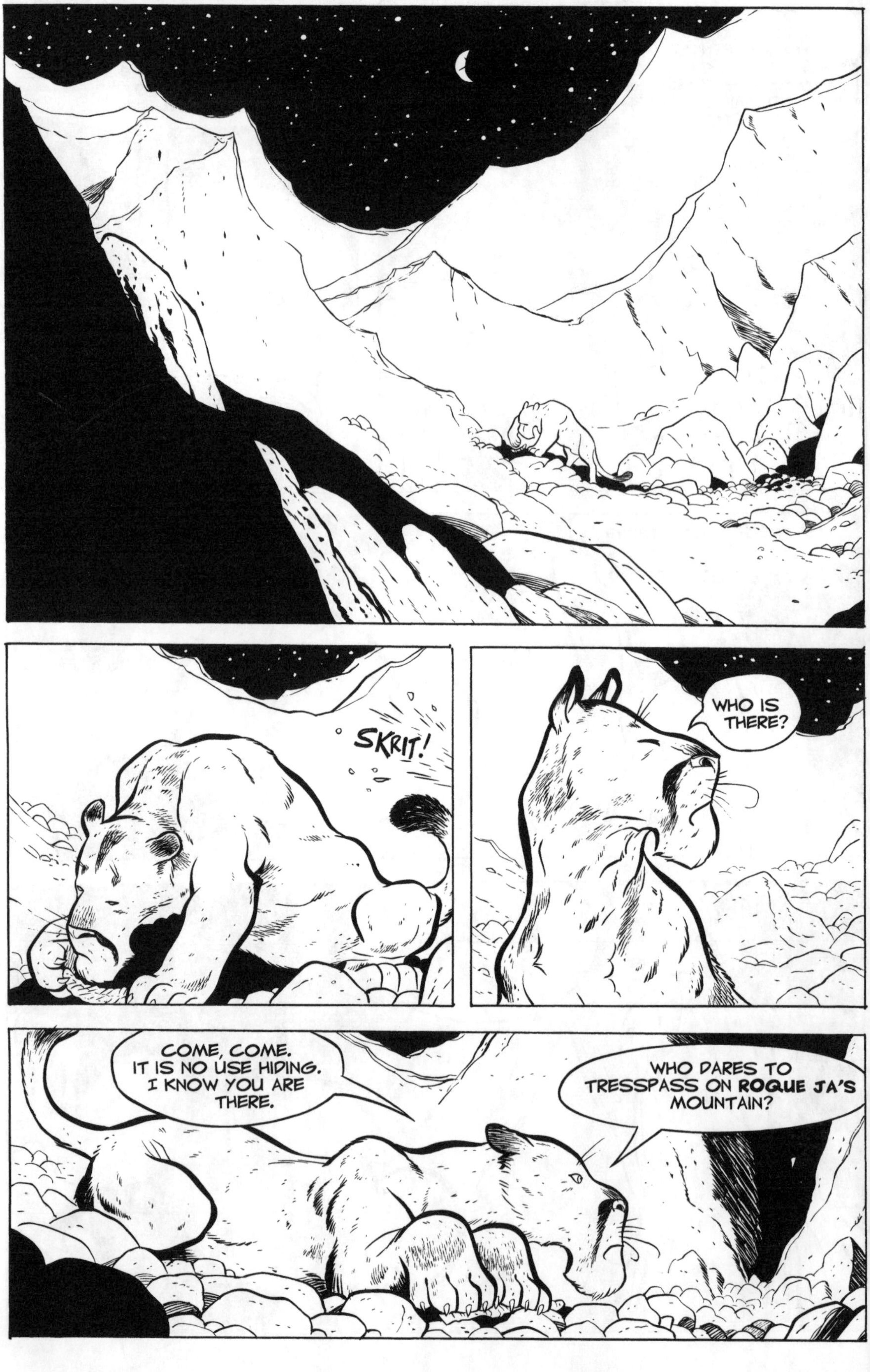
SKRIT!
WHO IS THERE?
COME, COME. IT IS NO USE HIDING. I KNOW YOU ARE THERE.
WHO DARES TO TRESSPASS ON **ROQUE JA'S** MOUNTAIN?

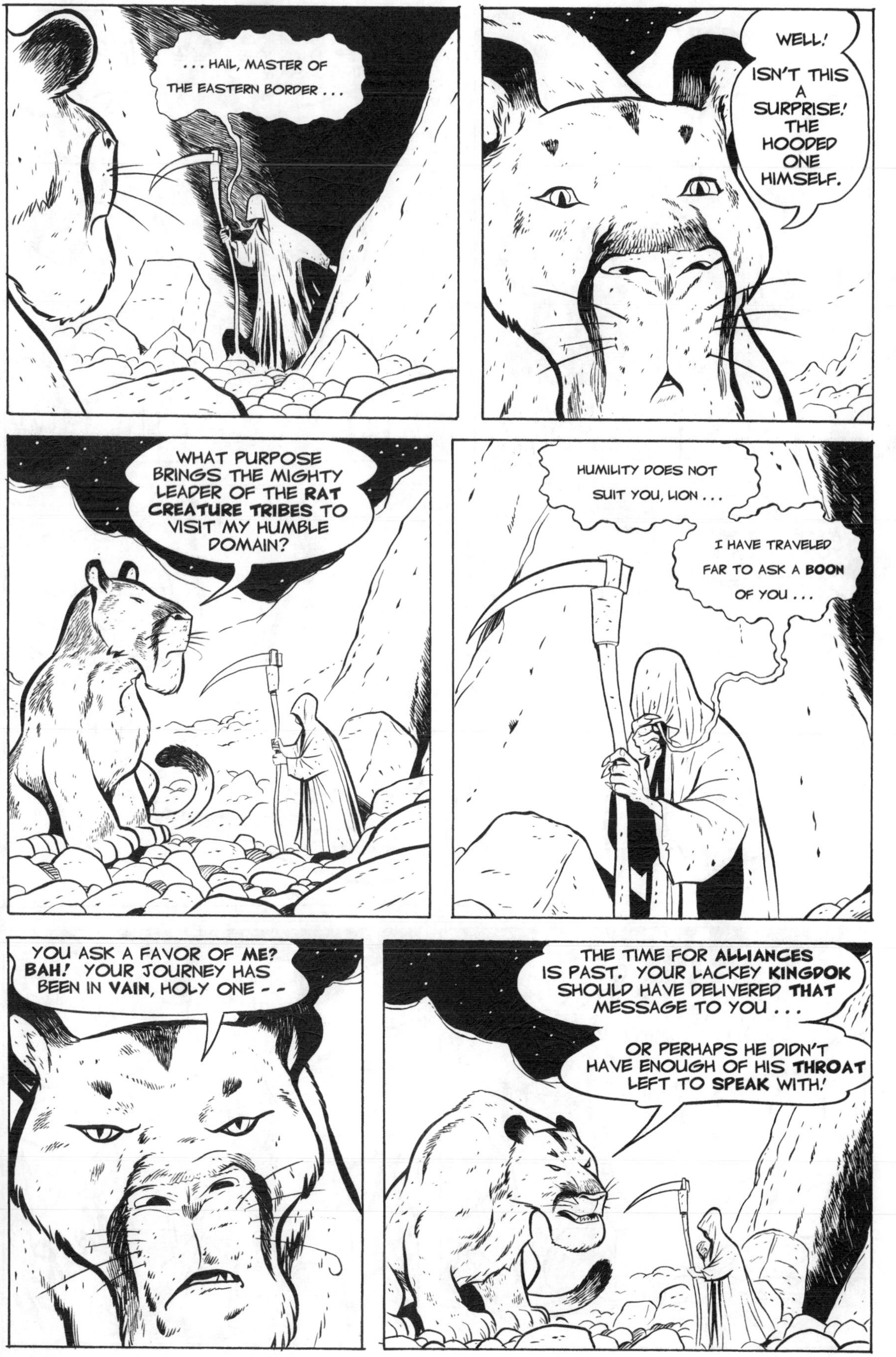
. . . HAIL, MASTER OF THE EASTERN BORDER . . .
WELL! ISN'T THIS A SURPRISE! THE HOODED ONE HIMSELF.
WHAT PURPOSE BRINGS THE MIGHTY LEADER OF THE RAT CREATURE TRIBES TO VISIT MY HUMBLE DOMAIN?
HUMILITY DOES NOT SUIT YOU, LION . . .
I HAVE TRAVELED FAR TO ASK A BOON OF YOU . . .
YOU ASK A FAVOR OF ME? BAH! YOUR JOURNEY HAS BEEN IN VAIN, HOLY ONE - -
THE TIME FOR ALLIANCES IS PAST. YOUR LACKEY KINGDOK SHOULD HAVE DELIVERED THAT MESSAGE TO YOU . . .
OR PERHAPS HE DIDN'T HAVE ENOUGH OF HIS THROAT LEFT TO SPEAK WITH!

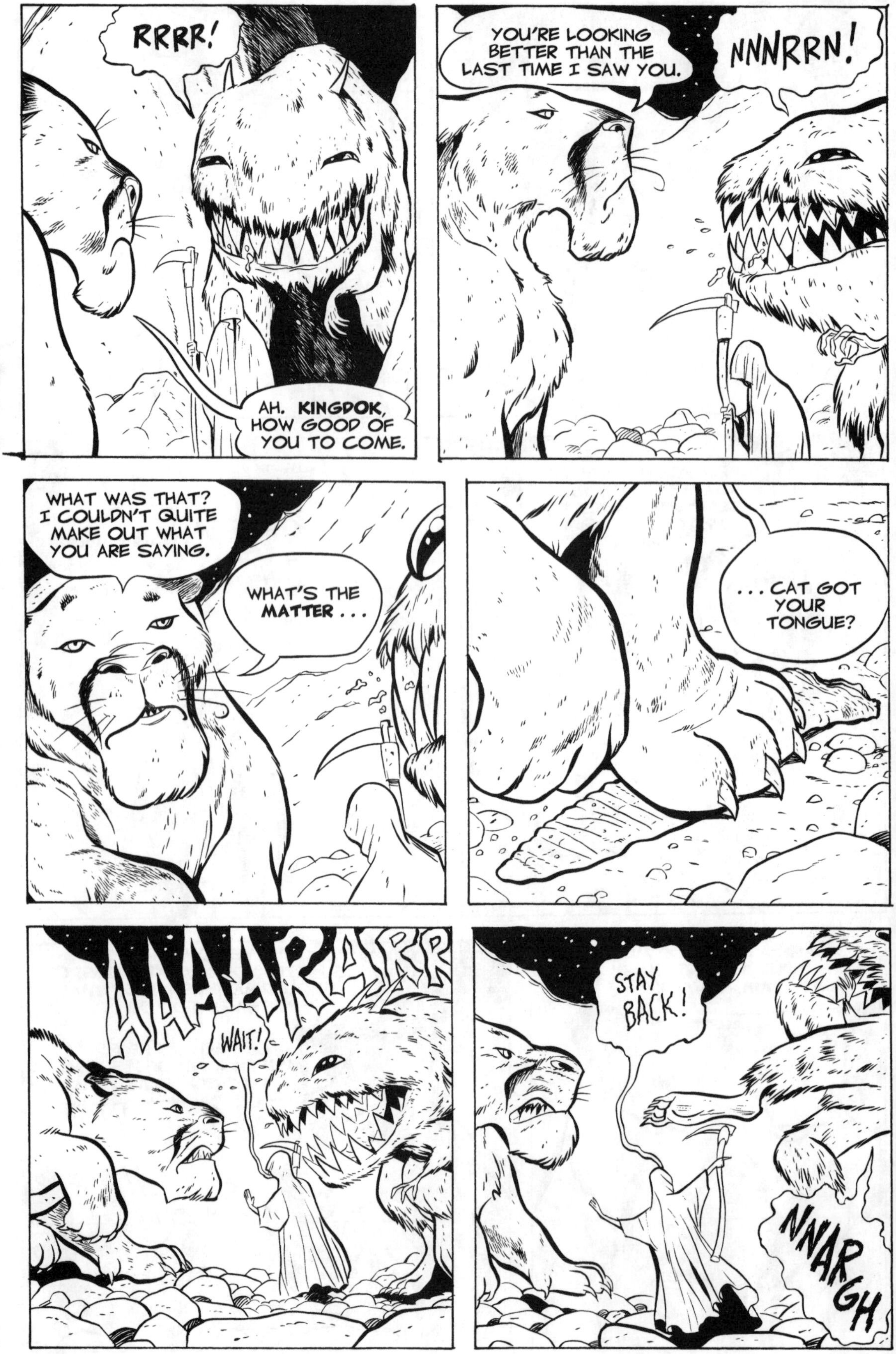
RRRR!
AH. KINGDOK, HOW GOOD OF YOU TO COME.
YOU'RE LOOKING BETTER THAN THE LAST TIME I SAW YOU.
NNNRRN!
WHAT WAS THAT? I COULDN'T QUITE MAKE OUT WHAT YOU ARE SAYING.
WHAT'S THE MATTER . . .
. . . CAT GOT YOUR TONGUE?
AAAARARR
WAIT!
STAY BACK!
NNARGH

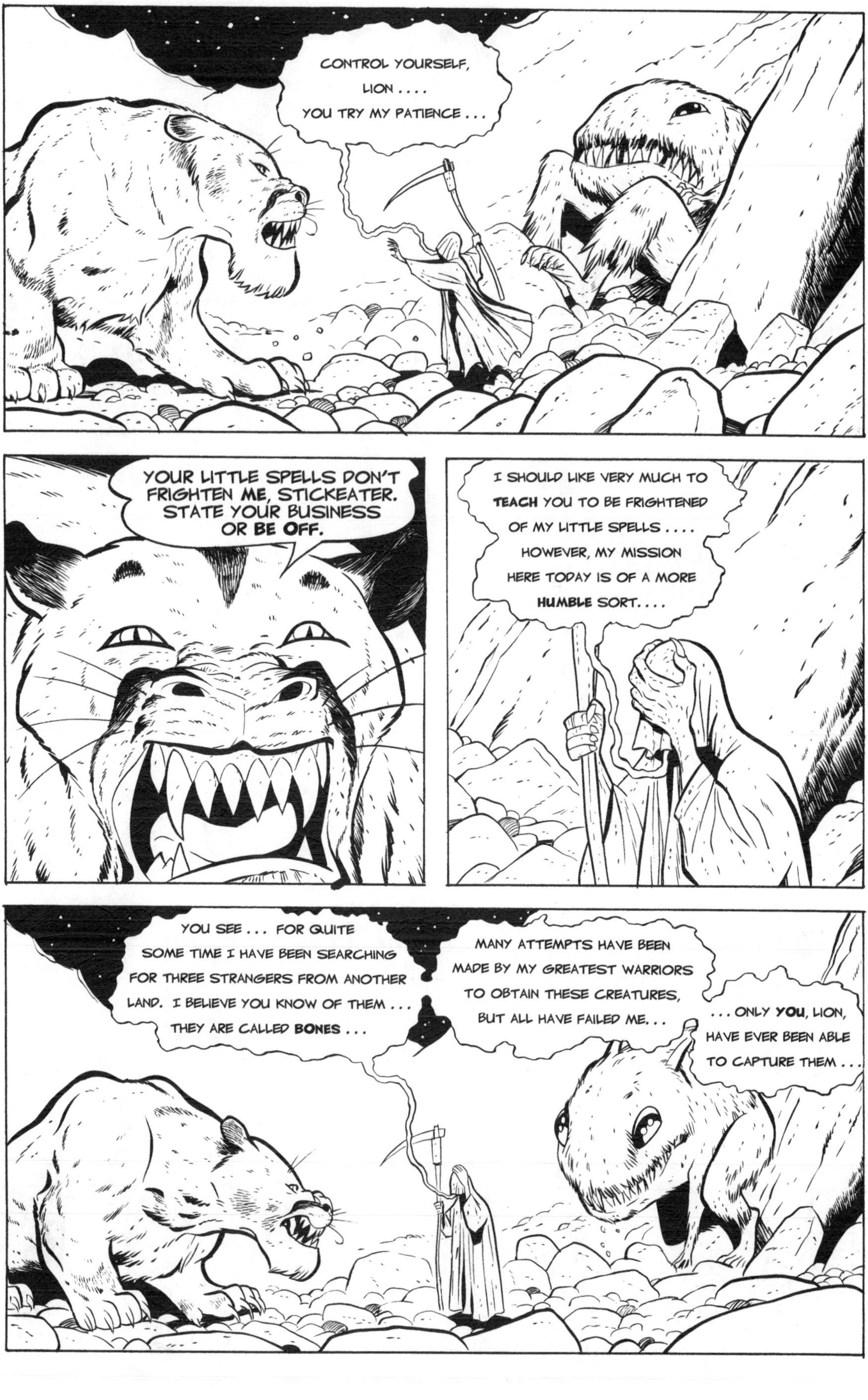
CONTROL YOURSELF, LION . . . . YOU TRY MY PATIENCE . . .
YOUR LITTLE SPELLS DON'T FRIGHTEN ME, STICKEATER. STATE YOUR BUSINESS OR BE OFF.
I SHOULD LIKE VERY MUCH TO TEACH YOU TO BE FRIGHTENED OF MY LITTLE SPELLS . . . . HOWEVER, MY MISSION HERE TODAY IS OF A MORE HUMBLE SORT. . . .
YOU SEE . . . FOR QUITE SOME TIME I HAVE BEEN SEARCHING FOR THREE STRANGERS FROM ANOTHER LAND. I BELIEVE YOU KNOW OF THEM . . . THEY ARE CALLED BONES . . .
MANY ATTEMPTS HAVE BEEN MADE BY MY GREATEST WARRIORS TO OBTAIN THESE CREATURES, BUT ALL HAVE FAILED ME. . .
. . . ONLY YOU, LION, HAVE EVER BEEN ABLE TO CAPTURE THEM . . .

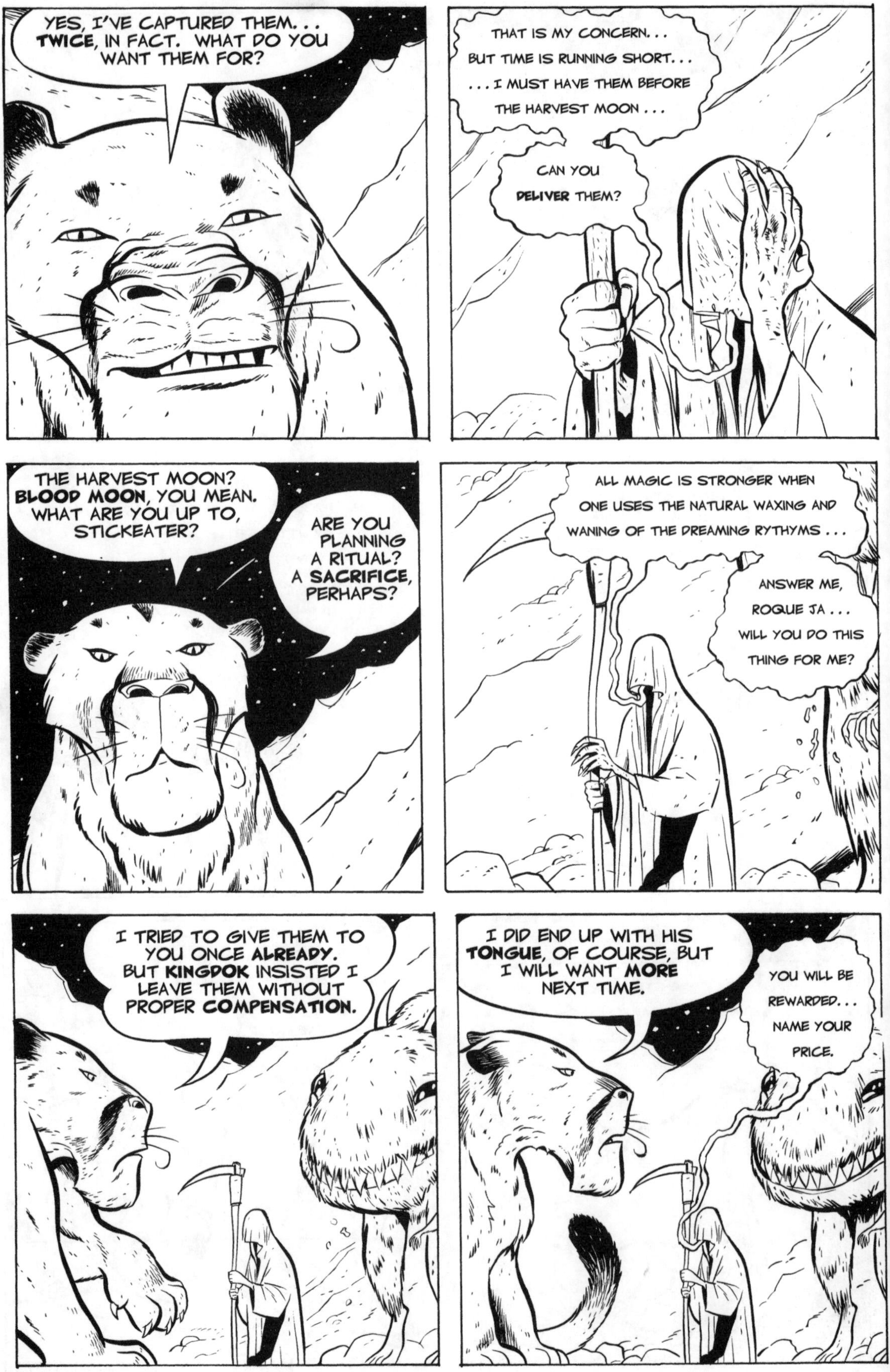
YES, I'VE CAPTURED THEM... **TWICE**, IN FACT. WHAT DO YOU WANT THEM FOR?
THAT IS MY CONCERN... BUT TIME IS RUNNING SHORT... ...I MUST HAVE THEM BEFORE THE HARVEST MOON...
CAN YOU **DELIVER** THEM?
THE HARVEST MOON? **BLOOD MOON**, YOU MEAN. WHAT ARE YOU UP TO, STICKEATER?
ARE YOU PLANNING A RITUAL? A **SACRIFICE**, PERHAPS?
ALL MAGIC IS STRONGER WHEN ONE USES THE NATURAL WAXING AND WANING OF THE DREAMING RYTHYMS...
ANSWER ME, ROQUE JA... WILL YOU DO THIS THING FOR ME?
I TRIED TO GIVE THEM TO YOU ONCE **ALREADY**. BUT **KINGDOK** INSISTED I LEAVE THEM WITHOUT PROPER **COMPENSATION**.
I DID END UP WITH HIS **TONGUE**, OF COURSE, BUT I WILL WANT **MORE** NEXT TIME.
YOU WILL BE REWARDED... NAME YOUR PRICE.

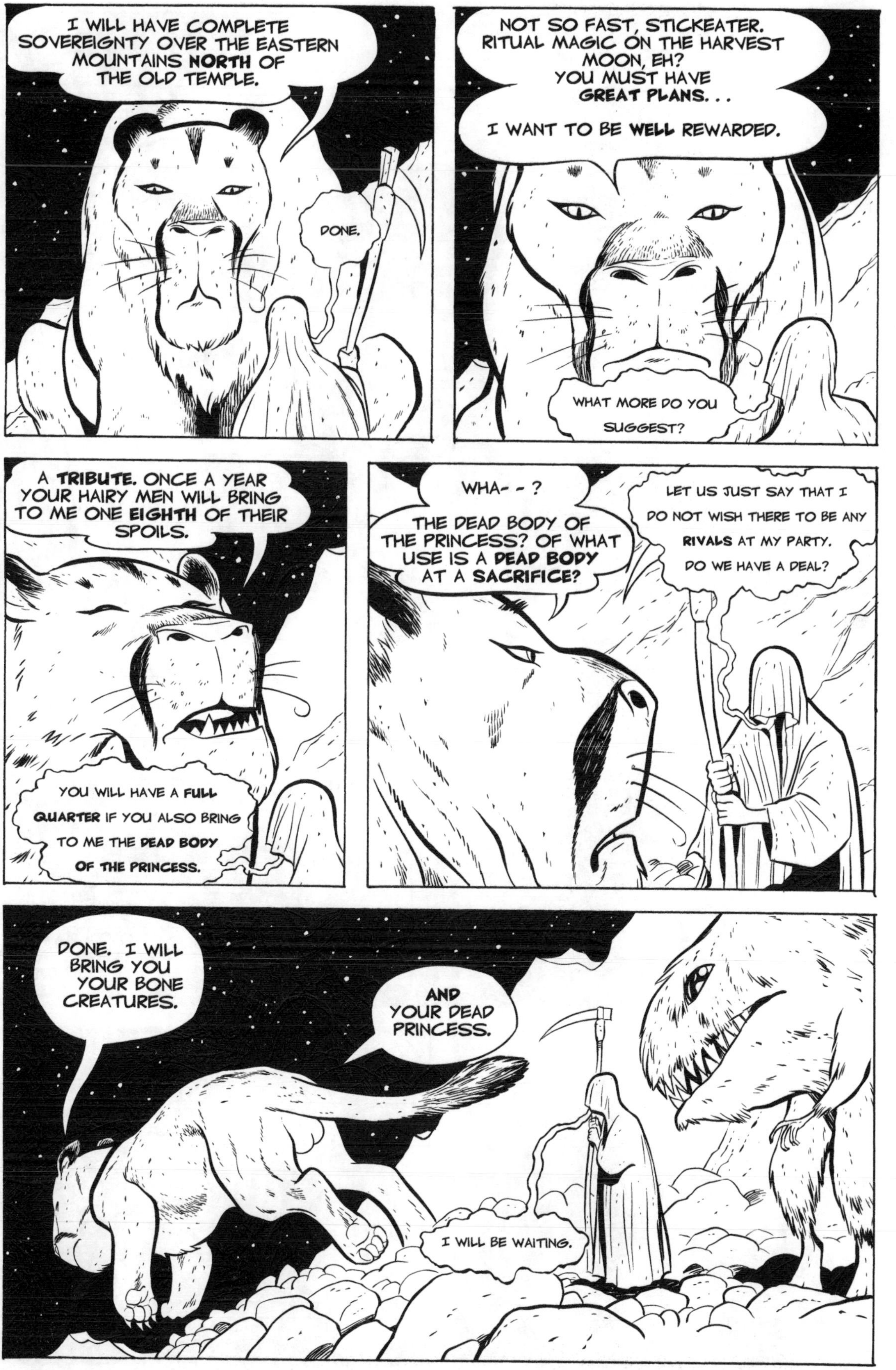
I WILL HAVE COMPLETE SOVEREIGNTY OVER THE EASTERN MOUNTAINS NORTH OF THE OLD TEMPLE.
DONE.
NOT SO FAST, STICKEATER. RITUAL MAGIC ON THE HARVEST MOON, EH? YOU MUST HAVE GREAT PLANS. . .
I WANT TO BE WELL REWARDED.
WHAT MORE DO YOU SUGGEST?
A TRIBUTE. ONCE A YEAR YOUR HAIRY MEN WILL BRING TO ME ONE EIGHTH OF THEIR SPOILS.
YOU WILL HAVE A FULL QUARTER IF YOU ALSO BRING TO ME THE DEAD BODY OF THE PRINCESS.
WHA- - ?
THE DEAD BODY OF THE PRINCESS? OF WHAT USE IS A DEAD BODY AT A SACRIFICE?
LET US JUST SAY THAT I DO NOT WISH THERE TO BE ANY RIVALS AT MY PARTY. DO WE HAVE A DEAL?
DONE. I WILL BRING YOU YOUR BONE CREATURES.
AND YOUR DEAD PRINCESS.
I WILL BE WAITING.

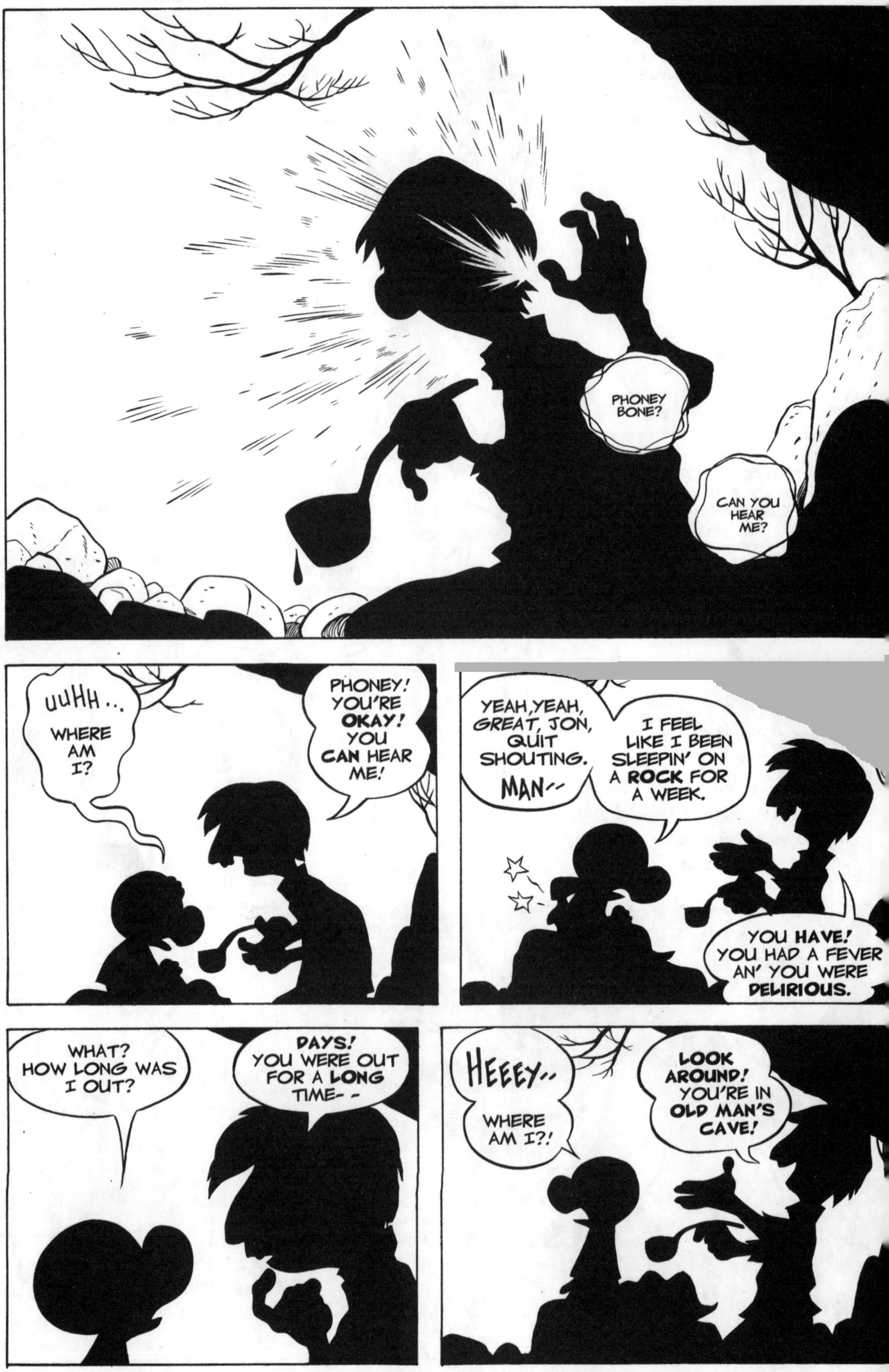
PHONEY BONE?
CAN YOU HEAR ME?
UUHH...
WHERE AM I?
PHONEY! YOU'RE **OKAY**! YOU **CAN** HEAR ME!
YEAH, YEAH, GREAT, JON, QUIT SHOUTING.
MAN--
I FEEL LIKE I BEEN SLEEPIN' ON A **ROCK** FOR A WEEK.
YOU **HAVE**! YOU HAD A FEVER AN' YOU WERE **DELIRIOUS**.
WHAT? HOW LONG WAS I OUT?
DAYS! YOU WERE OUT FOR A **LONG** TIME- -
HEEEY..
WHERE AM I?!
LOOK AROUND! YOU'RE IN **OLD MAN'S CAVE**!

ISN'T IT **EXCITING?** JUST LIKE TALES OF THE **OLDEN DAYS!**

BACK WHEN OLD MAN'S CAVE WAS THE MYSTICAL STRONGHOLD OF THE **VENI-YAN** WARRIORS!

WHOA.

YOU GOTTA BE KIDDIN' ME.

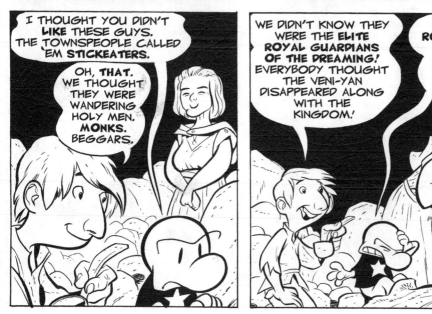

I THOUGHT YOU DIDN'T **LIKE** THESE GUYS. THE TOWNSPEOPLE CALLED 'EM **STICKEATERS.**

OH, **THAT.** WE THOUGHT THEY WERE WANDERING HOLY MEN. **MONKS.** BEGGARS.

WE DIDN'T KNOW THEY WERE THE **ELITE ROYAL GUARDIANS OF THE DREAMING!** EVERYBODY THOUGHT THE VENI-YAN DISAPPEARED ALONG WITH THE KINGDOM!

KINGDOM? **ROYAL** GUARDIANS?

UH, OH. WAIT A MINUTE -- IT'S ALL COMING BACK TO ME . . .

WELL, LOOK WHO'S FEELING BETTER! GOOD MORNING, PHONCIBLE!

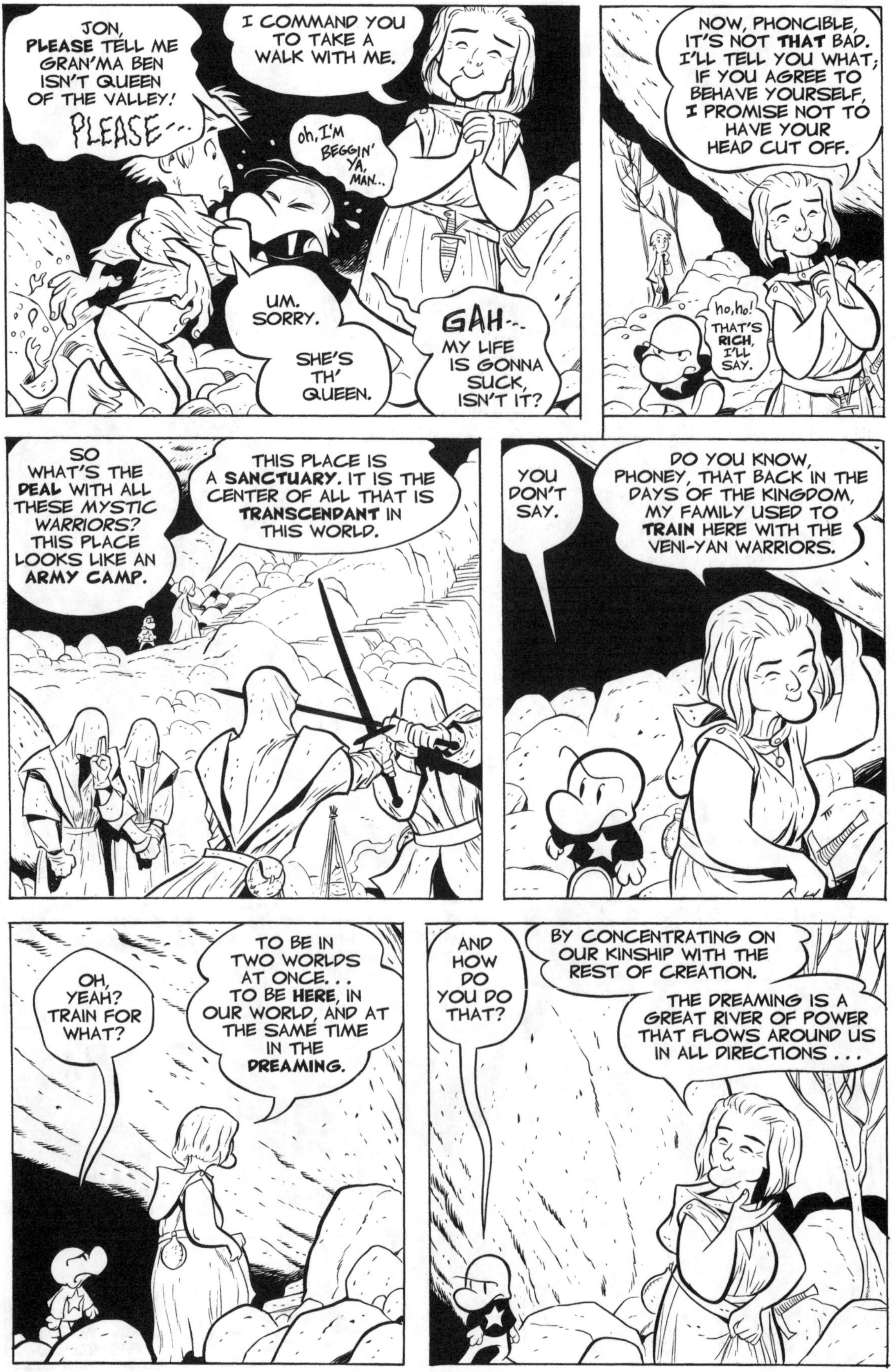
JON, PLEASE TELL ME GRAN'MA BEN ISN'T QUEEN OF THE VALLEY! PLEASE...
I COMMAND YOU TO TAKE A WALK WITH ME.
oh, I'M BEGGIN' YA, MAN...
UM. SORRY.
SHE'S TH' QUEEN.
GAH... MY LIFE IS GONNA SUCK, ISN'T IT?
NOW, PHONCIBLE, IT'S NOT THAT BAD. I'LL TELL YOU WHAT; IF YOU AGREE TO BEHAVE YOURSELF, I PROMISE NOT TO HAVE YOUR HEAD CUT OFF.
ho, ho! THAT'S RICH, I'LL SAY.
SO WHAT'S THE DEAL WITH ALL THESE MYSTIC WARRIORS? THIS PLACE LOOKS LIKE AN ARMY CAMP.
THIS PLACE IS A SANCTUARY. IT IS THE CENTER OF ALL THAT IS TRANSCENDANT IN THIS WORLD.
YOU DON'T SAY.
DO YOU KNOW, PHONEY, THAT BACK IN THE DAYS OF THE KINGDOM, MY FAMILY USED TO TRAIN HERE WITH THE VENI-YAN WARRIORS.
OH, YEAH? TRAIN FOR WHAT?
TO BE IN TWO WORLDS AT ONCE... TO BE HERE, IN OUR WORLD, AND AT THE SAME TIME IN THE DREAMING.
AND HOW DO YOU DO THAT?
BY CONCENTRATING ON OUR KINSHIP WITH THE REST OF CREATION.
THE DREAMING IS A GREAT RIVER OF POWER THAT FLOWS AROUND US IN ALL DIRECTIONS...

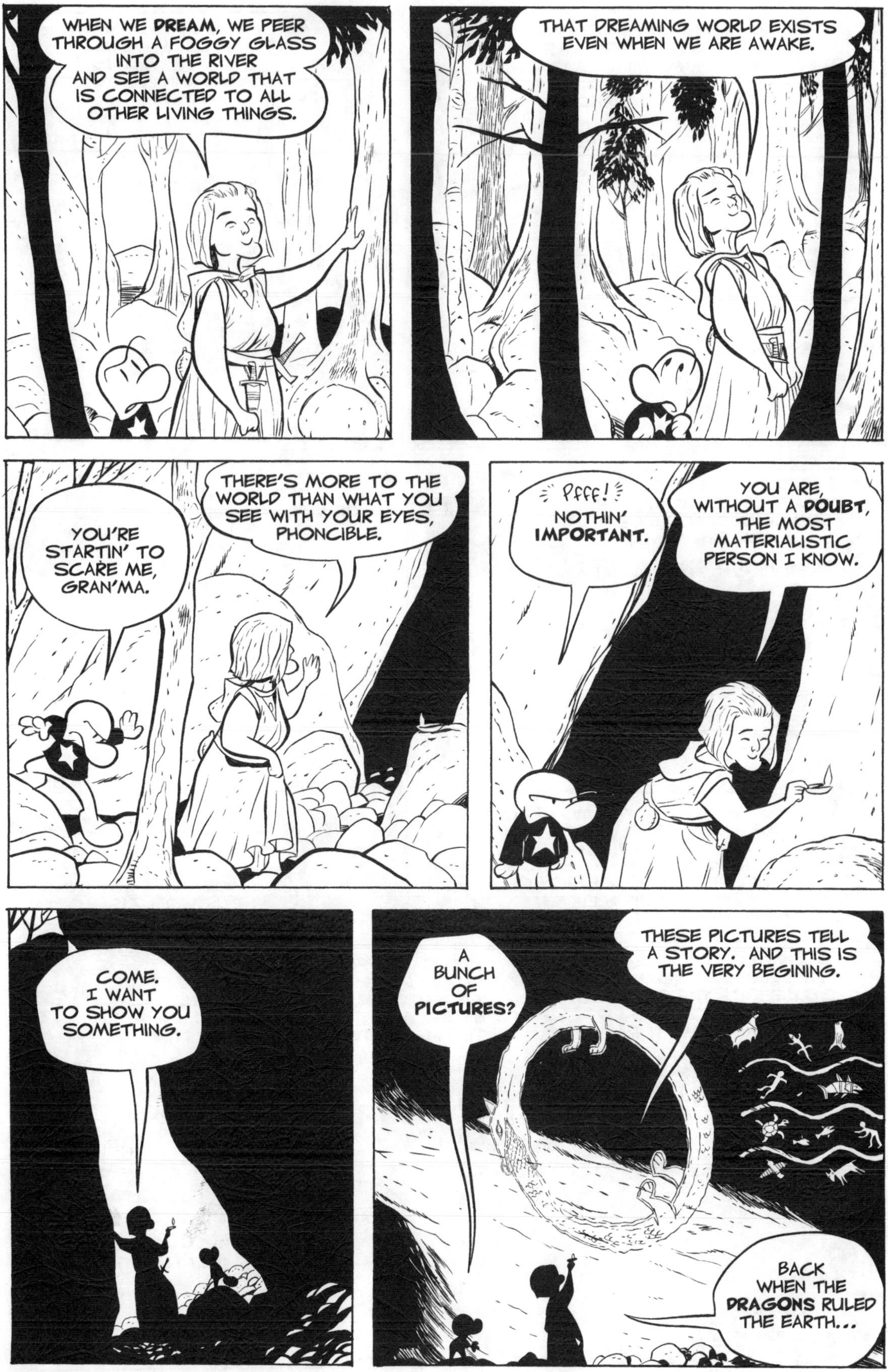
WHEN WE DREAM, WE PEER THROUGH A FOGGY GLASS INTO THE RIVER AND SEE A WORLD THAT IS CONNECTED TO ALL OTHER LIVING THINGS.
THAT DREAMING WORLD EXISTS EVEN WHEN WE ARE AWAKE.
YOU'RE STARTIN' TO SCARE ME, GRAN'MA.
THERE'S MORE TO THE WORLD THAN WHAT YOU SEE WITH YOUR EYES, PHONCIBLE.
Pfff! NOTHIN' IMPORTANT.
YOU ARE, WITHOUT A DOUBT, THE MOST MATERIALISTIC PERSON I KNOW.
COME. I WANT TO SHOW YOU SOMETHING.
A BUNCH OF PICTURES?
THESE PICTURES TELL A STORY. AND THIS IS THE VERY BEGINING.
BACK WHEN THE DRAGONS RULED THE EARTH...

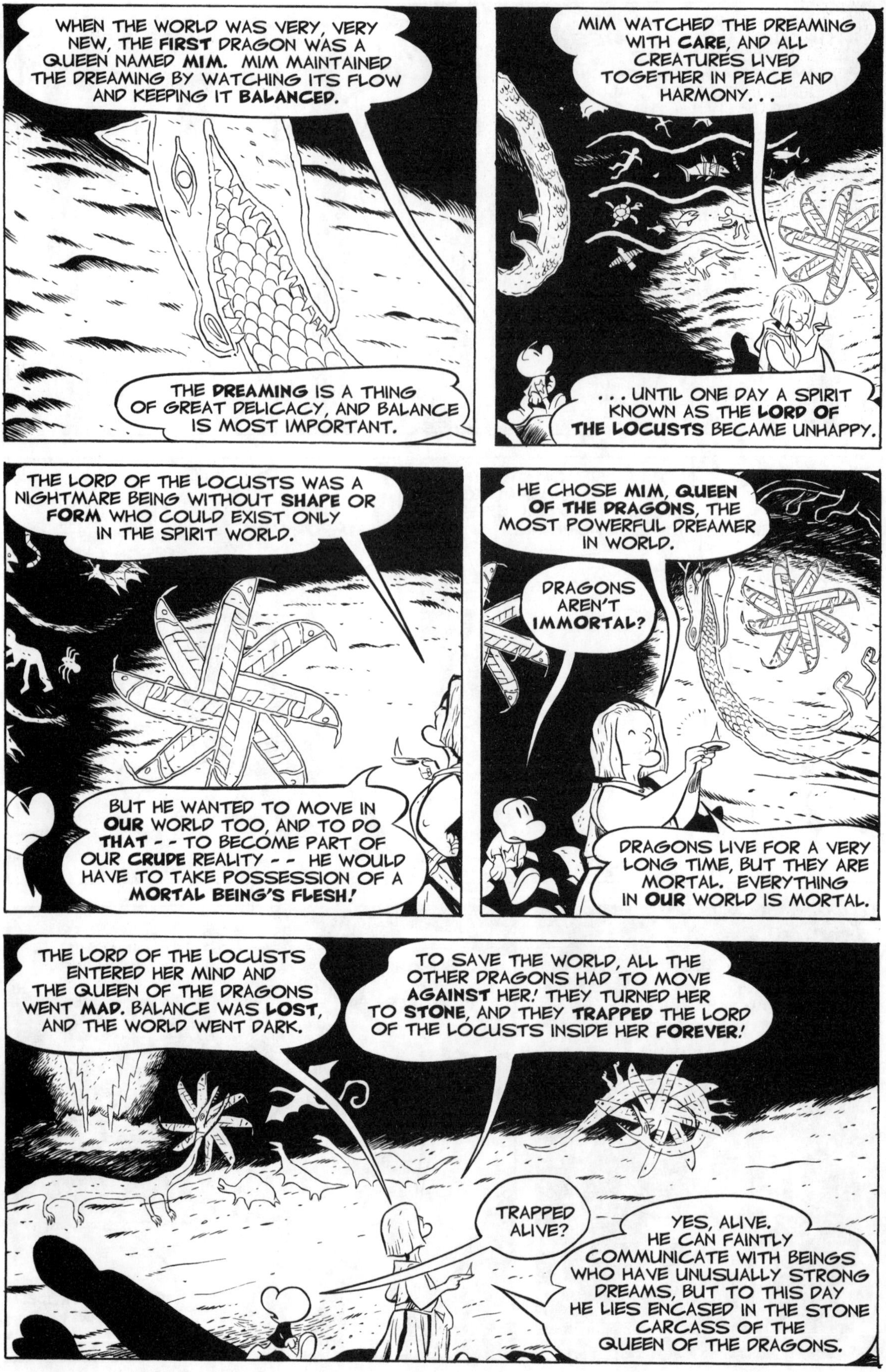
WHEN THE WORLD WAS VERY, VERY NEW, THE **FIRST** DRAGON WAS A QUEEN NAMED **MIM.** MIM MAINTAINED THE DREAMING BY WATCHING ITS FLOW AND KEEPING IT **BALANCED.**
THE **DREAMING** IS A THING OF GREAT DELICACY, AND BALANCE IS MOST IMPORTANT.
MIM WATCHED THE DREAMING WITH **CARE**, AND ALL CREATURES LIVED TOGETHER IN PEACE AND HARMONY. . .
. . . UNTIL ONE DAY A SPIRIT KNOWN AS THE **LORD OF THE LOCUSTS** BECAME UNHAPPY.
THE LORD OF THE LOCUSTS WAS A NIGHTMARE BEING WITHOUT **SHAPE** OR **FORM** WHO COULD EXIST ONLY IN THE SPIRIT WORLD.
BUT HE WANTED TO MOVE IN **OUR** WORLD TOO, AND TO DO **THAT** - - TO BECOME PART OF OUR **CRUDE** REALITY - - HE WOULD HAVE TO TAKE POSSESSION OF A **MORTAL BEING'S FLESH!**
HE CHOSE **MIM, QUEEN OF THE DRAGONS**, THE MOST POWERFUL DREAMER IN WORLD.
DRAGONS AREN'T **IMMORTAL?**
DRAGONS LIVE FOR A VERY LONG TIME, BUT THEY ARE MORTAL. EVERYTHING IN **OUR** WORLD IS MORTAL.
THE LORD OF THE LOCUSTS ENTERED HER MIND AND THE QUEEN OF THE DRAGONS WENT **MAD.** BALANCE WAS **LOST**, AND THE WORLD WENT DARK.
TO SAVE THE WORLD, ALL THE OTHER DRAGONS HAD TO MOVE **AGAINST** HER! THEY TURNED HER TO **STONE**, AND THEY **TRAPPED** THE LORD OF THE LOCUSTS INSIDE HER **FOREVER!**
TRAPPED ALIVE?
YES, ALIVE. HE CAN FAINTLY COMMUNICATE WITH BEINGS WHO HAVE UNUSUALLY STRONG DREAMS, BUT TO THIS DAY HE LIES ENCASED IN THE STONE CARCASS OF THE QUEEN OF THE DRAGONS.

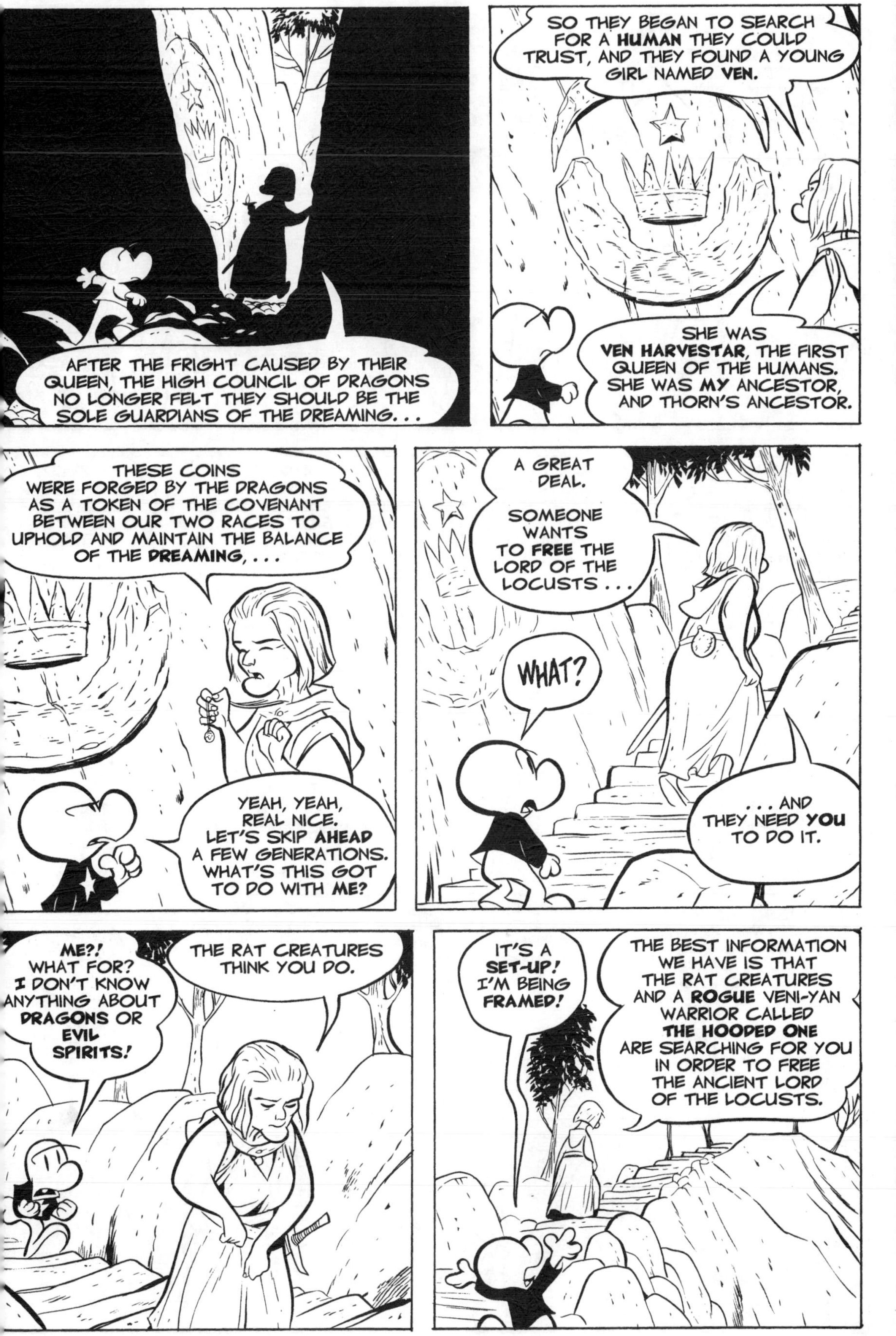

AFTER THE FRIGHT CAUSED BY THEIR QUEEN, THE HIGH COUNCIL OF DRAGONS NO LONGER FELT THEY SHOULD BE THE SOLE GUARDIANS OF THE DREAMING. . .
SO THEY BEGAN TO SEARCH FOR A **HUMAN** THEY COULD TRUST, AND THEY FOUND A YOUNG GIRL NAMED **VEN.**
SHE WAS **VEN HARVESTAR**, THE FIRST QUEEN OF THE HUMANS. SHE WAS **MY** ANCESTOR, AND THORN'S ANCESTOR.
THESE COINS WERE FORGED BY THE DRAGONS AS A TOKEN OF THE COVENANT BETWEEN OUR TWO RACES TO UPHOLD AND MAINTAIN THE BALANCE OF THE **DREAMING**, . . .
YEAH, YEAH, REAL NICE. LET'S SKIP **AHEAD** A FEW GENERATIONS. WHAT'S THIS GOT TO DO WITH **ME**?
A GREAT DEAL.
SOMEONE WANTS TO **FREE** THE LORD OF THE LOCUSTS . . .
WHAT?
. . . AND THEY NEED **YOU** TO DO IT.
ME?! WHAT FOR? **I** DON'T KNOW ANYTHING ABOUT **DRAGONS** OR **EVIL SPIRITS!**
THE RAT CREATURES THINK YOU DO.
IT'S A **SET-UP!** I'M BEING **FRAMED!**
THE BEST INFORMATION WE HAVE IS THAT THE RAT CREATURES AND A **ROGUE** VENI-YAN WARRIOR CALLED **THE HOODED ONE** ARE SEARCHING FOR YOU IN ORDER TO FREE THE ANCIENT LORD OF THE LOCUSTS.

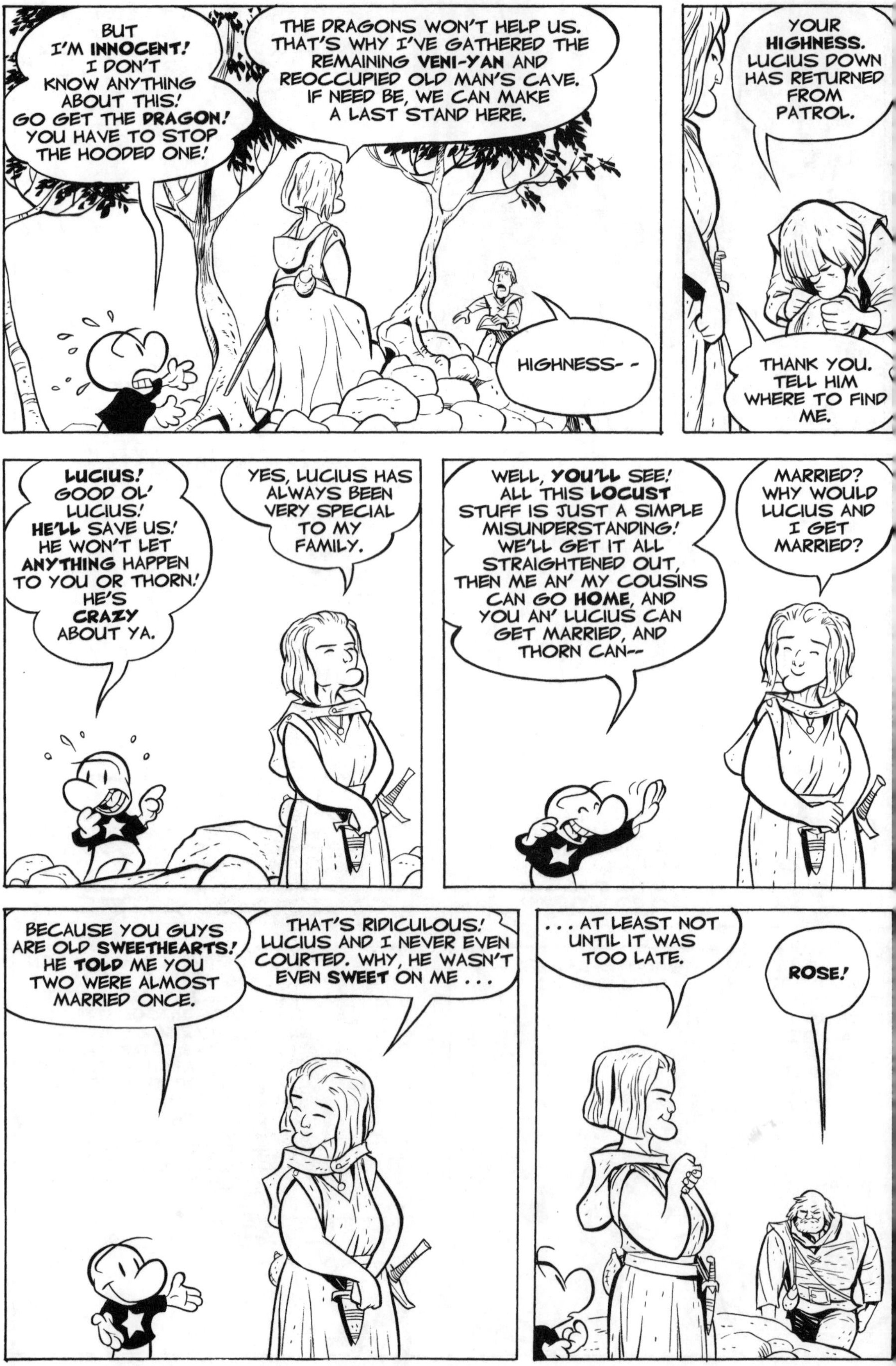
BUT I'M INNOCENT! I DON'T KNOW ANYTHING ABOUT THIS! GO GET THE DRAGON! YOU HAVE TO STOP THE HOODED ONE!
THE DRAGONS WON'T HELP US. THAT'S WHY I'VE GATHERED THE REMAINING VENI-YAN AND REOCCUPIED OLD MAN'S CAVE. IF NEED BE, WE CAN MAKE A LAST STAND HERE.
HIGHNESS--
YOUR HIGHNESS. LUCIUS DOWN HAS RETURNED FROM PATROL.
THANK YOU. TELL HIM WHERE TO FIND ME.
LUCIUS! GOOD OL' LUCIUS! HE'LL SAVE US! HE WON'T LET ANYTHING HAPPEN TO YOU OR THORN! HE'S CRAZY ABOUT YA.
YES, LUCIUS HAS ALWAYS BEEN VERY SPECIAL TO MY FAMILY.
WELL, YOU'LL SEE! ALL THIS LOCUST STUFF IS JUST A SIMPLE MISUNDERSTANDING! WE'LL GET IT ALL STRAIGHTENED OUT, THEN ME AN' MY COUSINS CAN GO HOME, AND YOU AN' LUCIUS CAN GET MARRIED, AND THORN CAN--
MARRIED? WHY WOULD LUCIUS AND I GET MARRIED?
BECAUSE YOU GUYS ARE OLD SWEETHEARTS! HE TOLD ME YOU TWO WERE ALMOST MARRIED ONCE.
THAT'S RIDICULOUS! LUCIUS AND I NEVER EVEN COURTED. WHY, HE WASN'T EVEN SWEET ON ME . . .
. . . AT LEAST NOT UNTIL IT WAS TOO LATE.
ROSE!

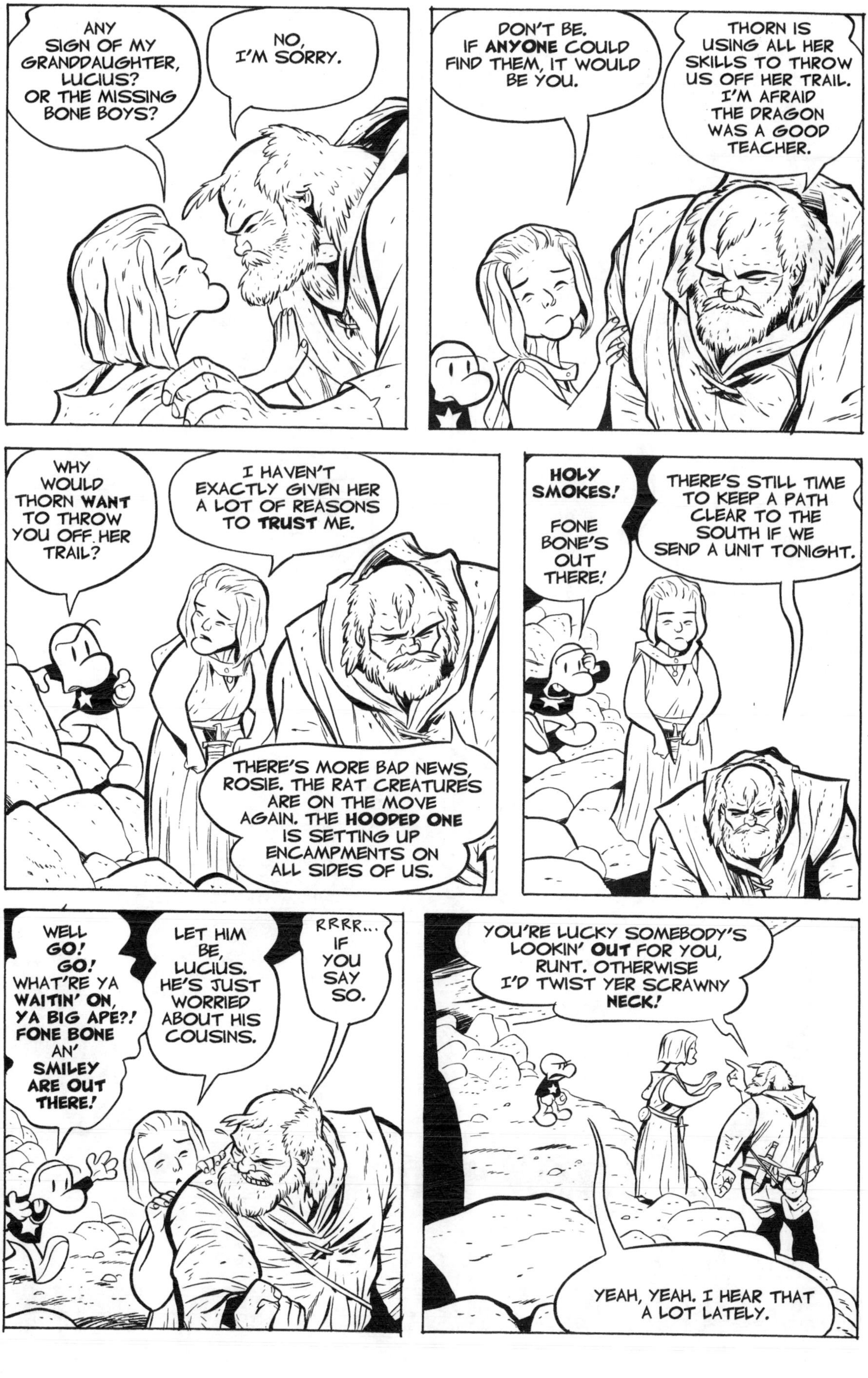
ANY SIGN OF MY GRANDDAUGHTER, LUCIUS? OR THE MISSING BONE BOYS?
NO, I'M SORRY.
DON'T BE. IF **ANYONE** COULD FIND THEM, IT WOULD BE YOU.
THORN IS USING ALL HER SKILLS TO THROW US OFF HER TRAIL. I'M AFRAID THE DRAGON WAS A GOOD TEACHER.
WHY WOULD THORN **WANT** TO THROW YOU OFF HER TRAIL?
I HAVEN'T EXACTLY GIVEN HER A LOT OF REASONS TO **TRUST** ME.
THERE'S MORE BAD NEWS, ROSIE. THE RAT CREATURES ARE ON THE MOVE AGAIN. THE **HOODED ONE** IS SETTING UP ENCAMPMENTS ON ALL SIDES OF US.
HOLY SMOKES!
FONE BONE'S OUT THERE!
THERE'S STILL TIME TO KEEP A PATH CLEAR TO THE SOUTH IF WE SEND A UNIT TONIGHT.
WELL **GO! GO!** WHAT'RE YA **WAITIN' ON, YA BIG APE?!** **FONE BONE** AN' **SMILEY ARE OUT THERE!**
LET HIM BE, LUCIUS. HE'S JUST WORRIED ABOUT HIS COUSINS.
RRRR... IF YOU SAY SO.
YOU'RE LUCKY SOMEBODY'S LOOKIN' **OUT** FOR YOU, RUNT. OTHERWISE I'D TWIST YER SCRAWNY **NECK!**
YEAH, YEAH. I HEAR THAT A LOT LATELY.

WHO **IS** THIS HOODED ONE ANYWAY?

I WISH I KNEW.

OKAY, OKAY, JUST FOR THE SAKE OF **ARGUMENT**, SUPPOSE ALL THIS DREAM STUFF IS **REAL**...

...WHAT WOULD **ACTUALLY HAPPEN** IF THE HOODED ONE MANAGED TO SET THE **LORD OF THE LOCUSTS** FREE?

WHY, THE END OF THE WORLD, OF COURSE.

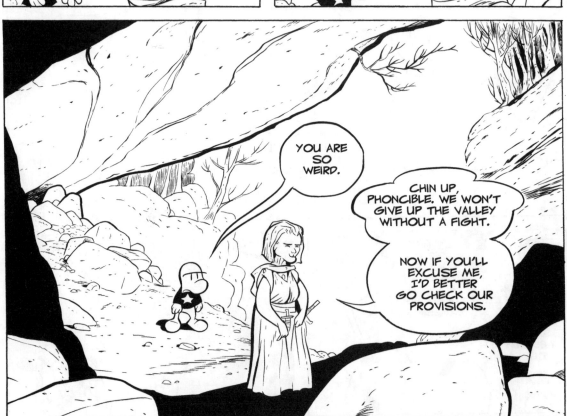

YOU ARE SO WEIRD.

CHIN UP, PHONCIBLE. WE WON'T GIVE UP THE VALLEY WITHOUT A FIGHT.

NOW IF YOU'LL EXCUSE ME, I'D BETTER GO CHECK OUR PROVISIONS.

NEXT: THE SIEGE

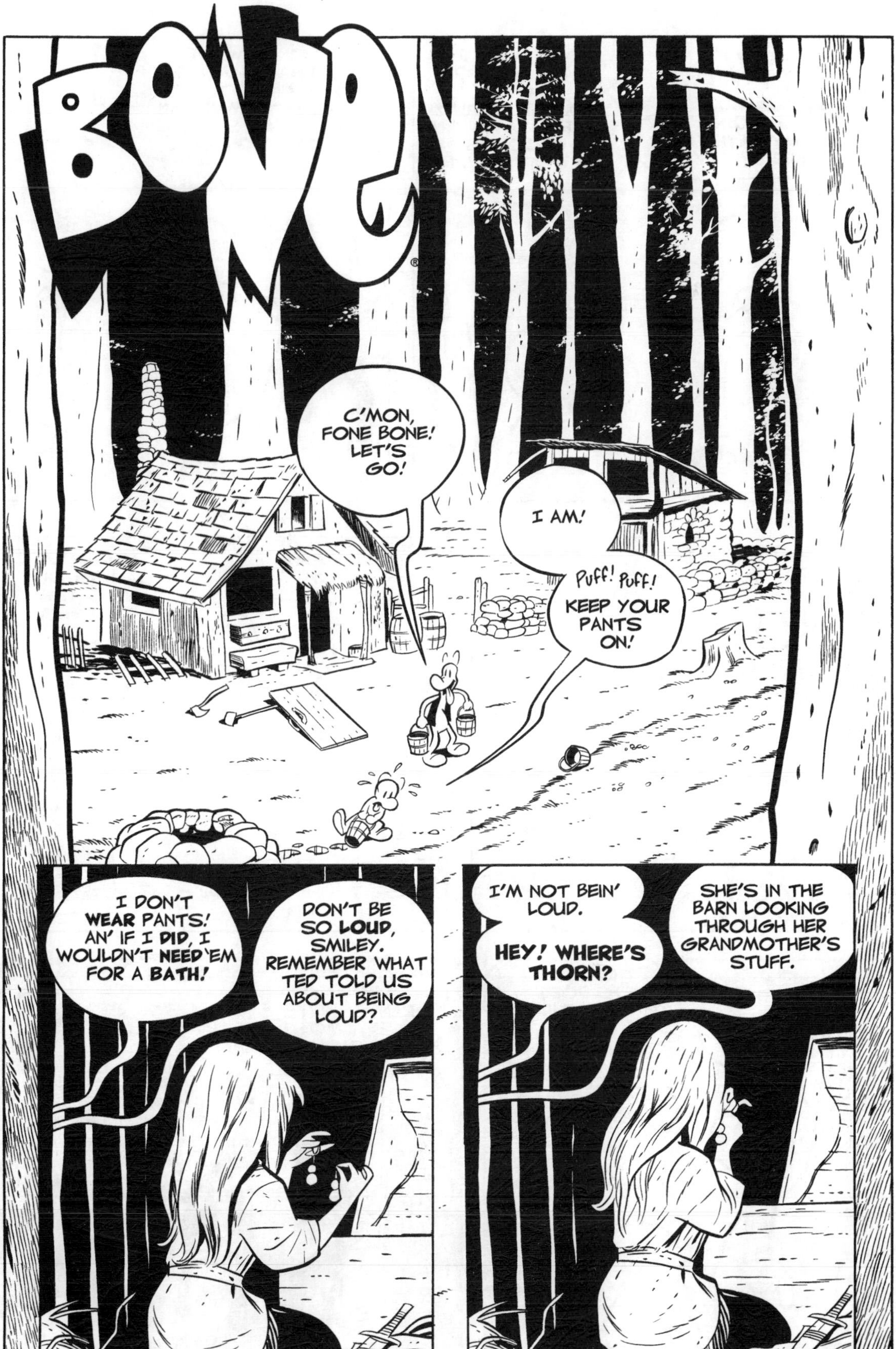
BONE®
C'MON, FONE BONE! LET'S GO!
I AM!
Puff! Puff! KEEP YOUR PANTS ON!
I DON'T **WEAR** PANTS! AN' IF I **DID**, I WOULDN'T **NEED** 'EM FOR A **BATH**!
DON'T BE SO **LOUD**, SMILEY. REMEMBER WHAT TED TOLD US ABOUT BEING LOUD?
I'M NOT BEIN' LOUD.
HEY! WHERE'S THORN?
SHE'S IN THE BARN LOOKING THROUGH HER GRANDMOTHER'S STUFF.

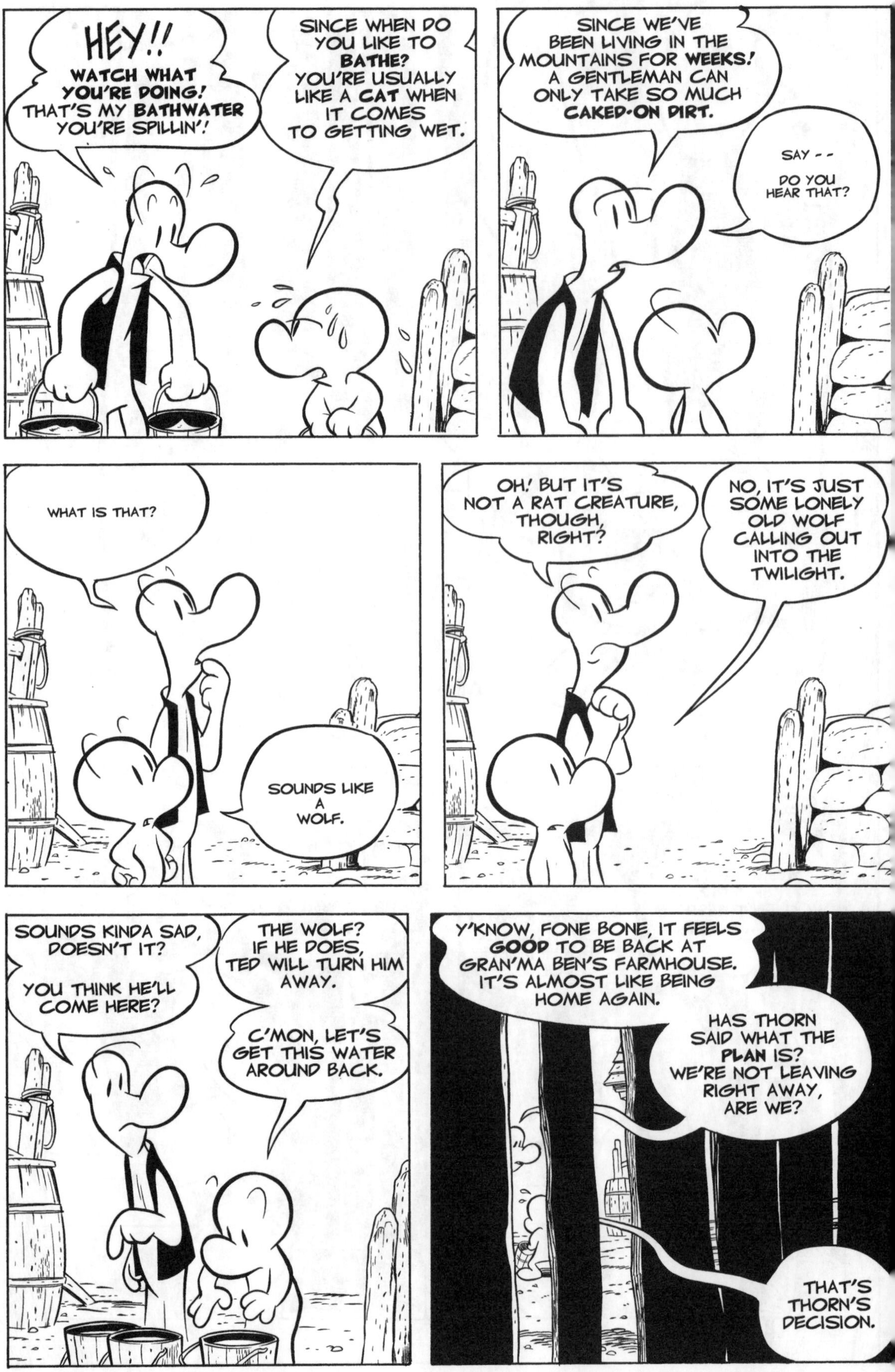
HEY!! WATCH WHAT YOU'RE DOING! THAT'S MY BATHWATER YOU'RE SPILLIN'!
SINCE WHEN DO YOU LIKE TO BATHE? YOU'RE USUALLY LIKE A CAT WHEN IT COMES TO GETTING WET.
SINCE WE'VE BEEN LIVING IN THE MOUNTAINS FOR WEEKS! A GENTLEMAN CAN ONLY TAKE SO MUCH CAKED-ON DIRT.
SAY - - DO YOU HEAR THAT?
WHAT IS THAT?
SOUNDS LIKE A WOLF.
OH! BUT IT'S NOT A RAT CREATURE, THOUGH, RIGHT?
NO, IT'S JUST SOME LONELY OLD WOLF CALLING OUT INTO THE TWILIGHT.
SOUNDS KINDA SAD, DOESN'T IT?
YOU THINK HE'LL COME HERE?
THE WOLF? IF HE DOES, TED WILL TURN HIM AWAY.
C'MON, LET'S GET THIS WATER AROUND BACK.
Y'KNOW, FONE BONE, IT FEELS GOOD TO BE BACK AT GRAN'MA BEN'S FARMHOUSE. IT'S ALMOST LIKE BEING HOME AGAIN.
HAS THORN SAID WHAT THE PLAN IS? WE'RE NOT LEAVING RIGHT AWAY, ARE WE?
THAT'S THORN'S DECISION.

WELL, WHAT DOES SHE **WANT**? ARE WE GONNA STAY HERE, OR ARE WE GONNA GO TO OLD MAN'S CAVE?

NEITHER.

SHE JUST WANTS TO GET SOME THINGS AND GO BACK TO THE MOUNTAINS.

IT'S GRAN'MA BEN, ISN'T IT? THORN DOESN'T TRUST HER ANYMORE.

NOPE. SHE DOESN'T TRUST HER.

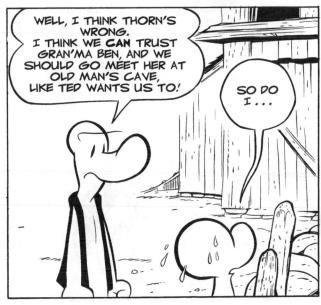

WELL, I THINK THORN'S WRONG. I THINK WE **CAN** TRUST GRAN'MA BEN, AND WE SHOULD GO MEET HER AT OLD MAN'S CAVE, LIKE TED WANTS US TO!

SO DO I...

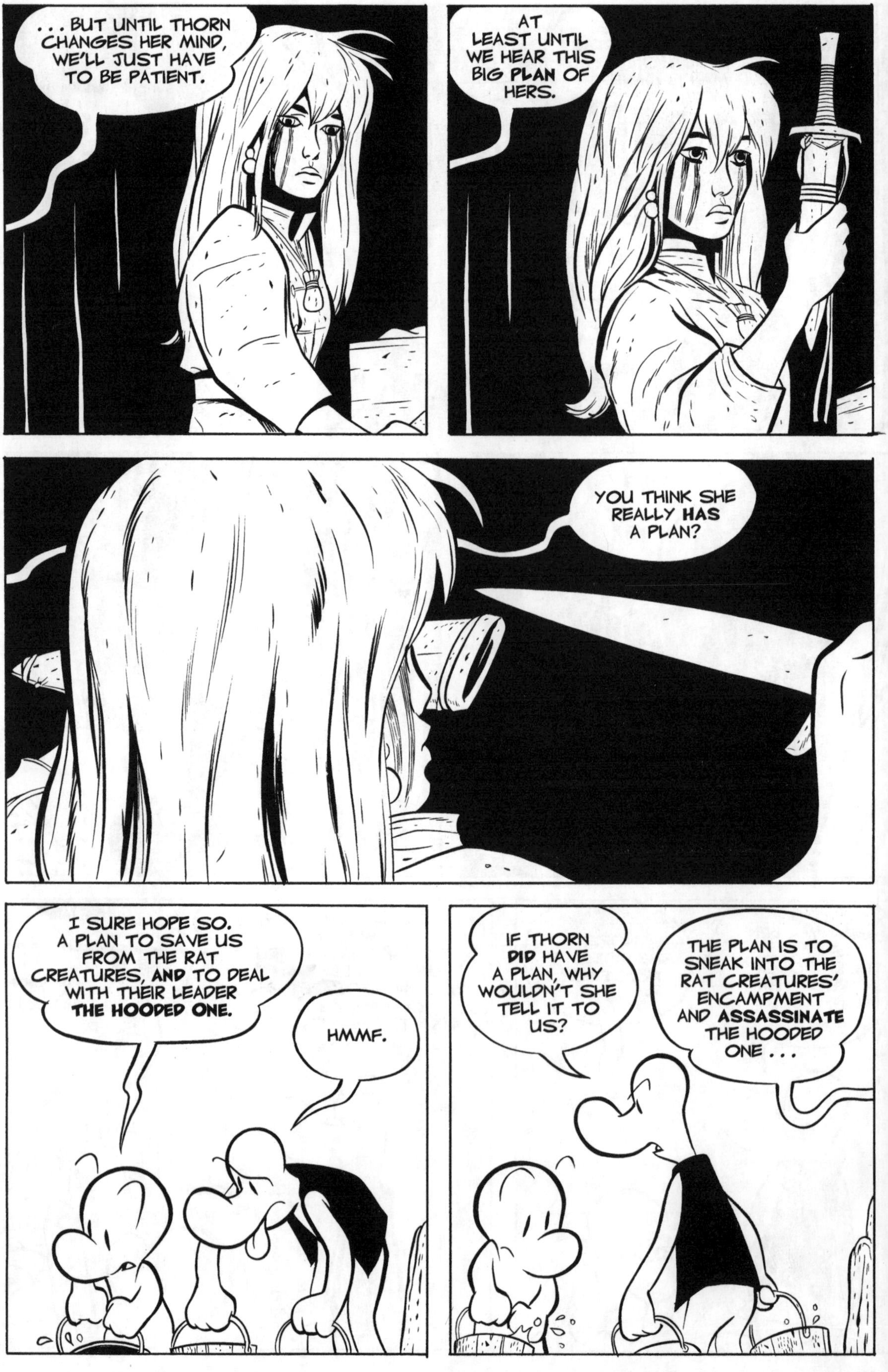
. . . BUT UNTIL THORN CHANGES HER MIND, WE'LL JUST HAVE TO BE PATIENT.
AT LEAST UNTIL WE HEAR THIS BIG **PLAN** OF HERS.
YOU THINK SHE REALLY **HAS** A PLAN?
I SURE HOPE SO. A PLAN TO SAVE US FROM THE RAT CREATURES, **AND** TO DEAL WITH THEIR LEADER **THE HOODED ONE.**
HMMF.
IF THORN **DID** HAVE A PLAN, WHY WOULDN'T SHE TELL IT TO US?
THE PLAN IS TO SNEAK INTO THE RAT CREATURES' ENCAMPMENT AND **ASSASSINATE** THE HOODED ONE . . .

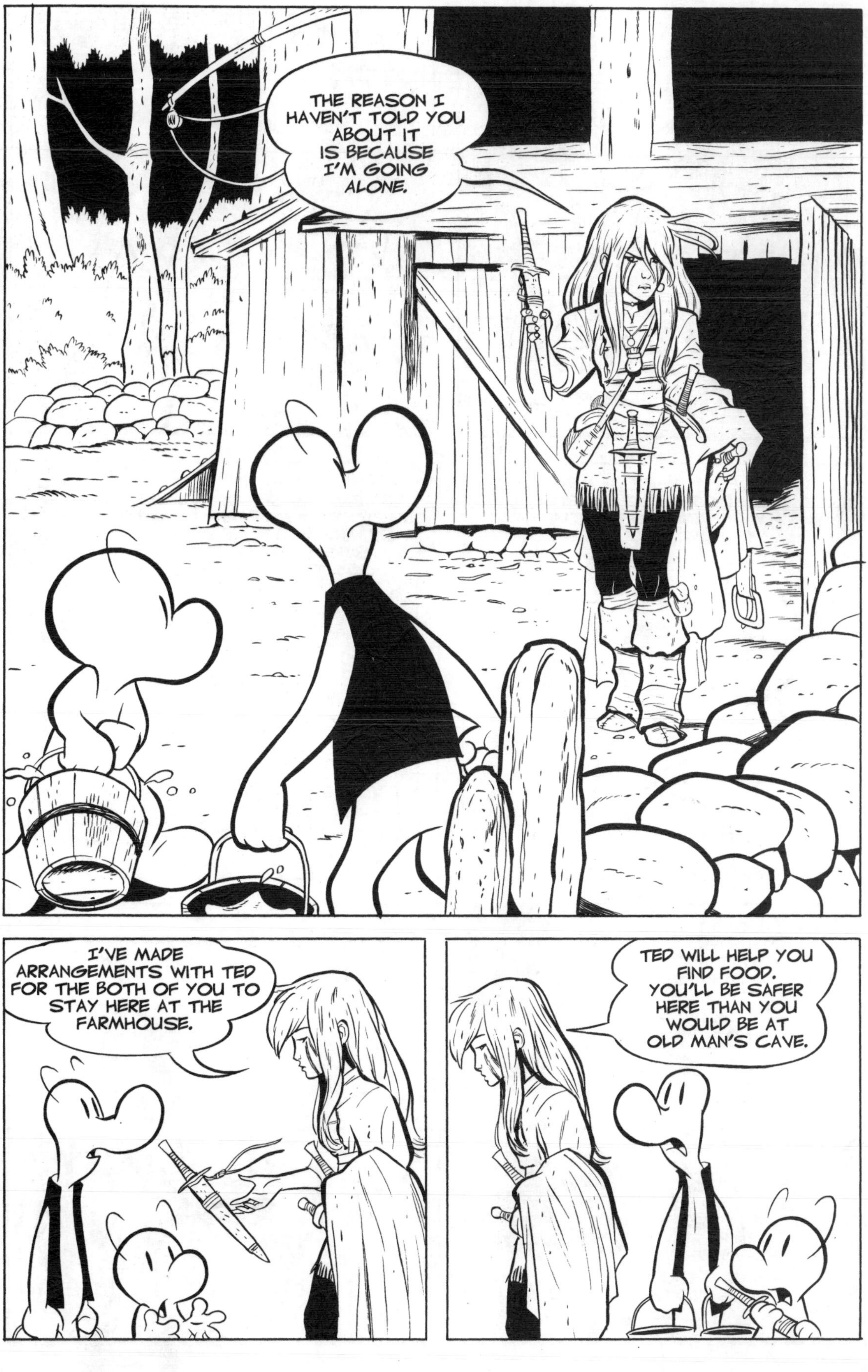
THE REASON I HAVEN'T TOLD YOU ABOUT IT IS BECAUSE I'M GOING ALONE.
I'VE MADE ARRANGEMENTS WITH TED FOR THE BOTH OF YOU TO STAY HERE AT THE FARMHOUSE.
TED WILL HELP YOU FIND FOOD. YOU'LL BE SAFER HERE THAN YOU WOULD BE AT OLD MAN'S CAVE.

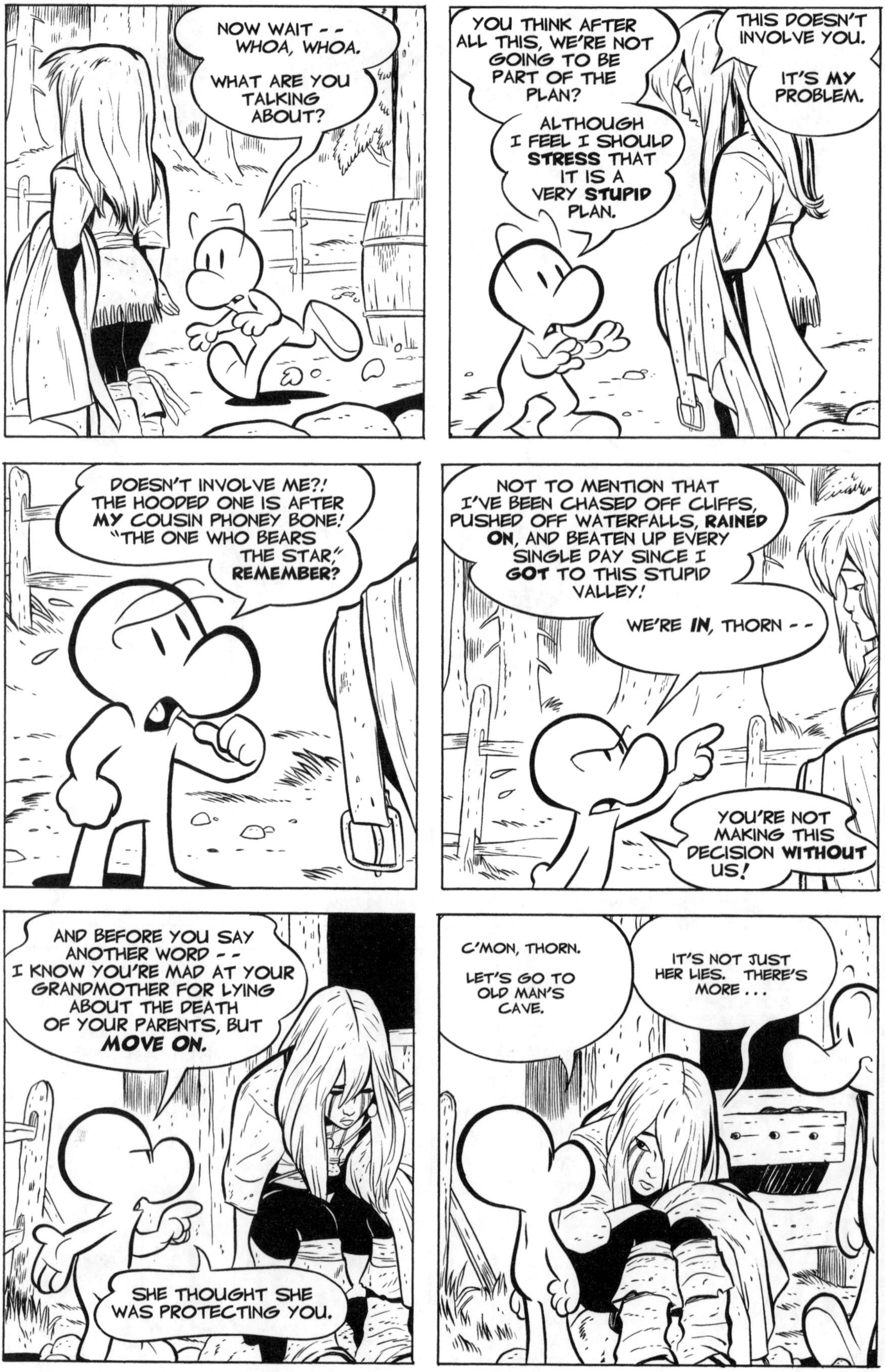
NOW WAIT - - WHOA, WHOA.
WHAT ARE YOU TALKING ABOUT?
YOU THINK AFTER ALL THIS, WE'RE NOT GOING TO BE PART OF THE PLAN?
ALTHOUGH I FEEL I SHOULD **STRESS** THAT IT IS A VERY **STUPID** PLAN.
THIS DOESN'T INVOLVE YOU.
IT'S **MY** PROBLEM.
DOESN'T INVOLVE ME?! THE HOODED ONE IS AFTER **MY** COUSIN PHONEY BONE! "THE ONE WHO BEARS THE STAR," **REMEMBER?**
NOT TO MENTION THAT I'VE BEEN CHASED OFF CLIFFS, PUSHED OFF WATERFALLS, **RAINED ON**, AND BEATEN UP EVERY SINGLE DAY SINCE I **GOT** TO THIS STUPID VALLEY!
WE'RE ***IN***, THORN - -
YOU'RE NOT MAKING THIS DECISION **WITHOUT** US!
AND BEFORE YOU SAY ANOTHER WORD - - I KNOW YOU'RE MAD AT YOUR GRANDMOTHER FOR LYING ABOUT THE DEATH OF YOUR PARENTS, BUT **MOVE ON.**
SHE THOUGHT SHE WAS PROTECTING YOU.
C'MON, THORN.
LET'S GO TO OLD MAN'S CAVE.
IT'S NOT JUST HER LIES. THERE'S MORE . . .

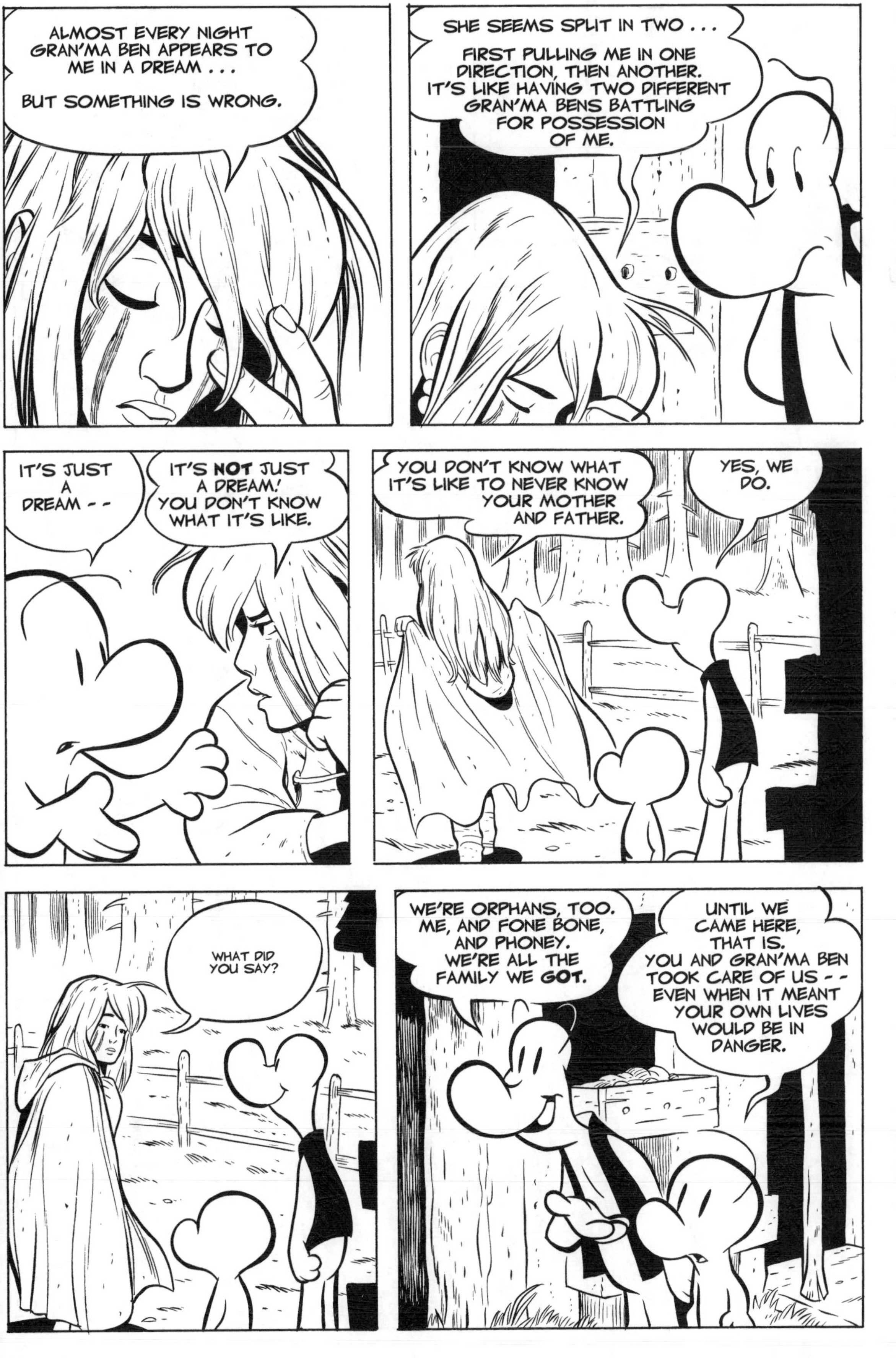
ALMOST EVERY NIGHT GRAN'MA BEN APPEARS TO ME IN A DREAM . . .
BUT SOMETHING IS WRONG.
SHE SEEMS SPLIT IN TWO . . .
FIRST PULLING ME IN ONE DIRECTION, THEN ANOTHER. IT'S LIKE HAVING TWO DIFFERENT GRAN'MA BENS BATTLING FOR POSSESSION OF ME.
IT'S JUST A DREAM - -
IT'S **NOT** JUST A DREAM! YOU DON'T KNOW WHAT IT'S LIKE.
YOU DON'T KNOW WHAT IT'S LIKE TO NEVER KNOW YOUR MOTHER AND FATHER.
YES, WE DO.
WHAT DID YOU SAY?
WE'RE ORPHANS, TOO. ME, AND FONE BONE, AND PHONEY. WE'RE ALL THE FAMILY WE **GOT**.
UNTIL WE CAME HERE, THAT IS. YOU AND GRAN'MA BEN TOOK CARE OF US - - EVEN WHEN IT MEANT YOUR OWN LIVES WOULD BE IN DANGER.

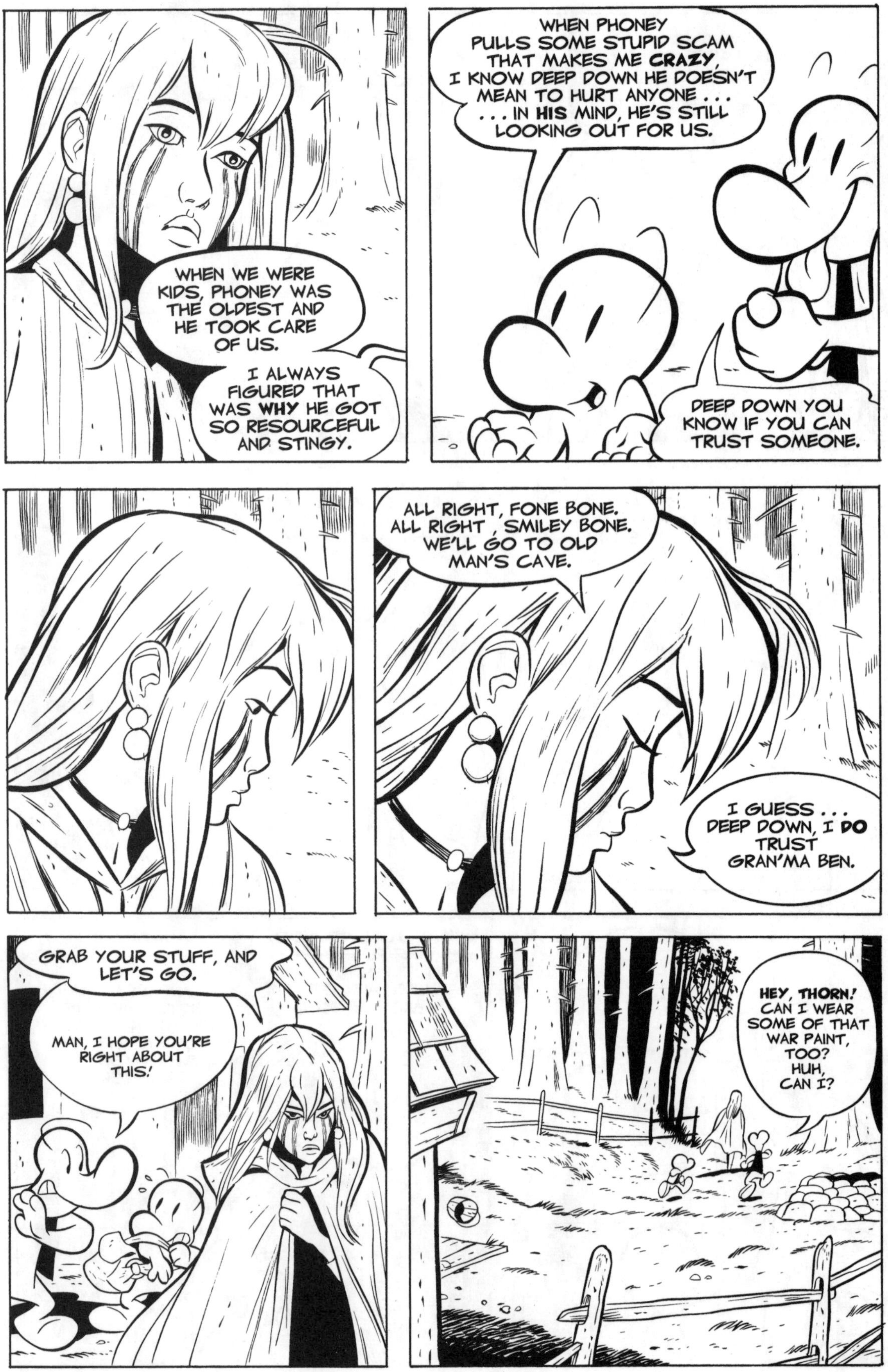
WHEN WE WERE KIDS, PHONEY WAS THE OLDEST AND HE TOOK CARE OF US.
I ALWAYS FIGURED THAT WAS **WHY** HE GOT SO RESOURCEFUL AND STINGY.
WHEN PHONEY PULLS SOME STUPID SCAM THAT MAKES ME **CRAZY**, I KNOW DEEP DOWN HE DOESN'T MEAN TO HURT ANYONE . . . . . . IN **HIS** MIND, HE'S STILL LOOKING OUT FOR US.
DEEP DOWN YOU KNOW IF YOU CAN TRUST SOMEONE.
ALL RIGHT, FONE BONE. ALL RIGHT, SMILEY BONE. WE'LL GO TO OLD MAN'S CAVE.
I GUESS . . . DEEP DOWN, I **DO** TRUST GRAN'MA BEN.
GRAB YOUR STUFF, AND LET'S GO.
MAN, I HOPE YOU'RE RIGHT ABOUT THIS!
HEY, THORN! CAN I WEAR SOME OF THAT WAR PAINT, TOO? HUH, CAN I?

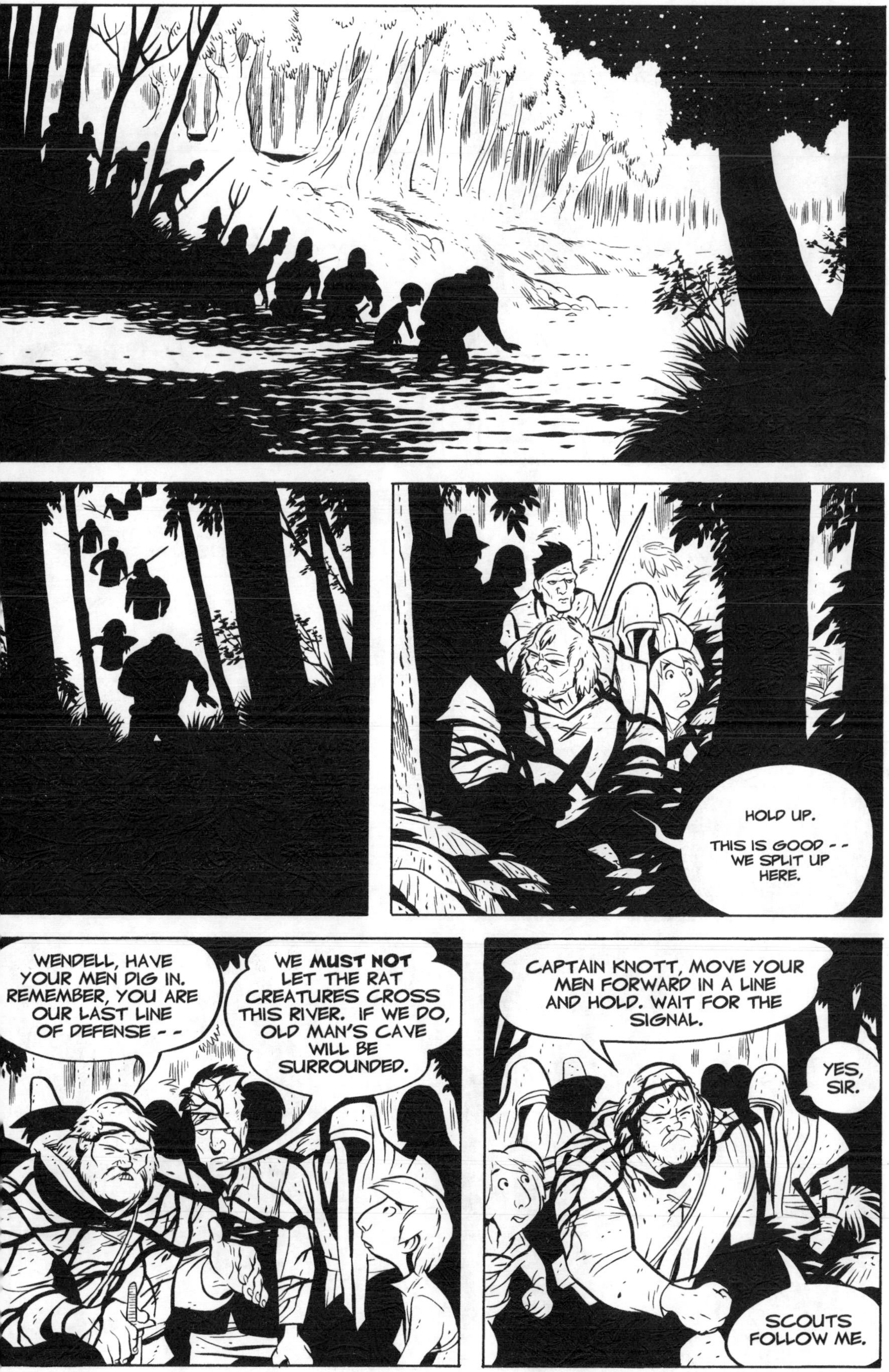
HOLD UP.
THIS IS GOOD -- WE SPLIT UP HERE.
WENDELL, HAVE YOUR MEN DIG IN. REMEMBER, YOU ARE OUR LAST LINE OF DEFENSE --
WE **MUST NOT** LET THE RAT CREATURES CROSS THIS RIVER. IF WE DO, OLD MAN'S CAVE WILL BE SURROUNDED.
CAPTAIN KNOTT, MOVE YOUR MEN FORWARD IN A LINE AND HOLD. WAIT FOR THE SIGNAL.
YES, SIR.
SCOUTS FOLLOW ME.

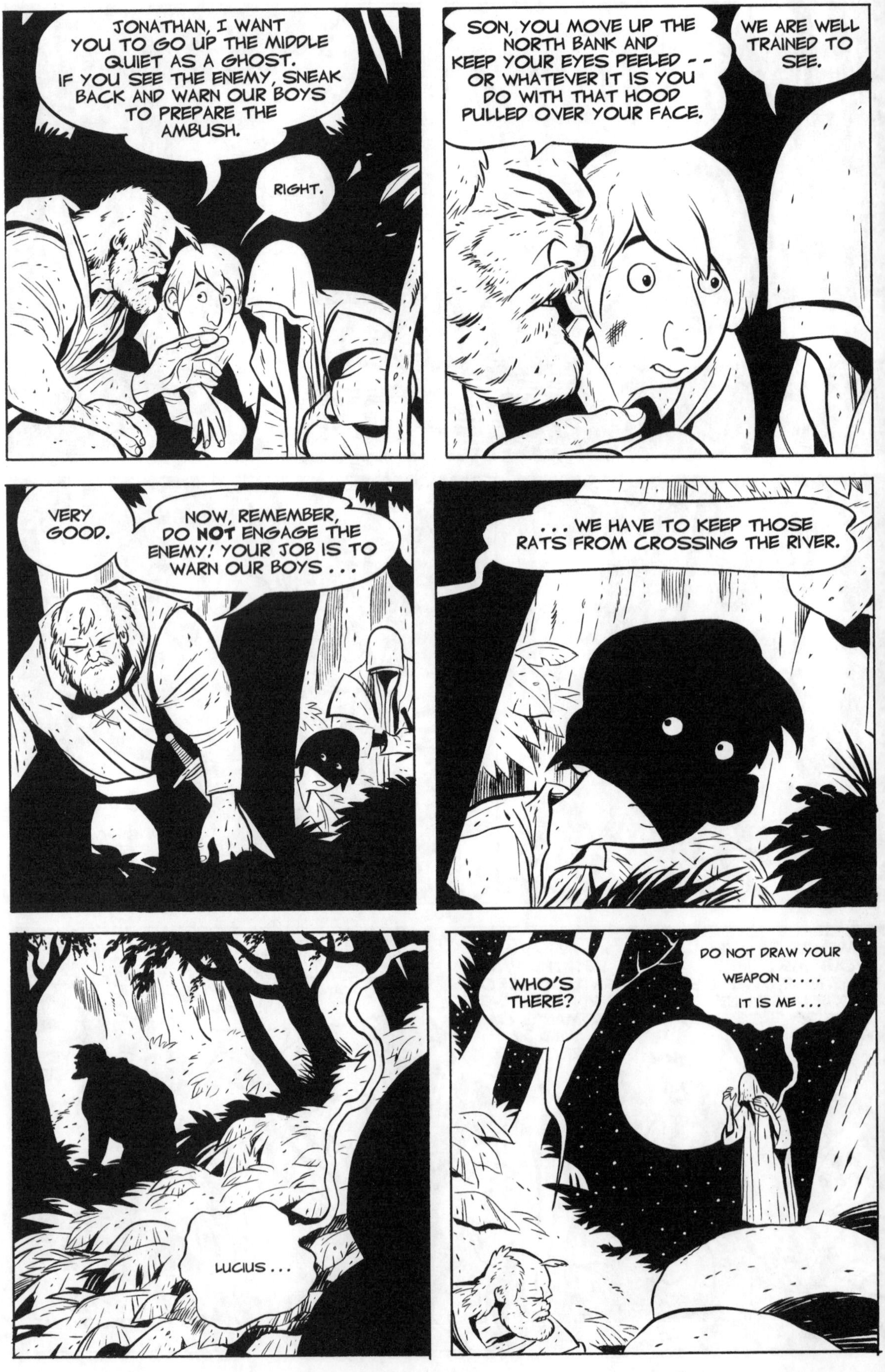
JONATHAN, I WANT YOU TO GO UP THE MIDDLE QUIET AS A GHOST. IF YOU SEE THE ENEMY, SNEAK BACK AND WARN OUR BOYS TO PREPARE THE AMBUSH.
RIGHT.
SON, YOU MOVE UP THE NORTH BANK AND KEEP YOUR EYES PEELED - - OR WHATEVER IT IS YOU DO WITH THAT HOOD PULLED OVER YOUR FACE.
WE ARE WELL TRAINED TO SEE.
VERY GOOD.
NOW, REMEMBER, DO **NOT** ENGAGE THE ENEMY! YOUR JOB IS TO WARN OUR BOYS . . .
. . . WE HAVE TO KEEP THOSE RATS FROM CROSSING THE RIVER.
LUCIUS . . .
WHO'S THERE?
DO NOT DRAW YOUR WEAPON . . . . . IT IS ME . . .

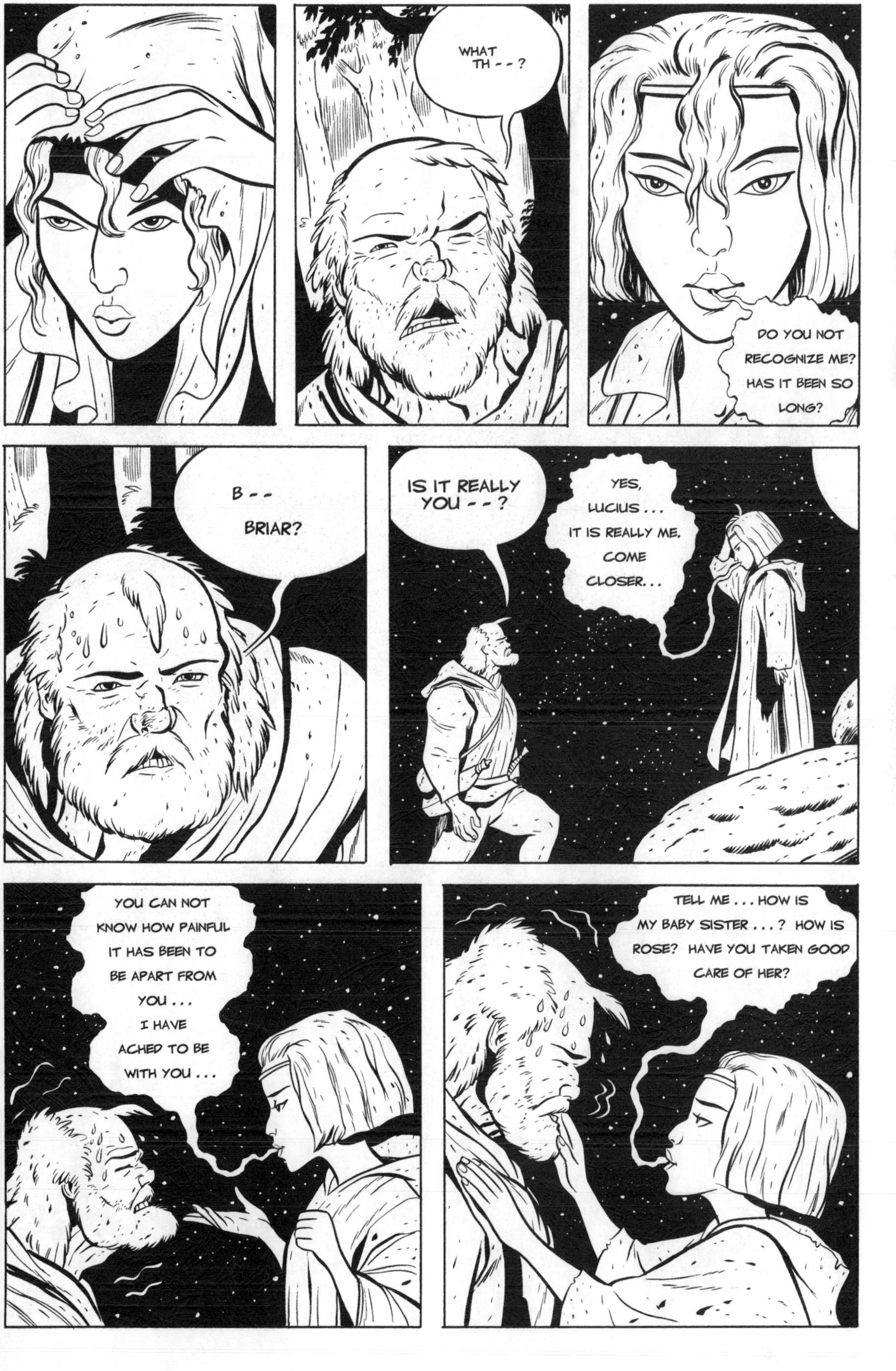
WHAT TH - - ?
DO YOU NOT RECOGNIZE ME? HAS IT BEEN SO LONG?
B - - BRIAR?
IS IT REALLY YOU - - ?
YES, LUCIUS . . . IT IS REALLY ME. COME CLOSER . . .
YOU CAN NOT KNOW HOW PAINFUL IT HAS BEEN TO BE APART FROM YOU . . . I HAVE ACHED TO BE WITH YOU . . .
TELL ME . . . HOW IS MY BABY SISTER . . . ? HOW IS ROSE? HAVE YOU TAKEN GOOD CARE OF HER?

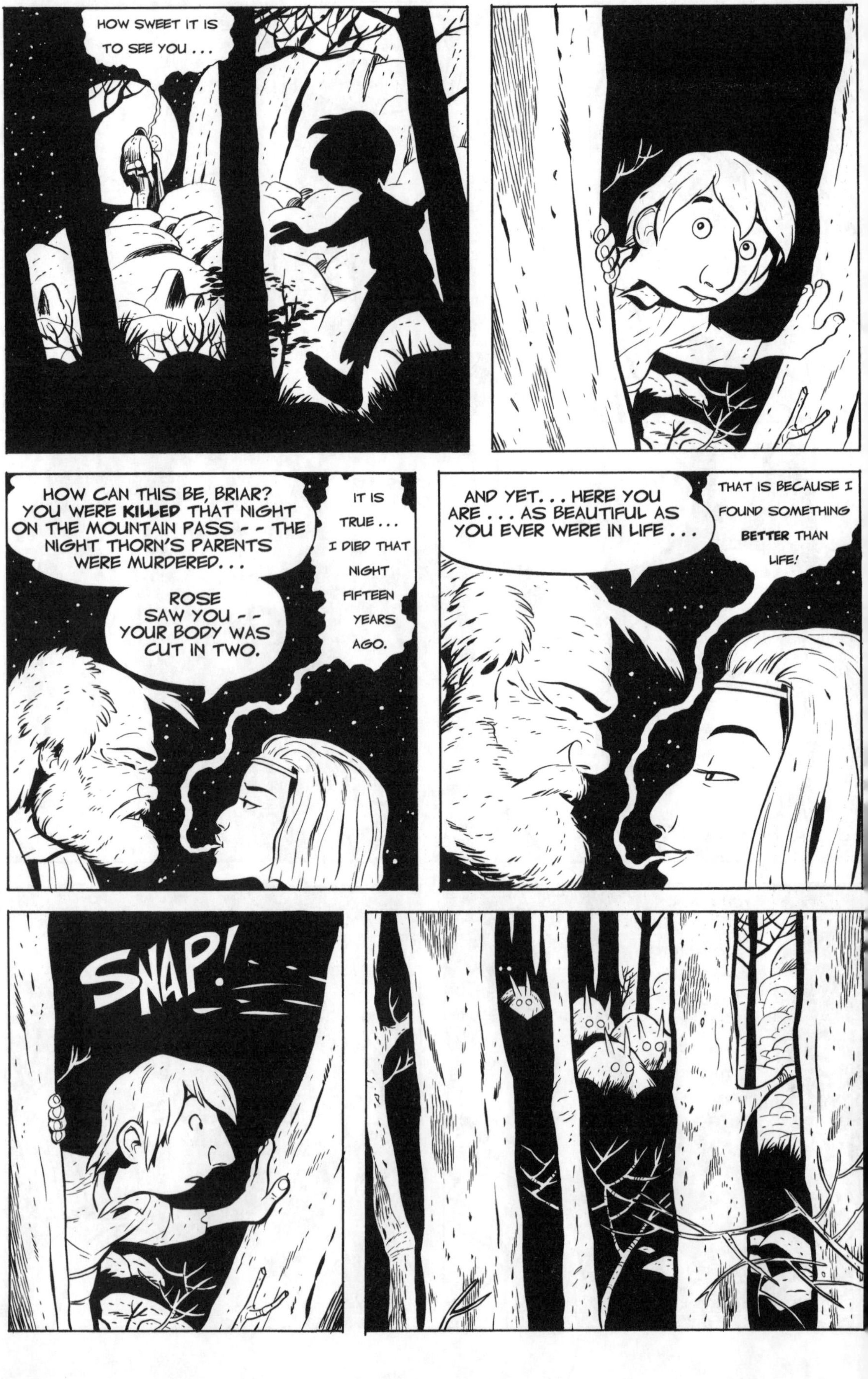
HOW SWEET IT IS TO SEE YOU . . .
HOW CAN THIS BE, BRIAR? YOU WERE **KILLED** THAT NIGHT ON THE MOUNTAIN PASS - - THE NIGHT THORN'S PARENTS WERE MURDERED. . .
ROSE SAW YOU - - YOUR BODY WAS CUT IN TWO.
IT IS TRUE . . . I DIED THAT NIGHT FIFTEEN YEARS AGO.
AND YET. . . HERE YOU ARE . . . AS BEAUTIFUL AS YOU EVER WERE IN LIFE . . .
THAT IS BECAUSE I FOUND SOMETHING **BETTER** THAN LIFE!
SNAP!

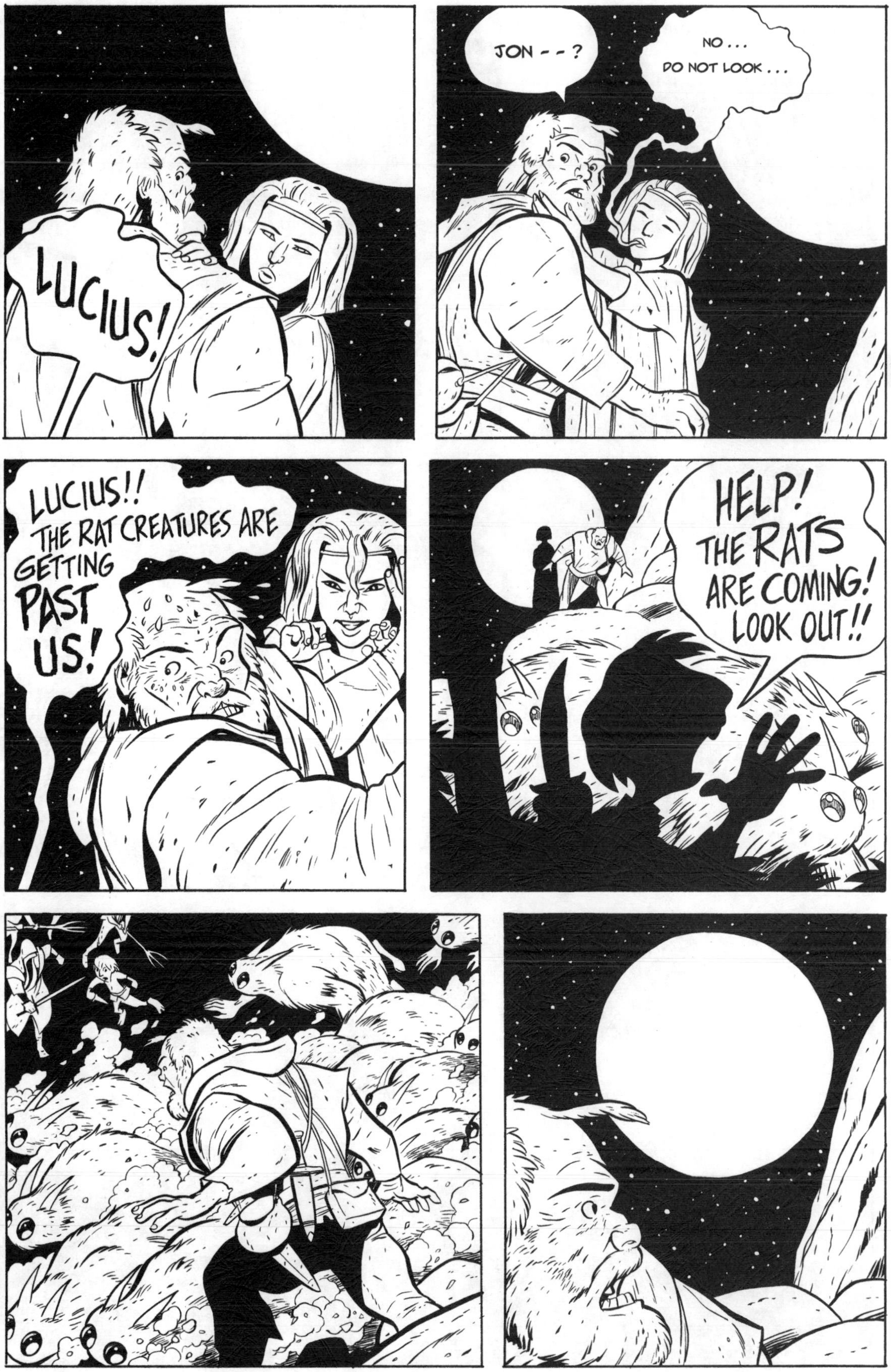
LUCIUS!
JON - - ?
NO . . .
DO NOT LOOK . . .
LUCIUS!! THE RAT CREATURES ARE GETTING PAST US!
HELP! THE RATS ARE COMING! LOOK OUT!!

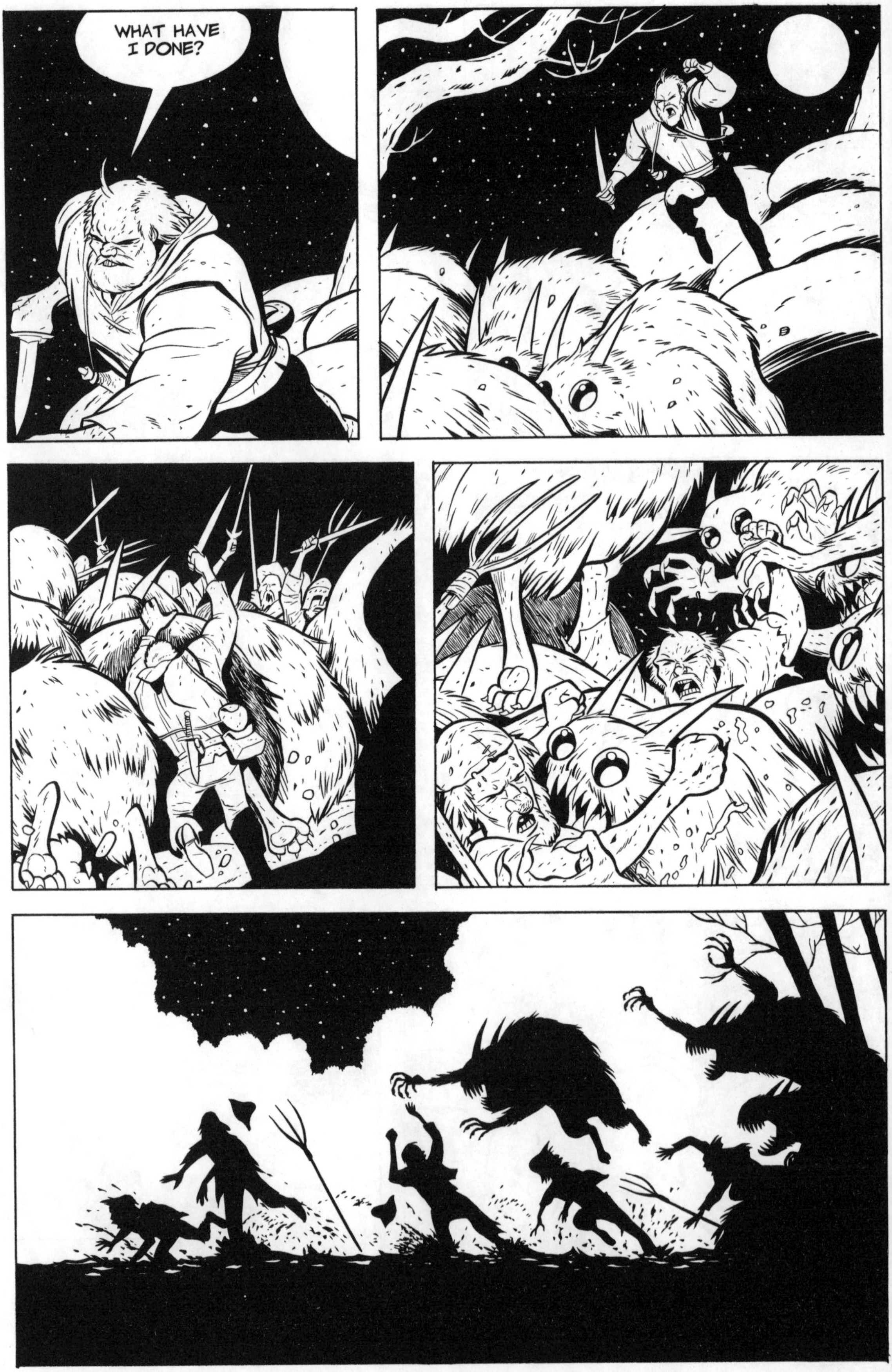
WHAT HAVE I DONE?

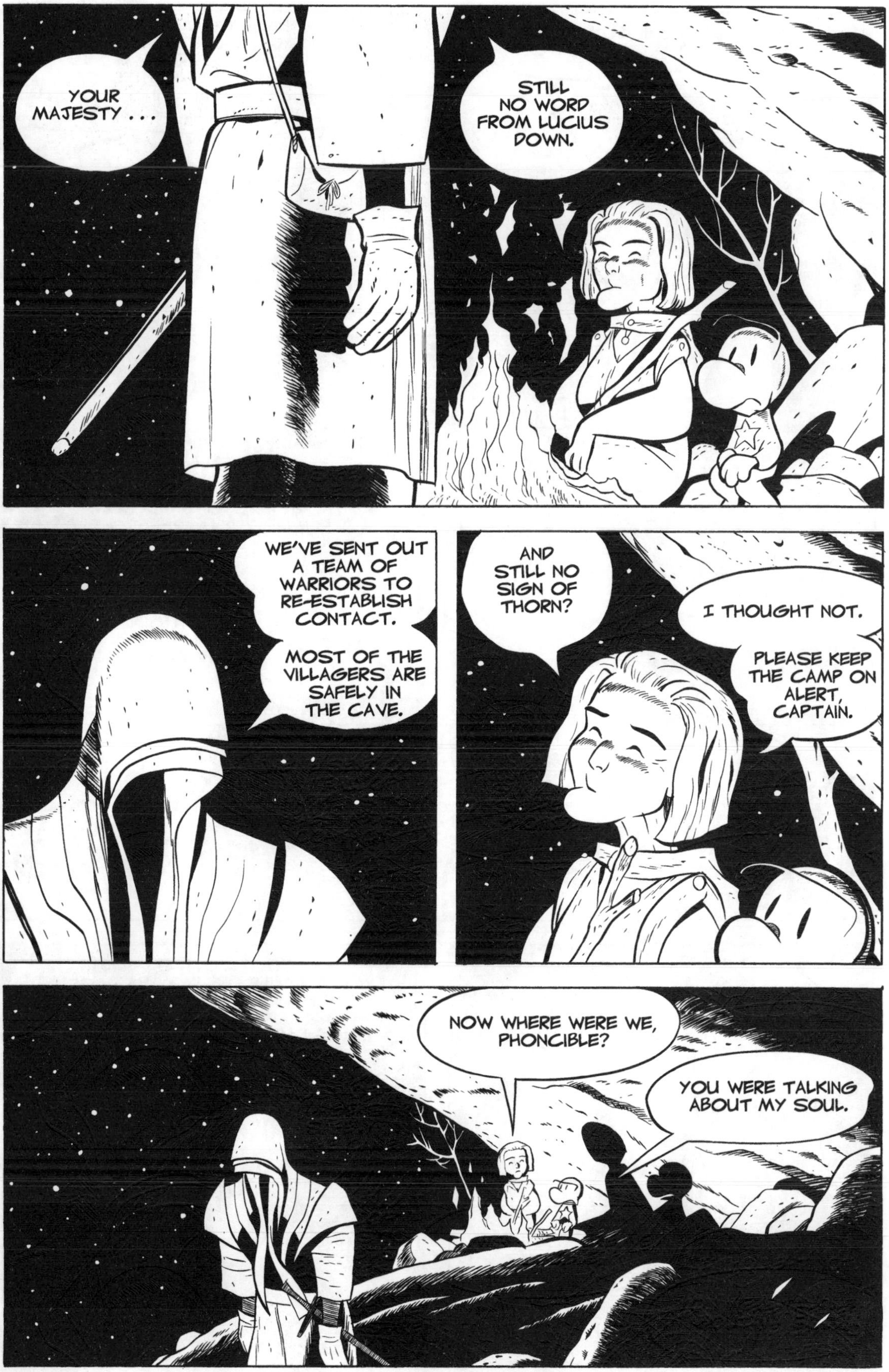
YOUR MAJESTY . . .
STILL NO WORD FROM LUCIUS DOWN.
WE'VE SENT OUT A TEAM OF WARRIORS TO RE-ESTABLISH CONTACT.
MOST OF THE VILLAGERS ARE SAFELY IN THE CAVE.
AND STILL NO SIGN OF THORN?
I THOUGHT NOT.
PLEASE KEEP THE CAMP ON ALERT, CAPTAIN.
NOW WHERE WERE WE, PHONCIBLE?
YOU WERE TALKING ABOUT MY SOUL.

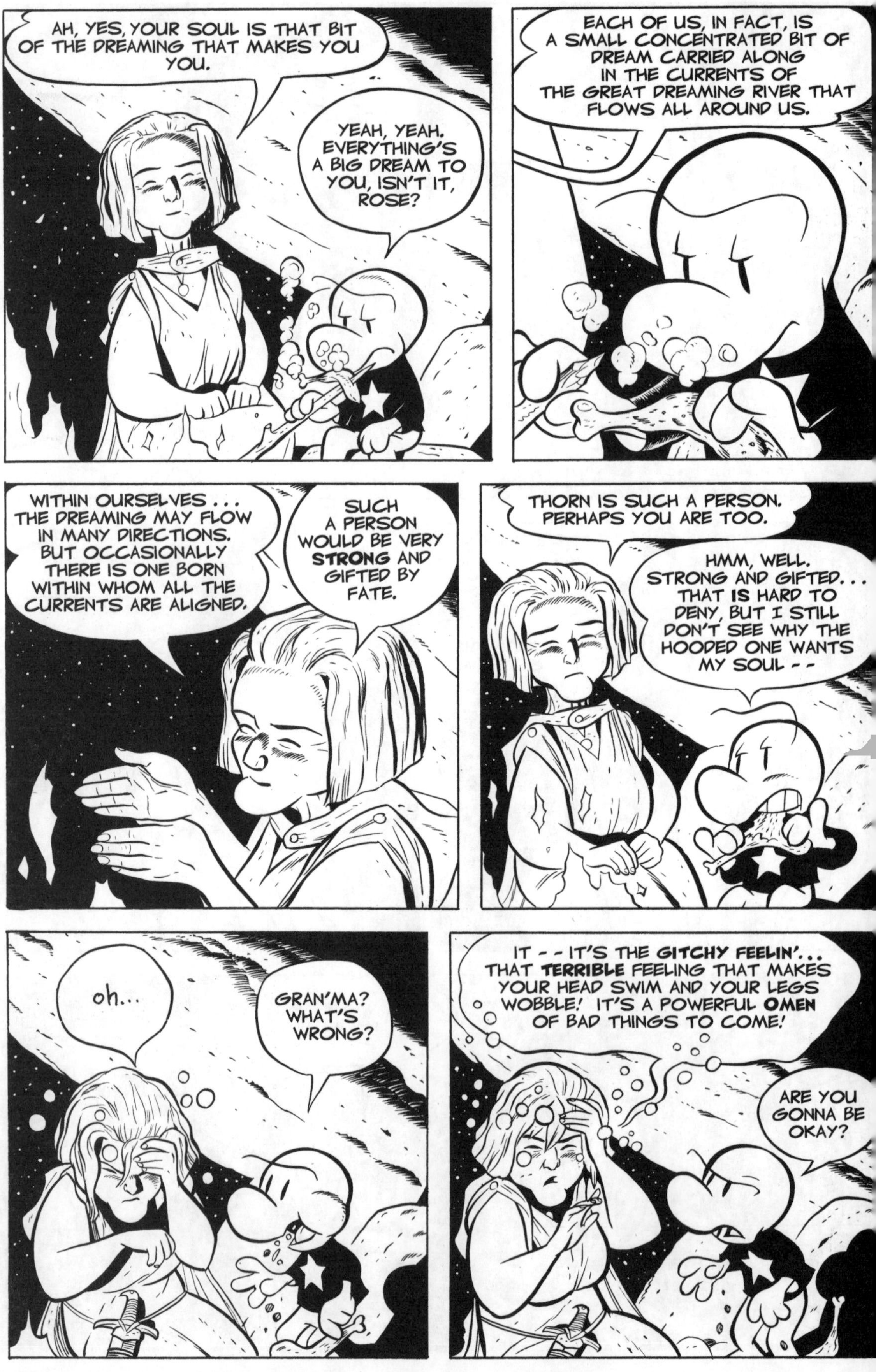
AH, YES, YOUR SOUL IS THAT BIT OF THE DREAMING THAT MAKES YOU YOU.
YEAH, YEAH. EVERYTHING'S A BIG DREAM TO YOU, ISN'T IT, ROSE?
EACH OF US, IN FACT, IS A SMALL CONCENTRATED BIT OF DREAM CARRIED ALONG IN THE CURRENTS OF THE GREAT DREAMING RIVER THAT FLOWS ALL AROUND US.
WITHIN OURSELVES . . . THE DREAMING MAY FLOW IN MANY DIRECTIONS. BUT OCCASIONALLY THERE IS ONE BORN WITHIN WHOM ALL THE CURRENTS ARE ALIGNED.
SUCH A PERSON WOULD BE VERY **STRONG** AND GIFTED BY FATE.
THORN IS SUCH A PERSON. PERHAPS YOU ARE TOO.
HMM, WELL. STRONG AND GIFTED . . . THAT **IS** HARD TO DENY, BUT I STILL DON'T SEE WHY THE HOODED ONE WANTS MY SOUL - -
oh...
GRAN'MA? WHAT'S WRONG?
IT - - IT'S THE **GITCHY FEELIN'**... THAT **TERRIBLE** FEELING THAT MAKES YOUR HEAD SWIM AND YOUR LEGS WOBBLE! IT'S A POWERFUL **OMEN** OF BAD THINGS TO COME!
ARE YOU GONNA BE OKAY?

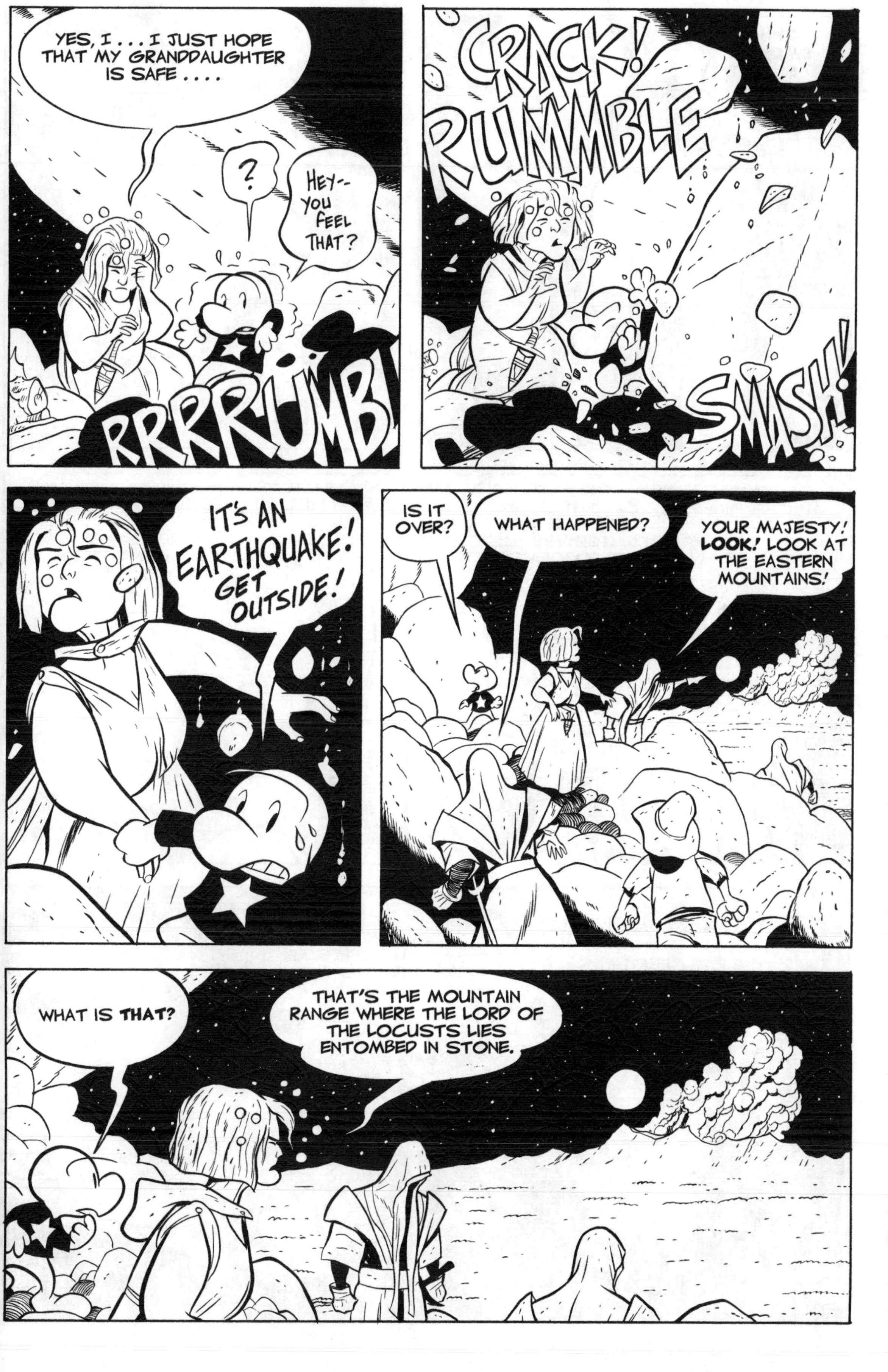
YES, I . . . I JUST HOPE THAT MY GRANDDAUGHTER IS SAFE . . . .
?
HEY-- YOU FEEL THAT?
RRRRUMB
CRACK!
RUMMBLE
SMASH!
IT'S AN EARTHQUAKE! GET OUTSIDE!
IS IT OVER?
WHAT HAPPENED?
YOUR MAJESTY! LOOK! LOOK AT THE EASTERN MOUNTAINS!
WHAT IS THAT?
THAT'S THE MOUNTAIN RANGE WHERE THE LORD OF THE LOCUSTS LIES ENTOMBED IN STONE.

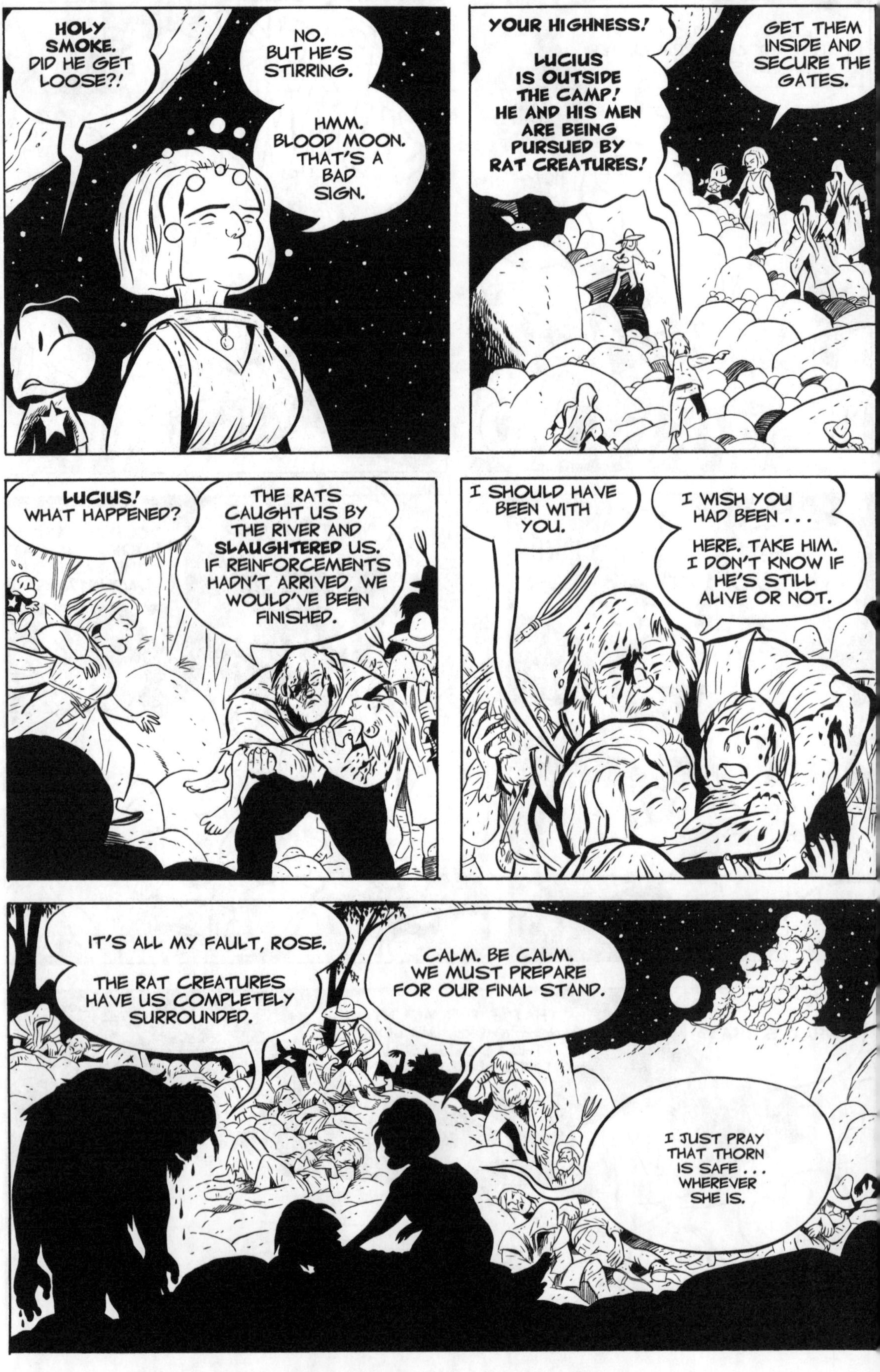
HOLY SMOKE. DID HE GET LOOSE?!
NO. BUT HE'S STIRRING.
HMM. BLOOD MOON. THAT'S A BAD SIGN.
YOUR HIGHNESS! LUCIUS IS OUTSIDE THE CAMP! HE AND HIS MEN ARE BEING PURSUED BY RAT CREATURES!
GET THEM INSIDE AND SECURE THE GATES.
LUCIUS! WHAT HAPPENED?
THE RATS CAUGHT US BY THE RIVER AND SLAUGHTERED US. IF REINFORCEMENTS HADN'T ARRIVED, WE WOULD'VE BEEN FINISHED.
I SHOULD HAVE BEEN WITH YOU.
I WISH YOU HAD BEEN . . .
HERE. TAKE HIM. I DON'T KNOW IF HE'S STILL ALIVE OR NOT.
IT'S ALL MY FAULT, ROSE.
THE RAT CREATURES HAVE US COMPLETELY SURROUNDED.
CALM. BE CALM. WE MUST PREPARE FOR OUR FINAL STAND.
I JUST PRAY THAT THORN IS SAFE . . . WHEREVER SHE IS.

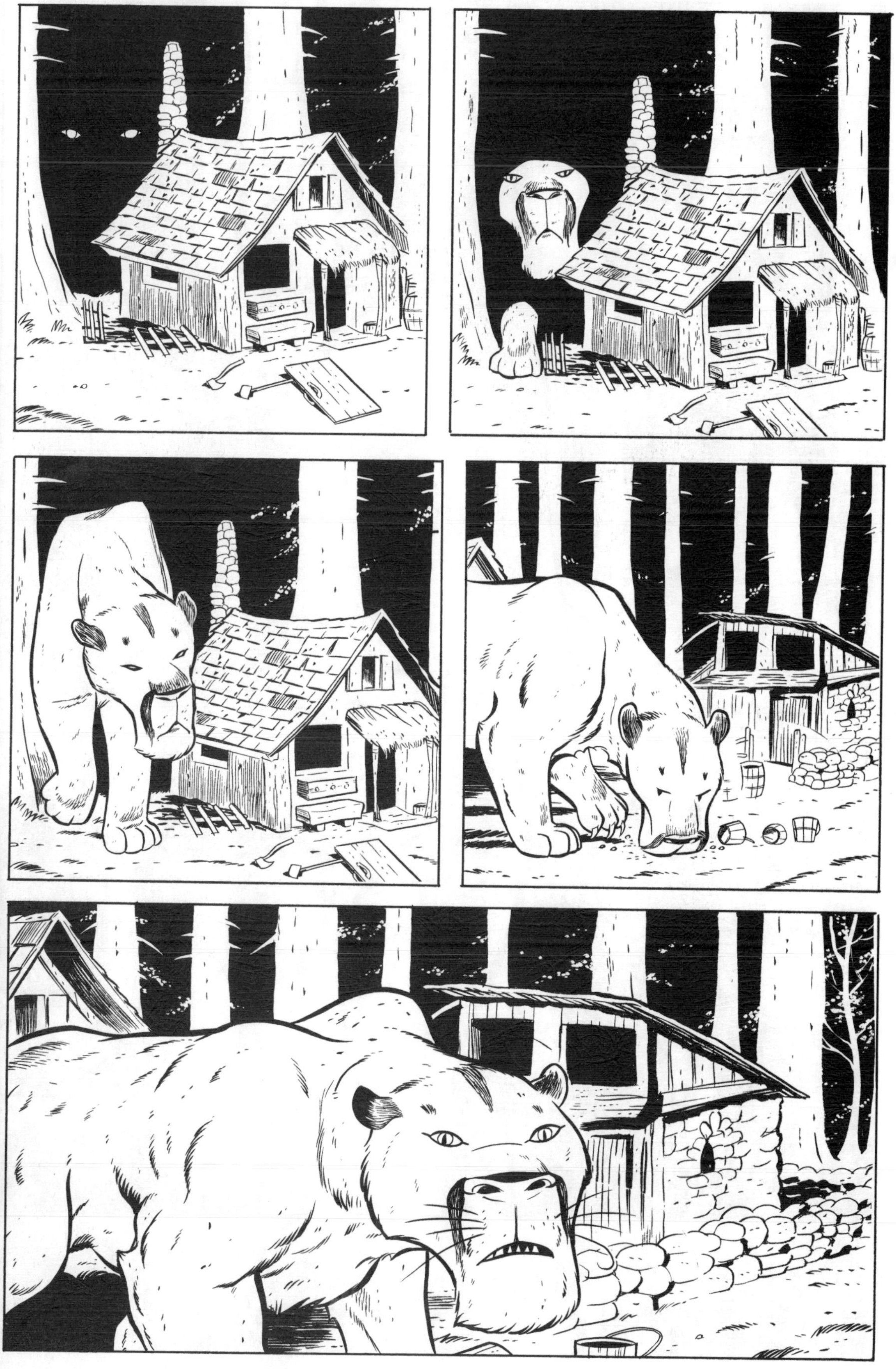

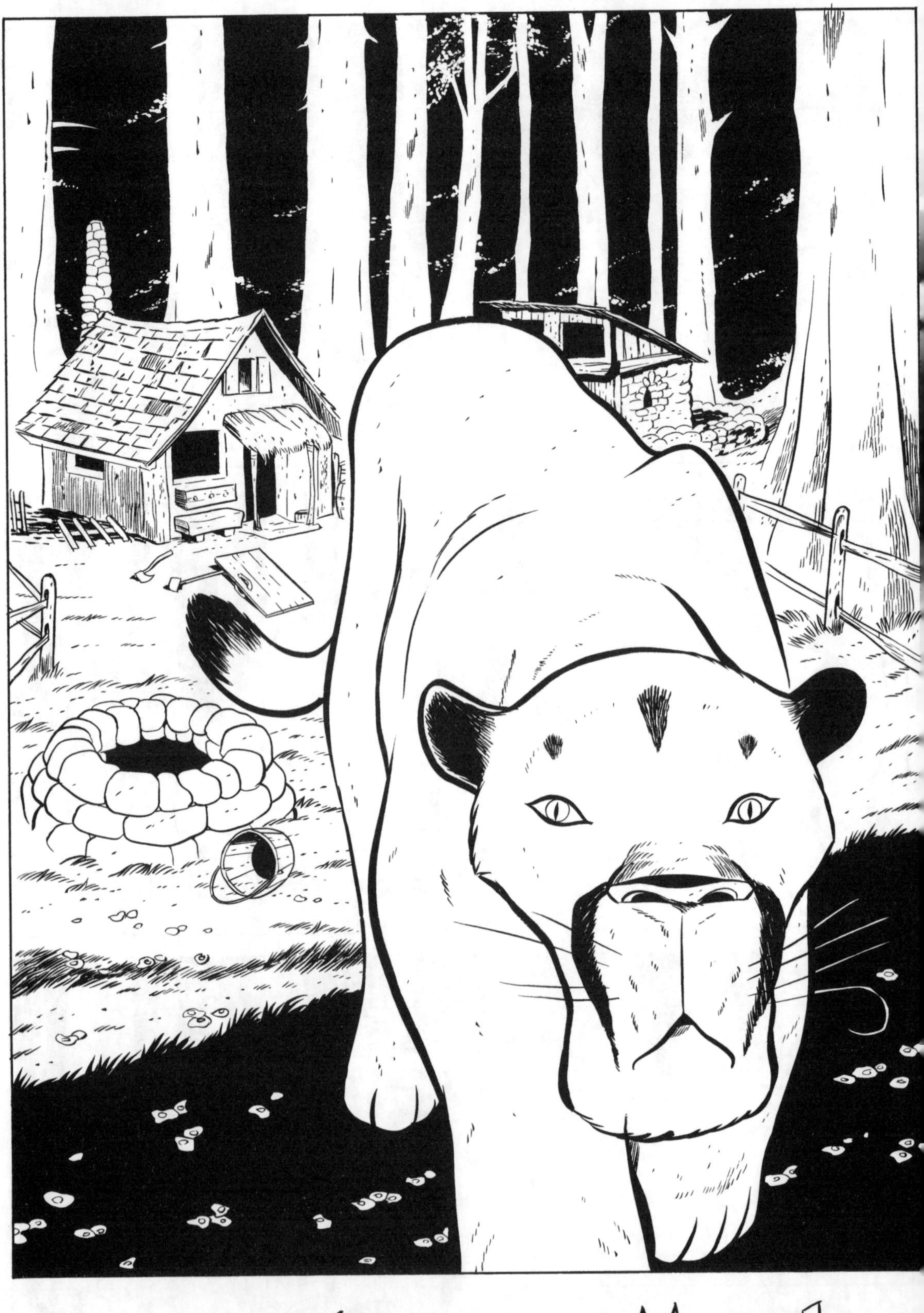

NEXT: HARVEST MOON

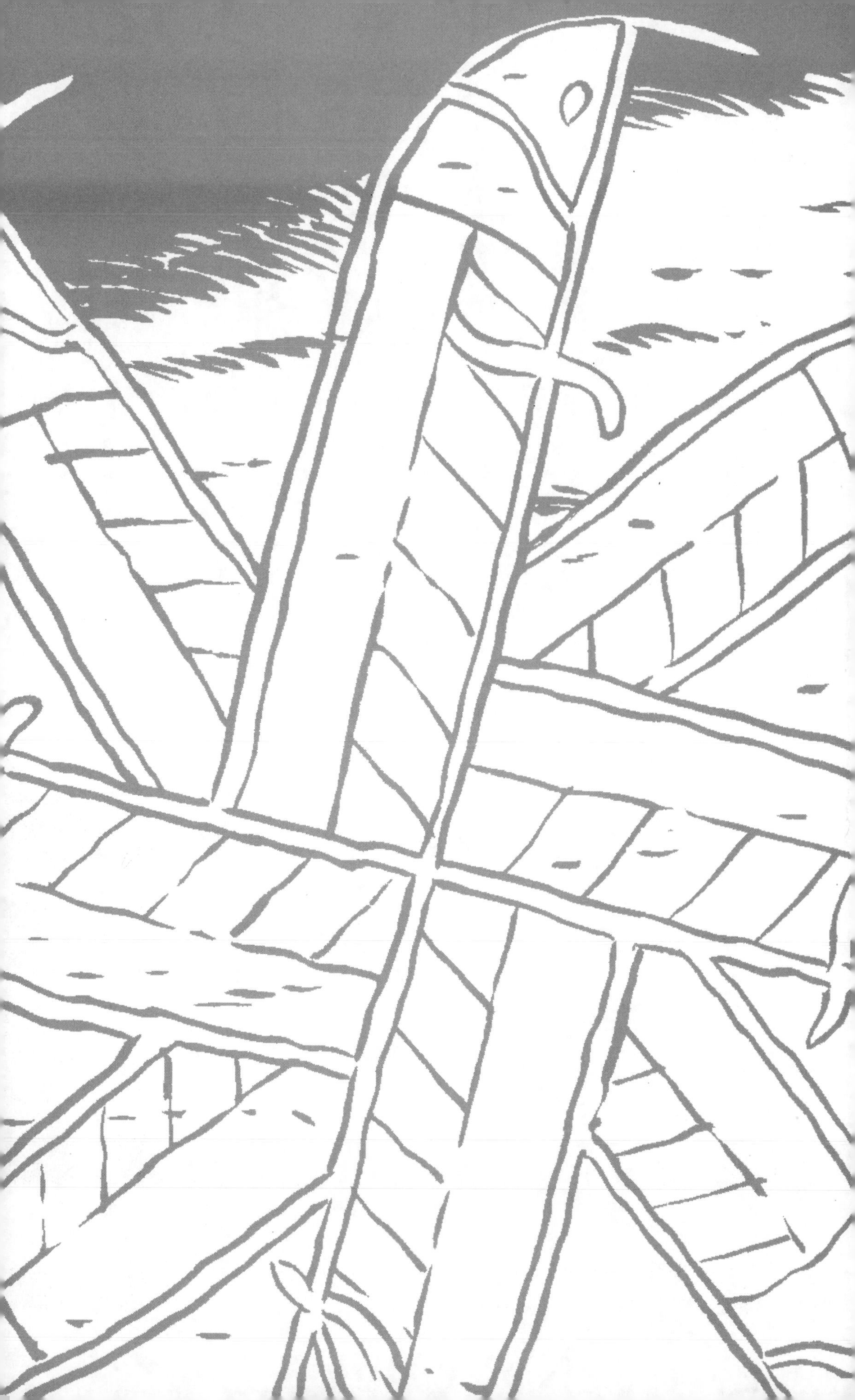

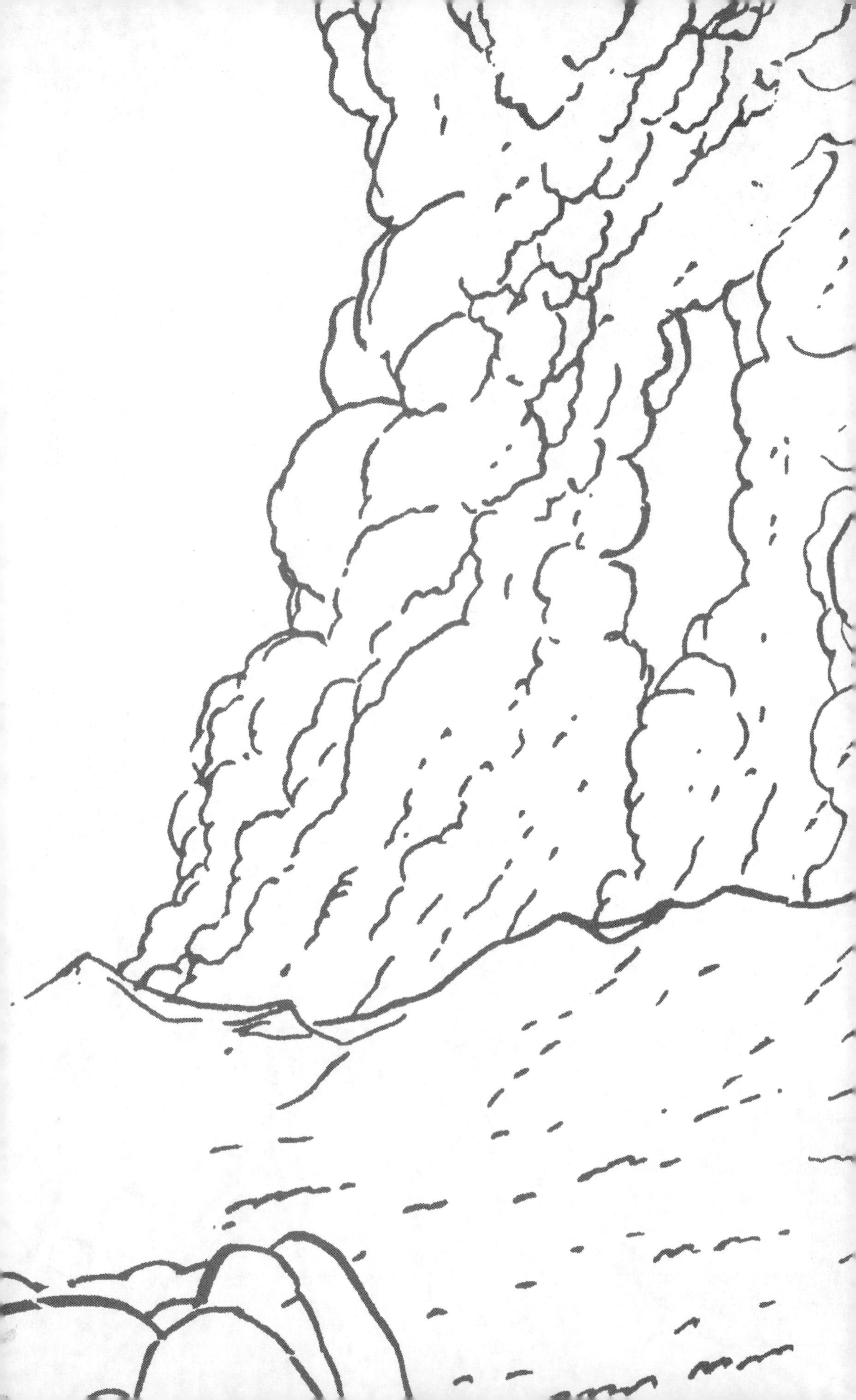

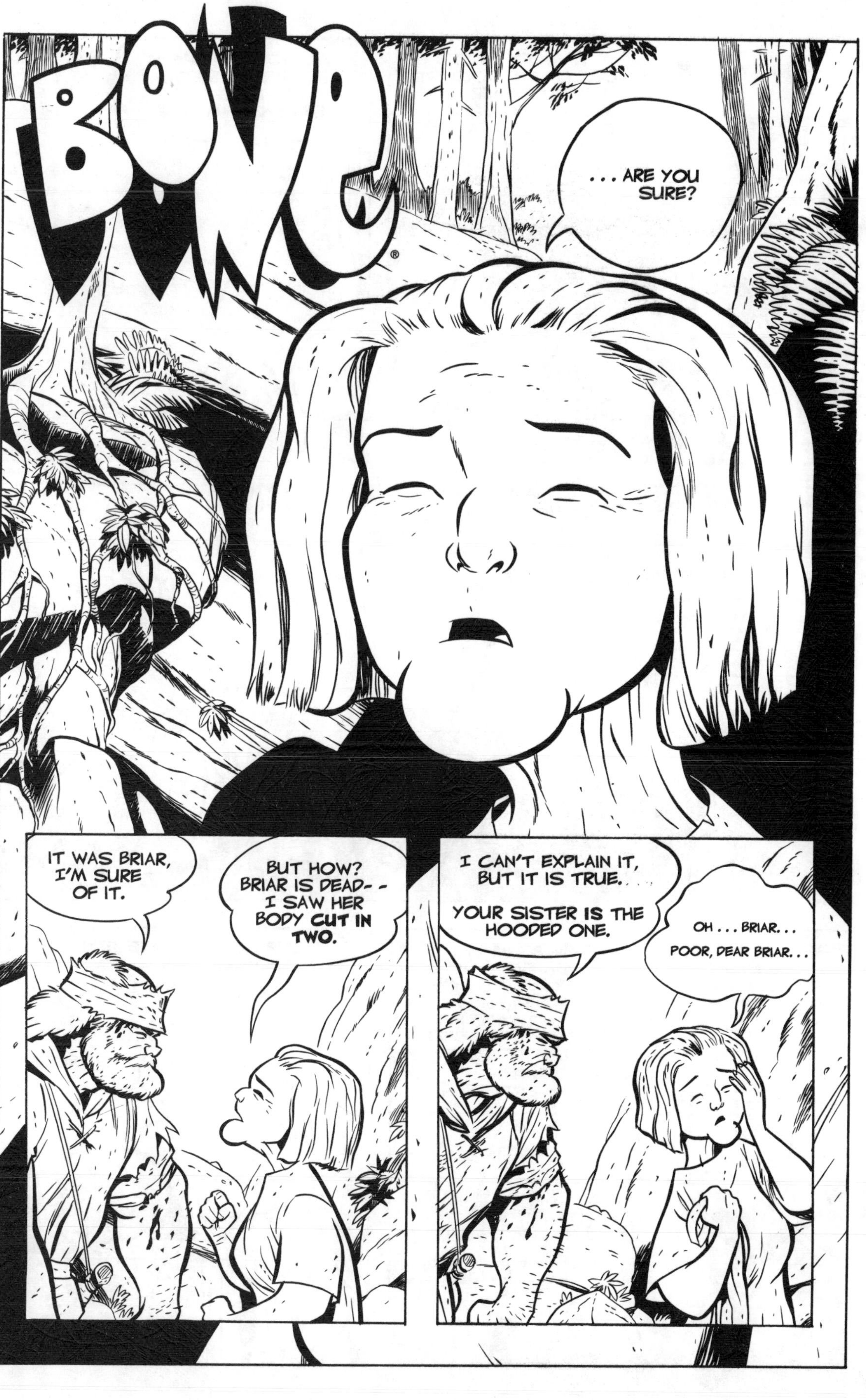
BONE®
. . . ARE YOU SURE?
IT WAS BRIAR, I'M SURE OF IT.
BUT HOW? BRIAR IS DEAD- - I SAW HER BODY **CUT IN TWO.**
I CAN'T EXPLAIN IT, BUT IT IS TRUE.
YOUR SISTER **IS** THE HOODED ONE.
OH . . . BRIAR . . .
POOR, DEAR BRIAR . . .

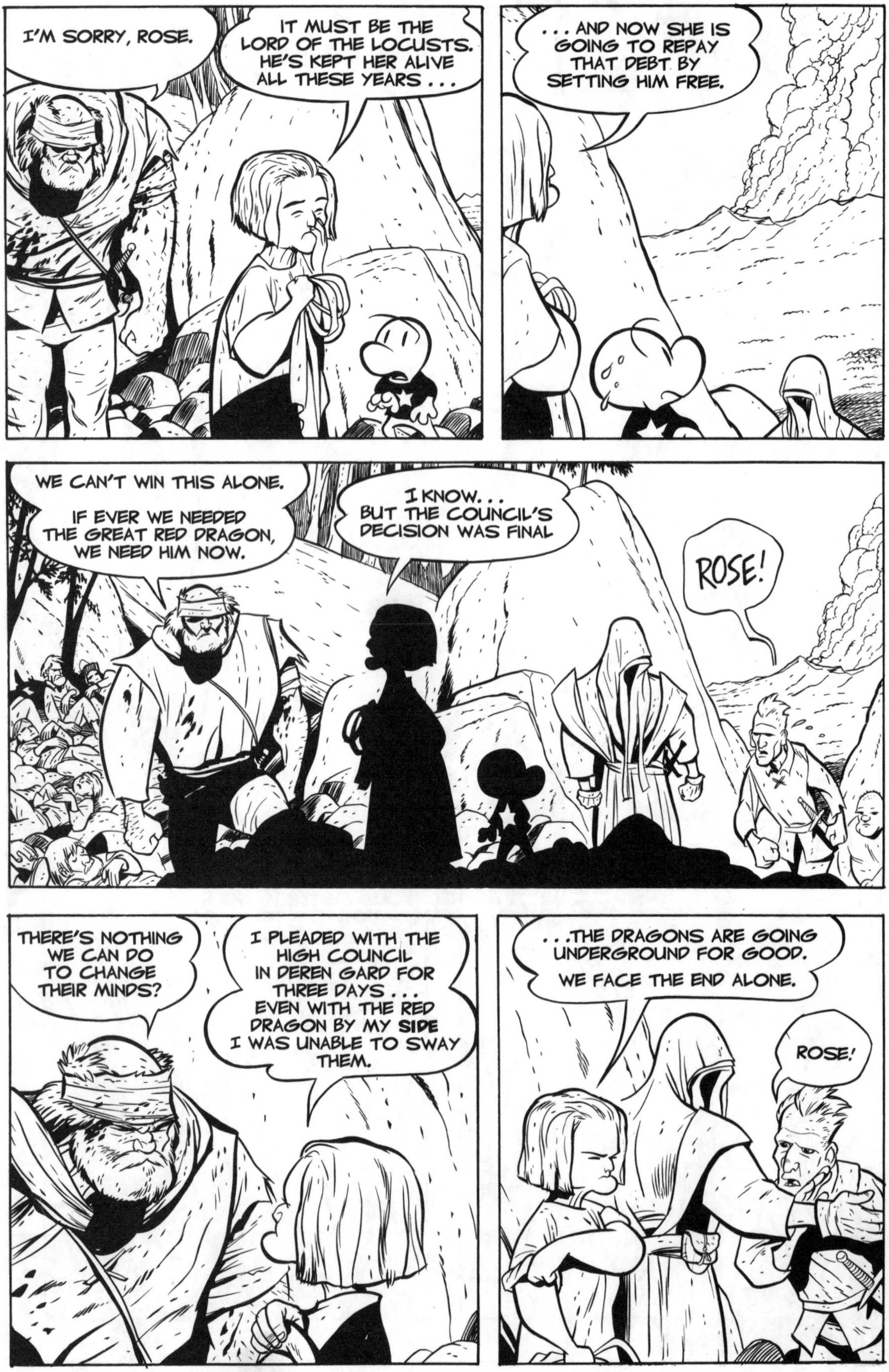
I'M SORRY, ROSE.
IT MUST BE THE LORD OF THE LOCUSTS. HE'S KEPT HER ALIVE ALL THESE YEARS . . .
. . . AND NOW SHE IS GOING TO REPAY THAT DEBT BY SETTING HIM FREE.
WE CAN'T WIN THIS ALONE.
IF EVER WE NEEDED THE GREAT RED DRAGON, WE NEED HIM NOW.
I KNOW. . . BUT THE COUNCIL'S DECISION WAS FINAL
ROSE!
THERE'S NOTHING WE CAN DO TO CHANGE THEIR MINDS?
I PLEADED WITH THE HIGH COUNCIL IN DEREN GARD FOR THREE DAYS . . . EVEN WITH THE RED DRAGON BY MY **SIDE** I WAS UNABLE TO SWAY THEM.
. . .THE DRAGONS ARE GOING UNDERGROUND FOR GOOD.
WE FACE THE END ALONE.
ROSE!

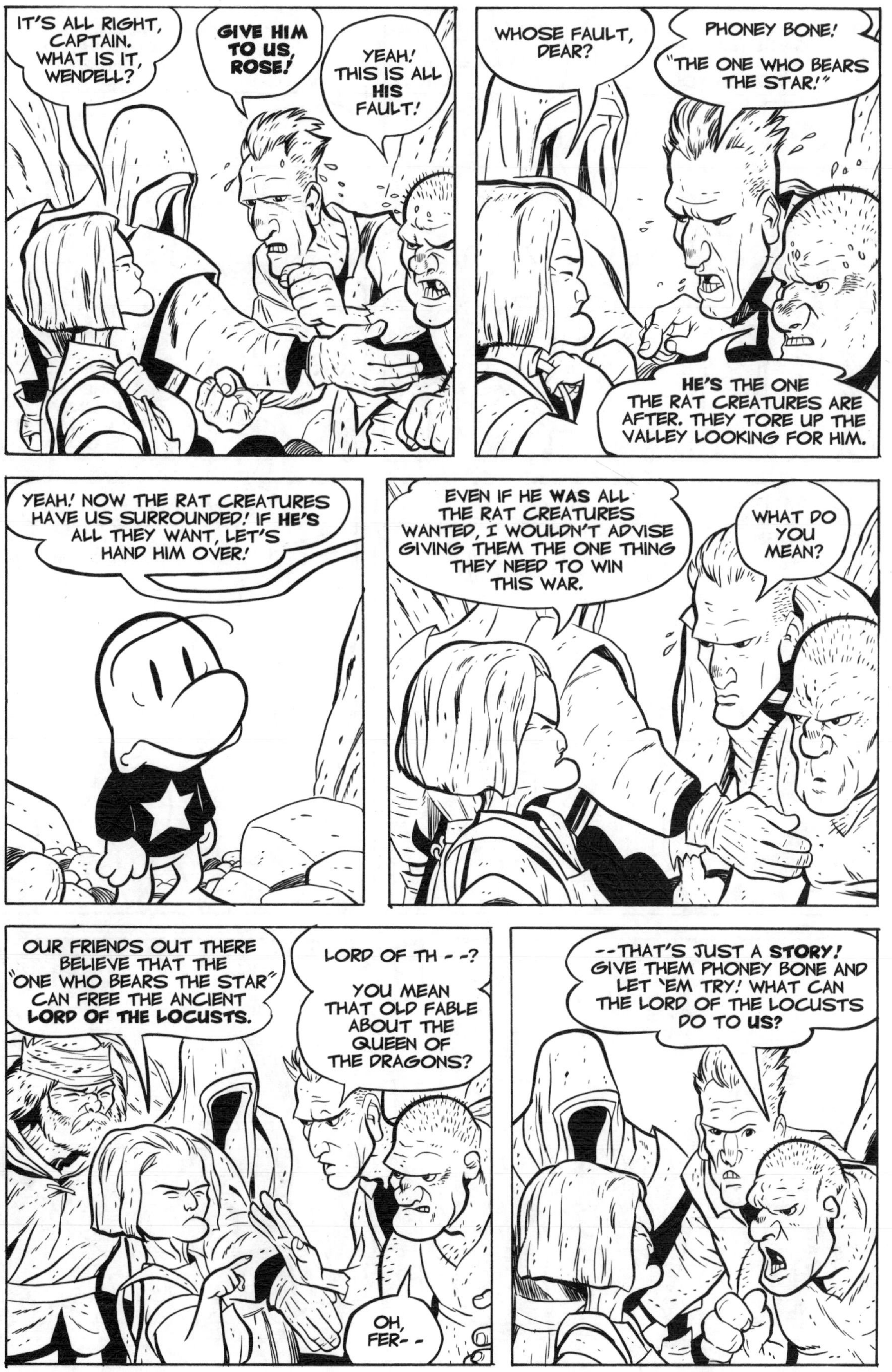
IT'S ALL RIGHT, CAPTAIN. WHAT IS IT, WENDELL?
GIVE HIM TO US, ROSE!
YEAH! THIS IS ALL HIS FAULT!
WHOSE FAULT, DEAR?
PHONEY BONE! "THE ONE WHO BEARS THE STAR!"
HE'S THE ONE THE RAT CREATURES ARE AFTER. THEY TORE UP THE VALLEY LOOKING FOR HIM.
YEAH! NOW THE RAT CREATURES HAVE US SURROUNDED! IF HE'S ALL THEY WANT, LET'S HAND HIM OVER!
EVEN IF HE WAS ALL THE RAT CREATURES WANTED, I WOULDN'T ADVISE GIVING THEM THE ONE THING THEY NEED TO WIN THIS WAR.
WHAT DO YOU MEAN?
OUR FRIENDS OUT THERE BELIEVE THAT THE "ONE WHO BEARS THE STAR" CAN FREE THE ANCIENT LORD OF THE LOCUSTS.
LORD OF TH - -?
YOU MEAN THAT OLD FABLE ABOUT THE QUEEN OF THE DRAGONS?
OH, FER- -
--THAT'S JUST A STORY! GIVE THEM PHONEY BONE AND LET 'EM TRY! WHAT CAN THE LORD OF THE LOCUSTS DO TO US?

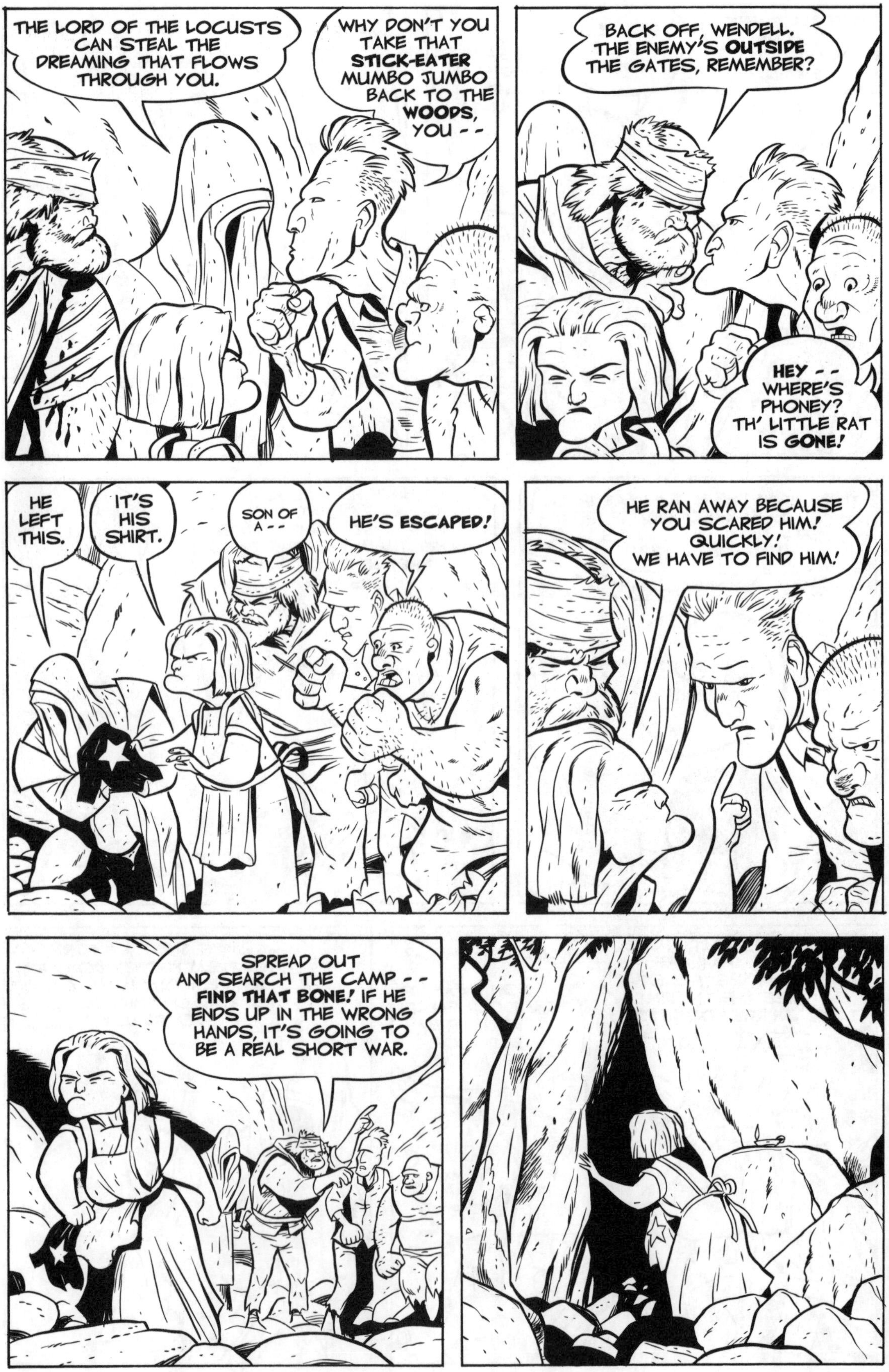
THE LORD OF THE LOCUSTS CAN STEAL THE DREAMING THAT FLOWS THROUGH YOU.
WHY DON'T YOU TAKE THAT **STICK-EATER** MUMBO JUMBO BACK TO THE **WOODS**, YOU - -
BACK OFF, WENDELL. THE ENEMY'S **OUTSIDE** THE GATES, REMEMBER?
HEY - - WHERE'S PHONEY? TH' LITTLE RAT IS **GONE**!
HE LEFT THIS.
IT'S HIS SHIRT.
SON OF A - -
HE'S **ESCAPED**!
HE RAN AWAY BECAUSE YOU SCARED HIM! QUICKLY! WE HAVE TO FIND HIM!
SPREAD OUT AND SEARCH THE CAMP - - **FIND THAT BONE!** IF HE ENDS UP IN THE WRONG HANDS, IT'S GOING TO BE A REAL SHORT WAR.

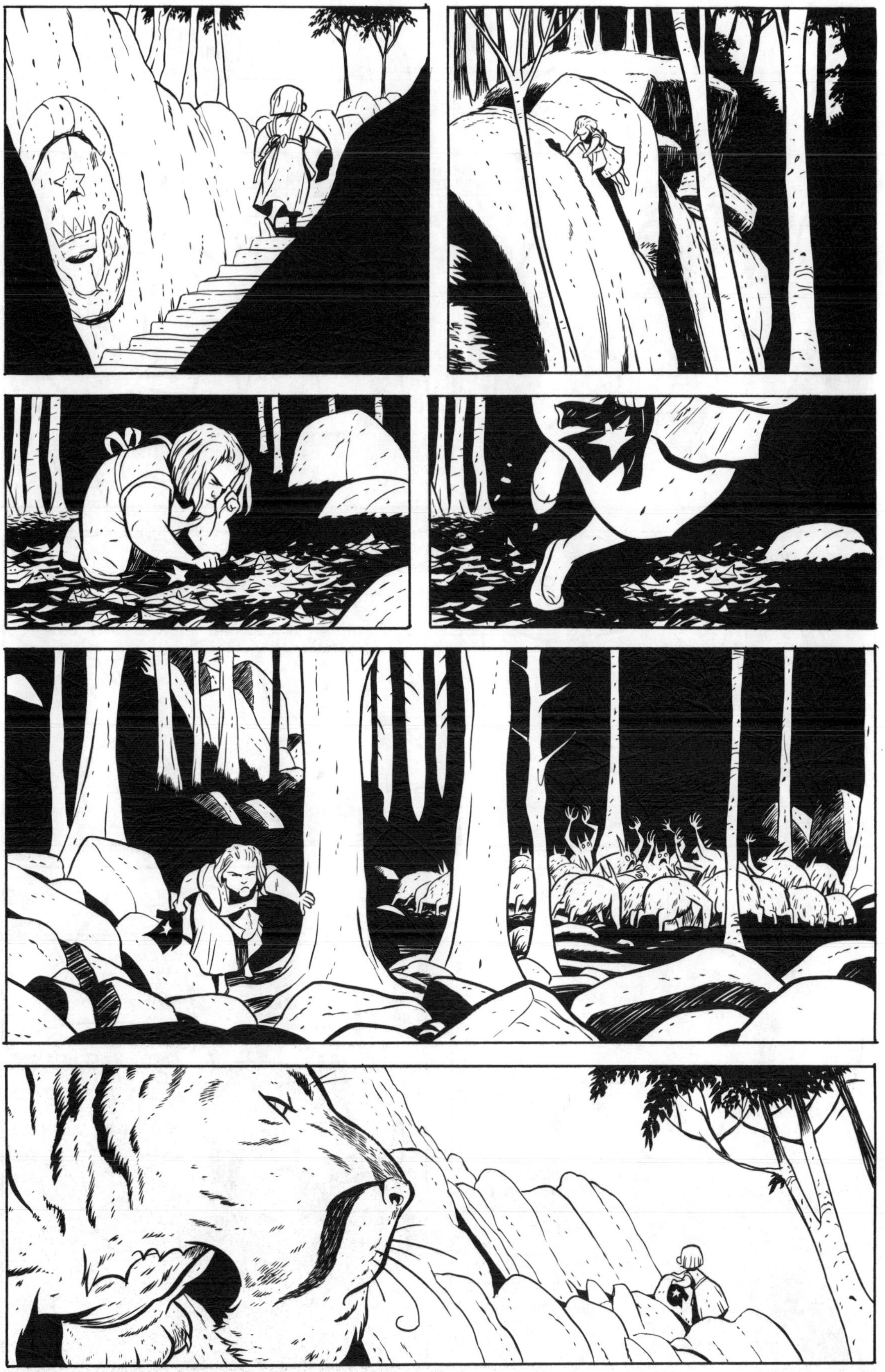

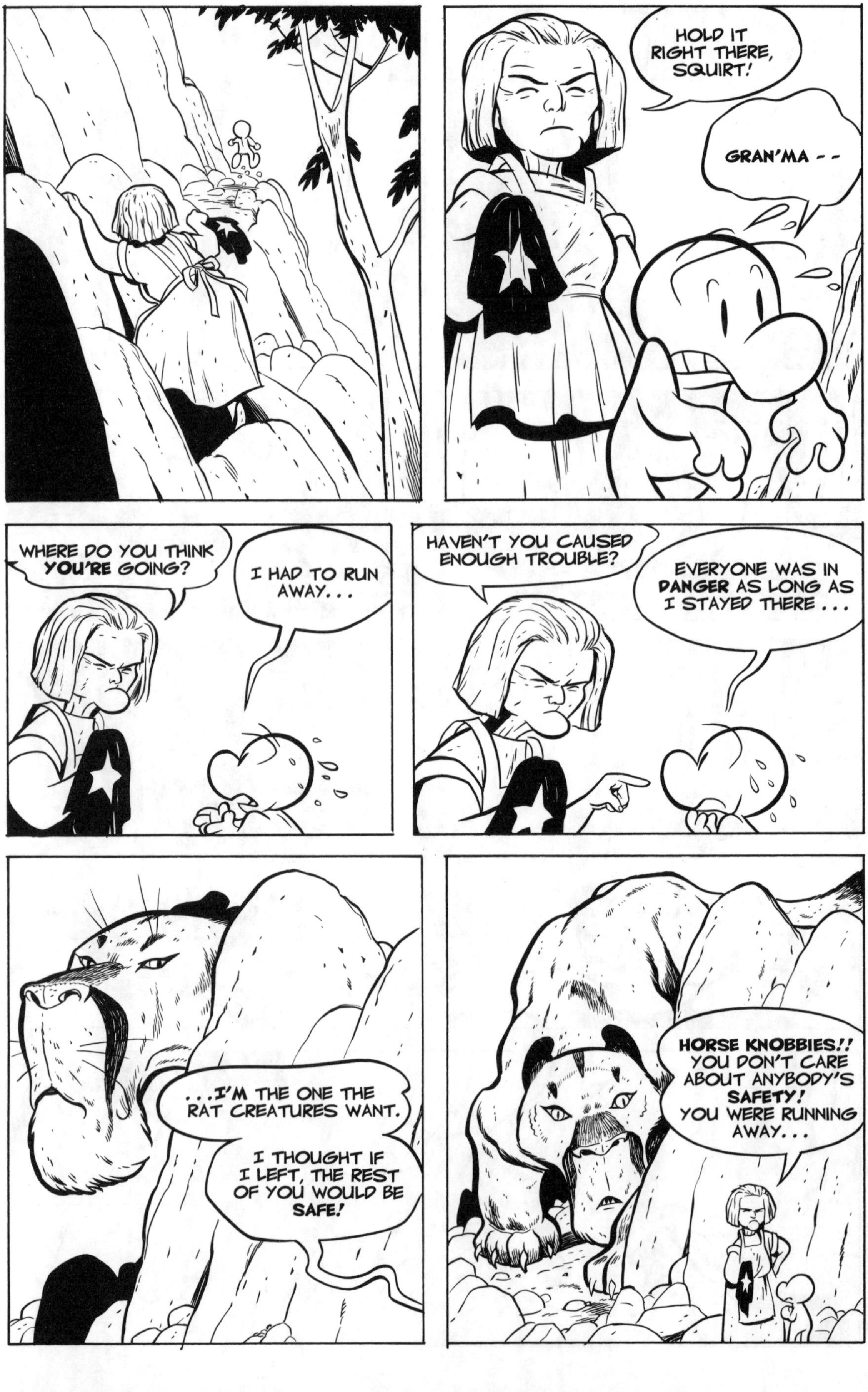
HOLD IT RIGHT THERE, SQUIRT!
GRAN'MA - -
WHERE DO YOU THINK **YOU'RE** GOING?
I HAD TO RUN AWAY...
HAVEN'T YOU CAUSED ENOUGH TROUBLE?
EVERYONE WAS IN **DANGER** AS LONG AS I STAYED THERE...
...**I'M** THE ONE THE RAT CREATURES WANT.
I THOUGHT IF I LEFT, THE REST OF YOU WOULD BE **SAFE!**
HORSE KNOBBIES!! YOU DON'T CARE ABOUT ANYBODY'S **SAFETY!** YOU WERE RUNNING AWAY...

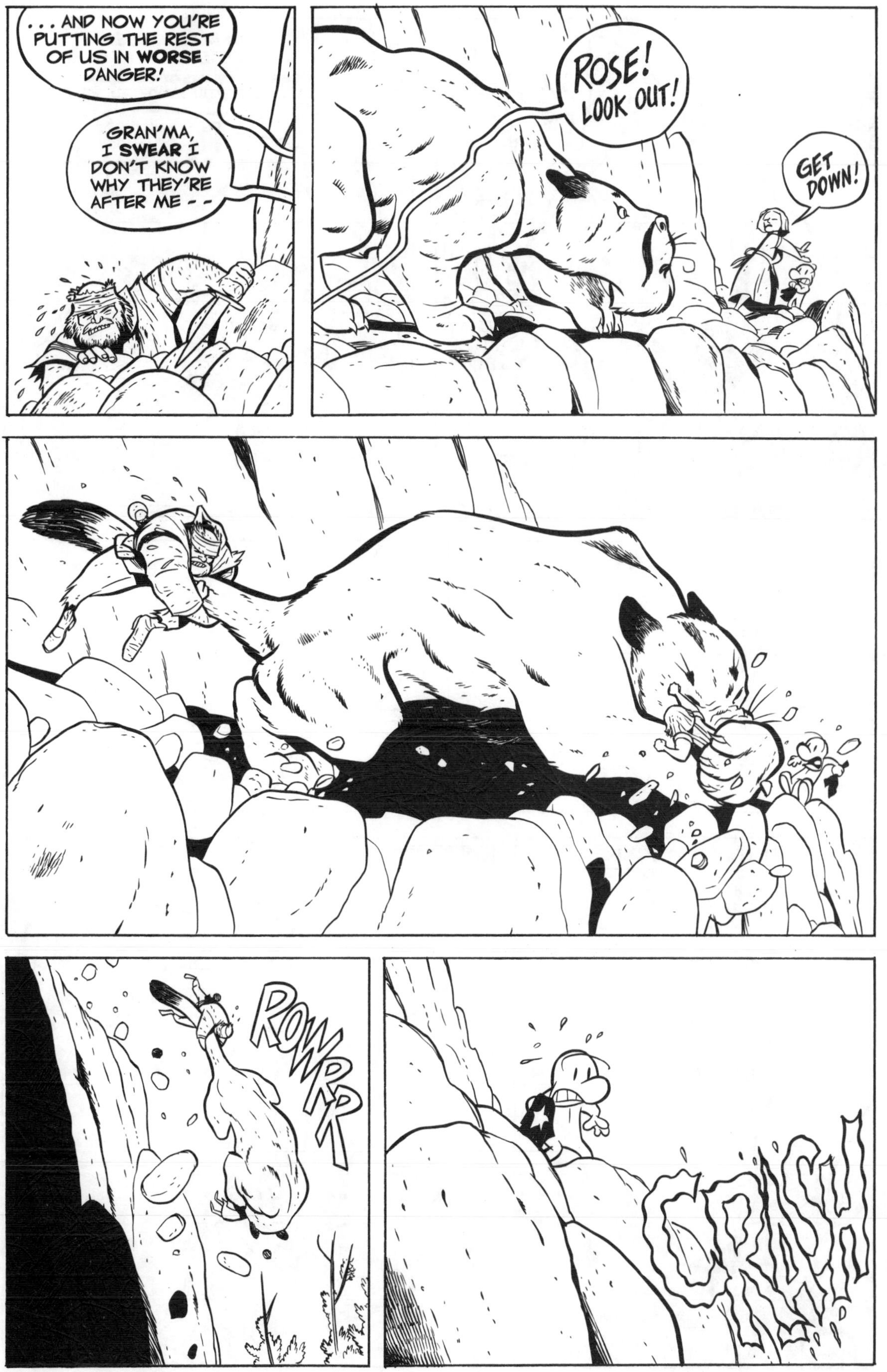

. . . AND NOW YOU'RE PUTTING THE REST OF US IN **WORSE** DANGER!
GRAN'MA, I **SWEAR** I DON'T KNOW WHY THEY'RE AFTER ME - -
ROSE! LOOK OUT!
GET DOWN!
ROWRRR
CRASH!

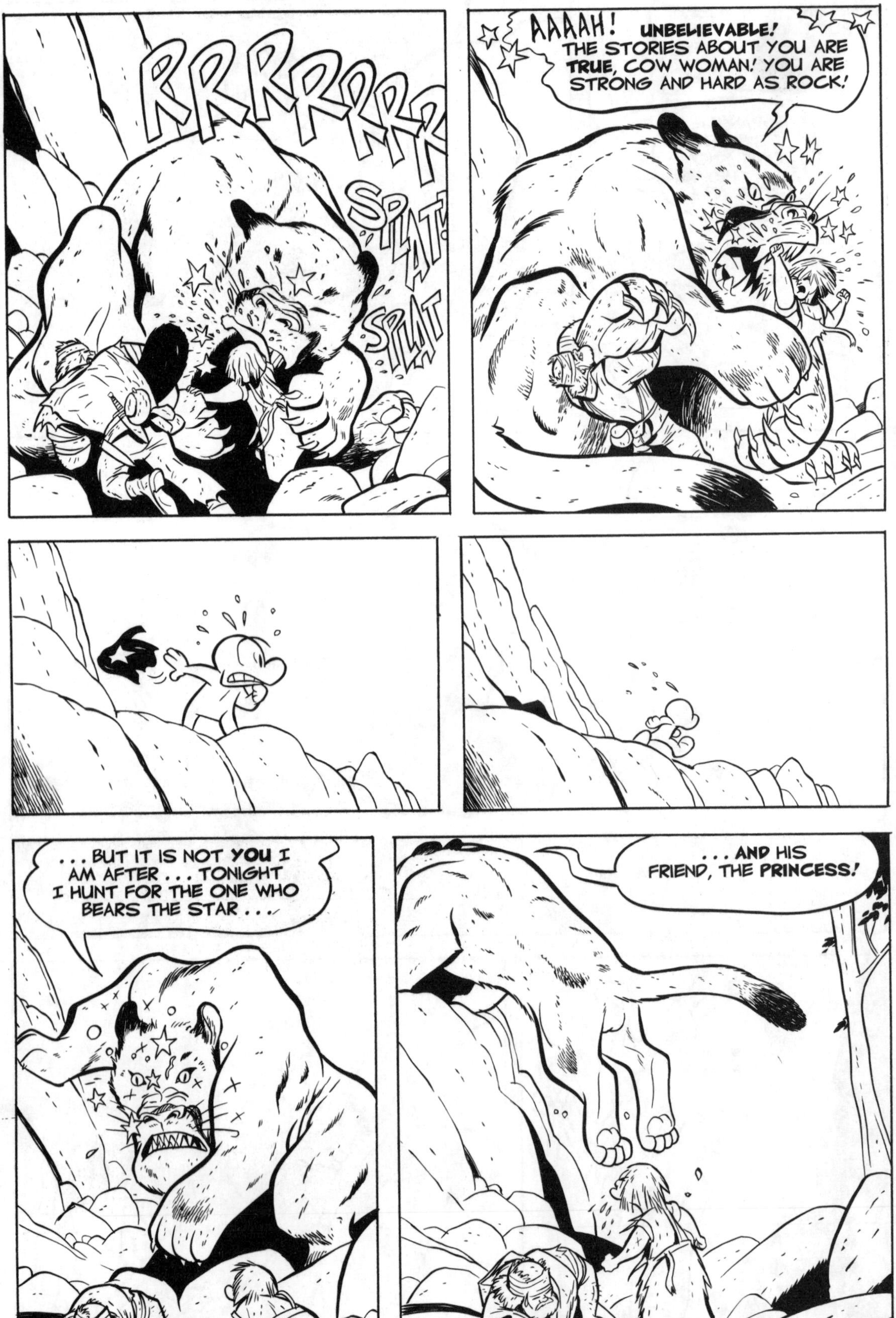
RRRRRRRR
SPLAT!
SPLAT
AAAAH! UNBELIEVABLE! THE STORIES ABOUT YOU ARE TRUE, COW WOMAN! YOU ARE STRONG AND HARD AS ROCK!
. . . BUT IT IS NOT YOU I AM AFTER . . . TONIGHT I HUNT FOR THE ONE WHO BEARS THE STAR . . .
. . . AND HIS FRIEND, THE PRINCESS!

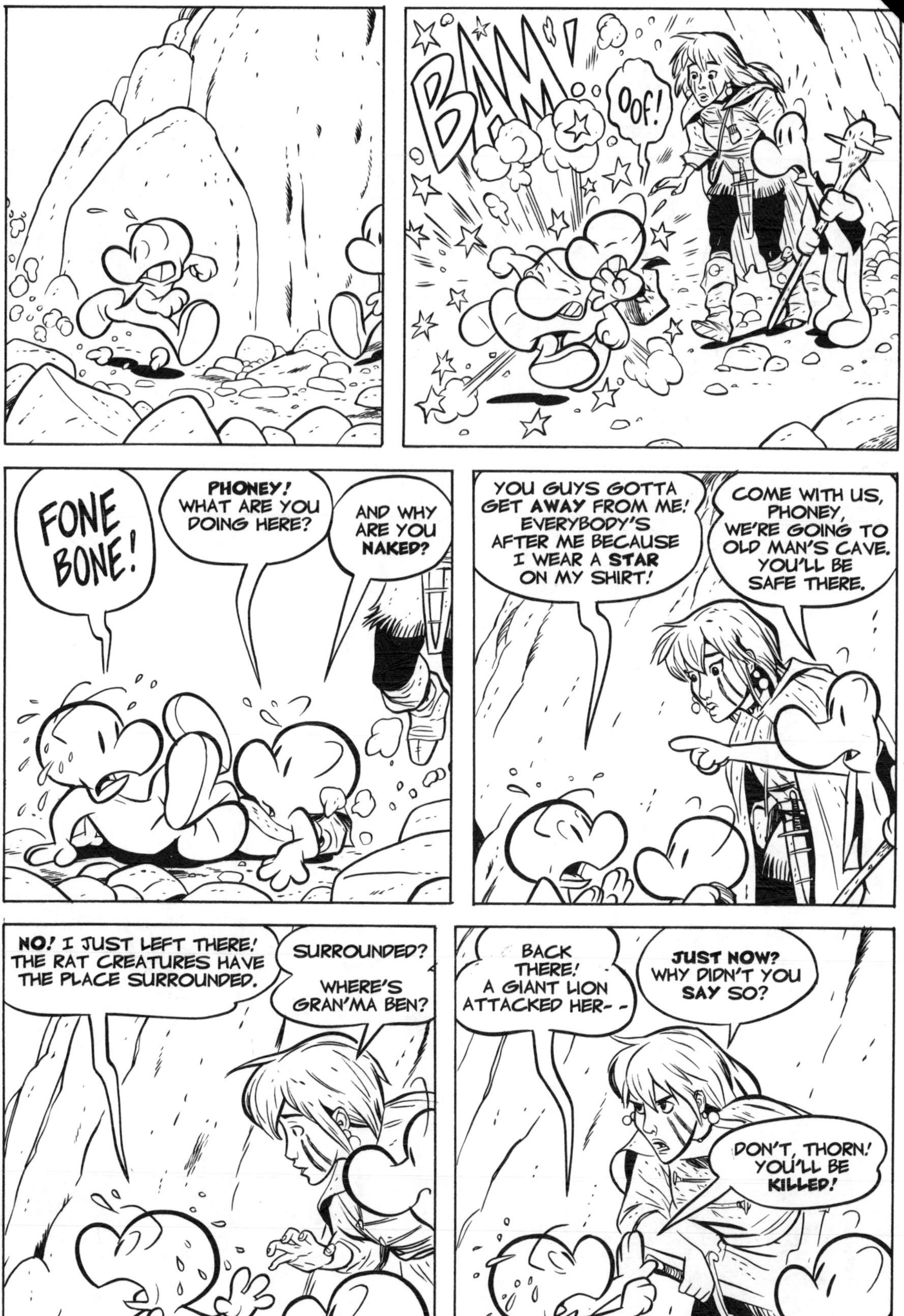
BAM!
OOF!
FONE BONE!
PHONEY! WHAT ARE YOU DOING HERE?
AND WHY ARE YOU NAKED?
YOU GUYS GOTTA GET AWAY FROM ME! EVERYBODY'S AFTER ME BECAUSE I WEAR A STAR ON MY SHIRT!
COME WITH US, PHONEY, WE'RE GOING TO OLD MAN'S CAVE. YOU'LL BE SAFE THERE.
NO! I JUST LEFT THERE! THE RAT CREATURES HAVE THE PLACE SURROUNDED.
SURROUNDED?
WHERE'S GRAN'MA BEN?
BACK THERE! A GIANT LION ATTACKED HER--
JUST NOW? WHY DIDN'T YOU SAY SO?
DON'T, THORN! YOU'LL BE KILLED!

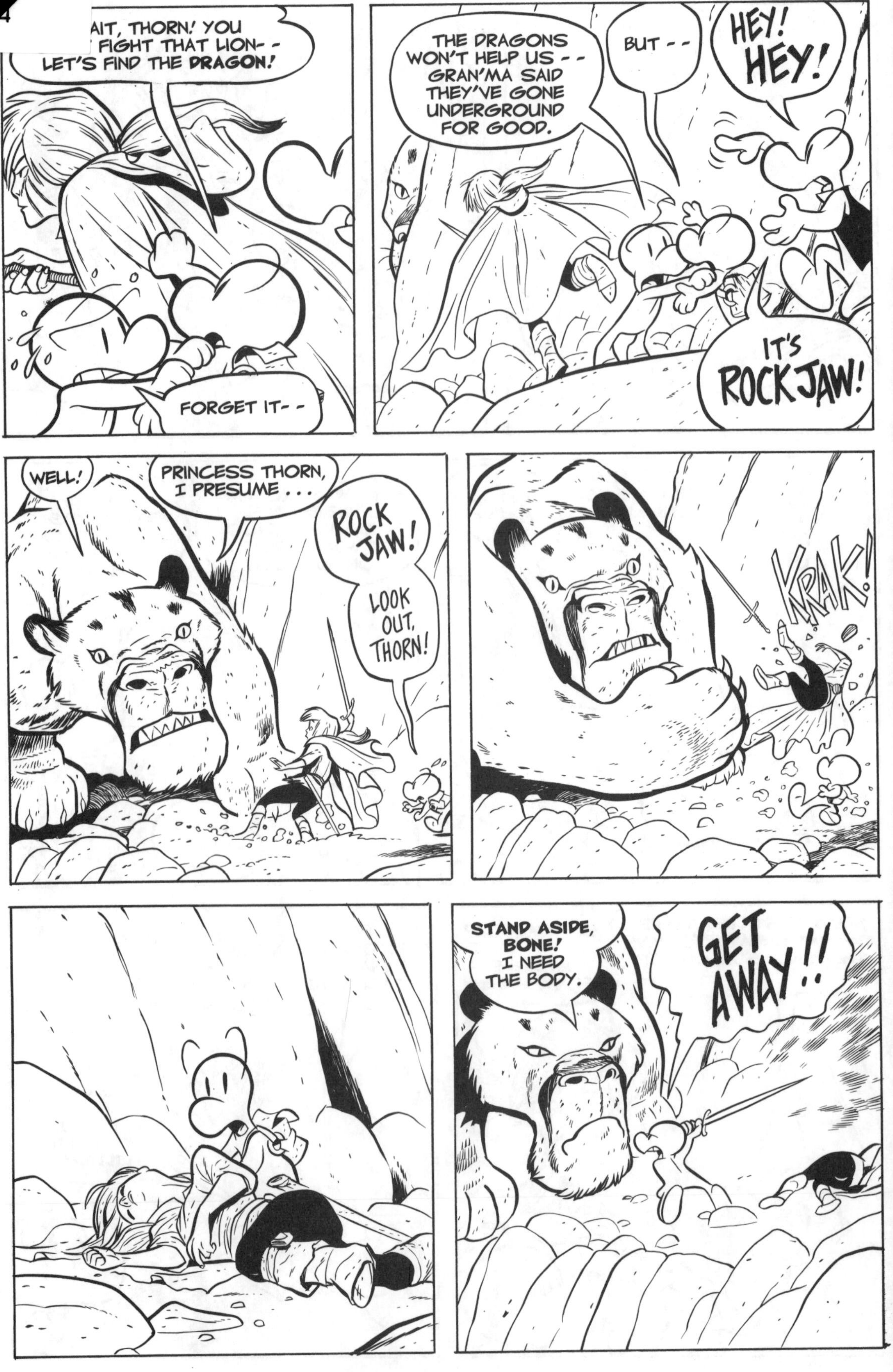
AIT, THORN! YOU FIGHT THAT LION- - LET'S FIND THE **DRAGON**!
FORGET IT- -
THE DRAGONS WON'T HELP US - - GRAN'MA SAID THEY'VE GONE UNDERGROUND FOR GOOD.
BUT - -
HEY! HEY!
IT'S ROCK JAW!
WELL!
PRINCESS THORN, I PRESUME . . .
ROCK JAW!
LOOK OUT, THORN!
KRAK!
STAND ASIDE, BONE! I NEED THE BODY.
GET AWAY!!

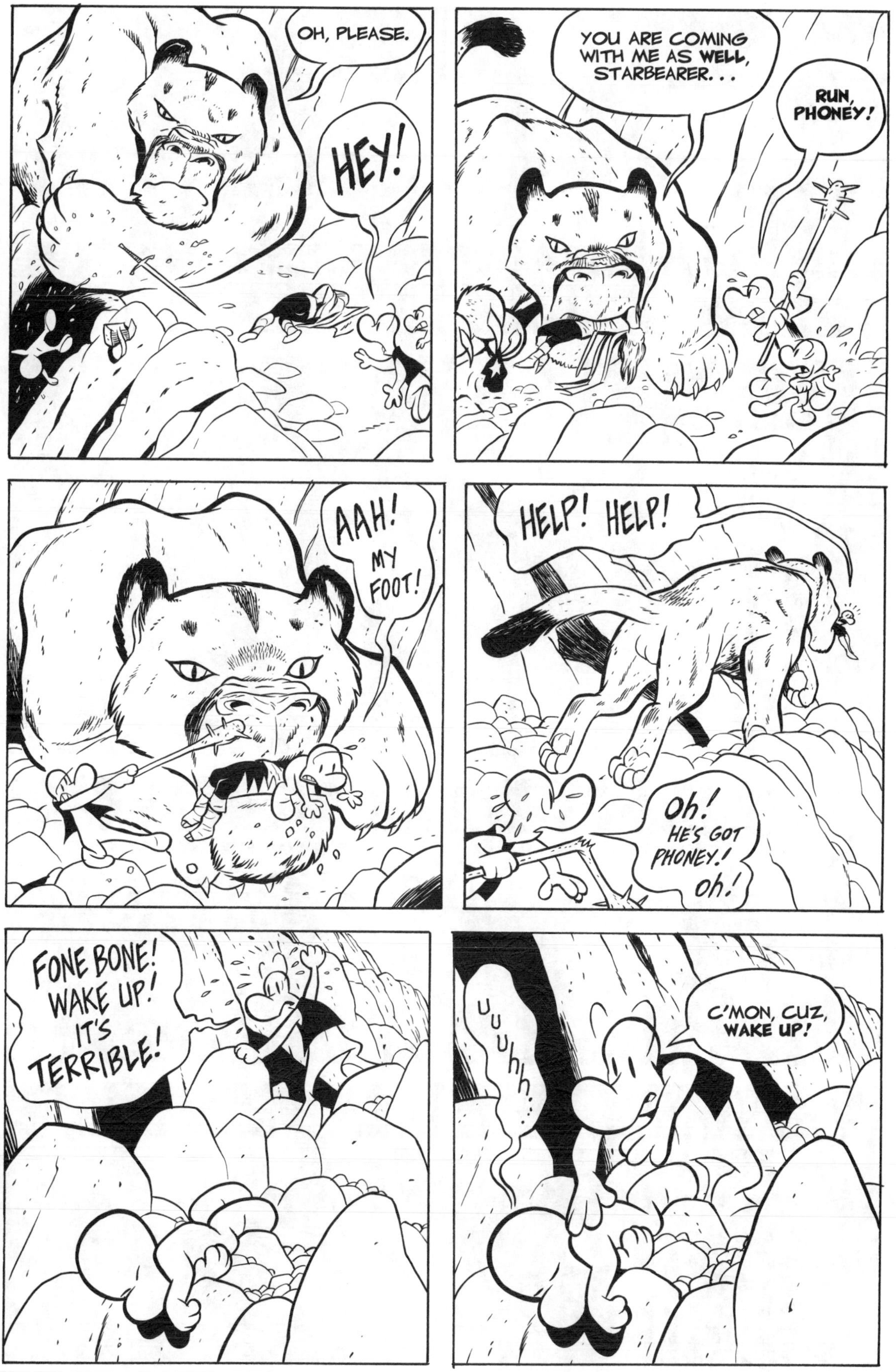
OH, PLEASE.
HEY!
YOU ARE COMING WITH ME AS WELL, STARBEARER...
RUN, PHONEY!
AAH! MY FOOT!
HELP! HELP!
Oh! HE'S GOT PHONEY! oh!
FONE BONE! WAKE UP! IT'S TERRIBLE!
Uuuhh...
C'MON, CUZ, WAKE UP!

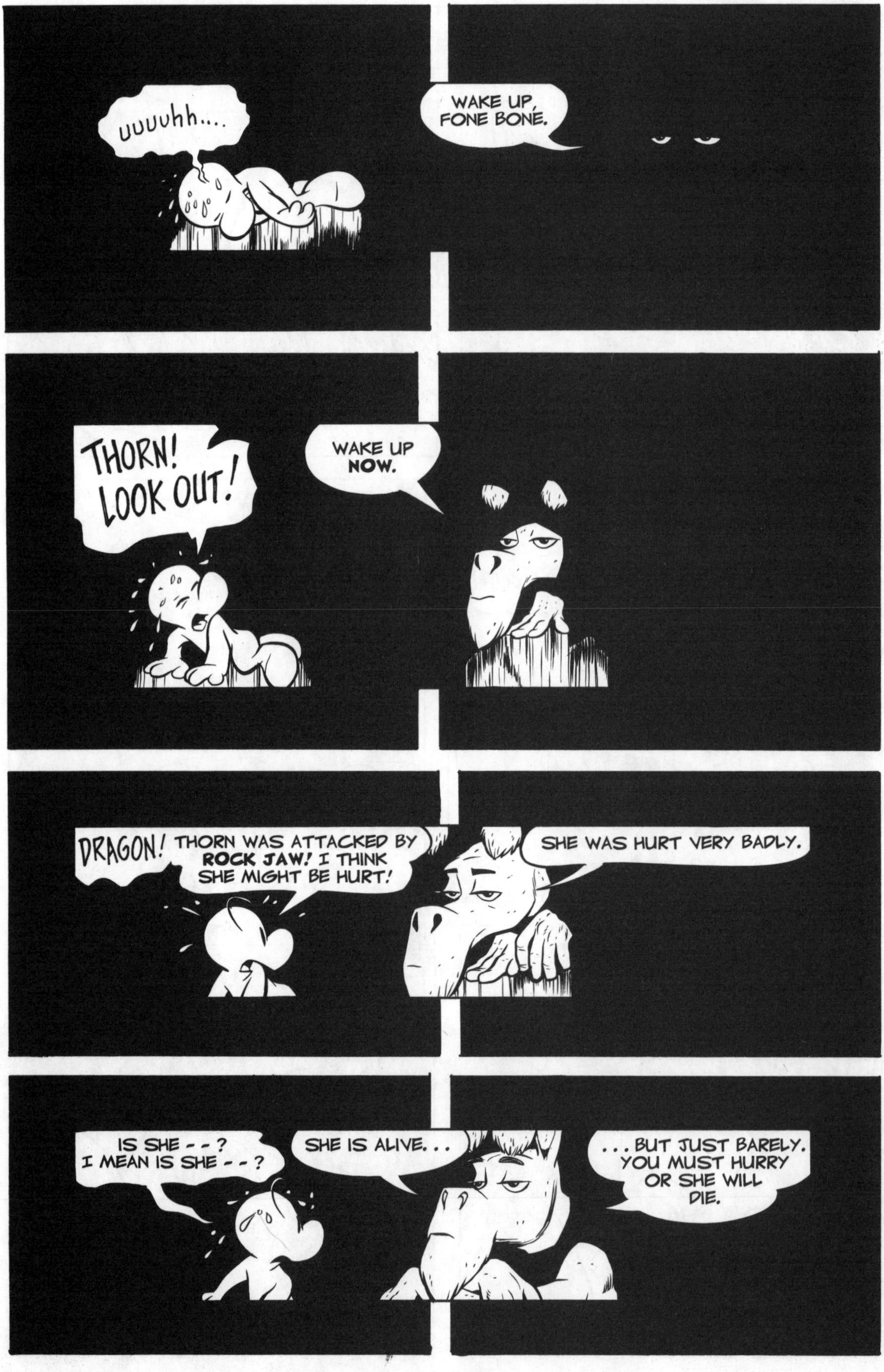
uuuuhh....
WAKE UP, FONE BONE.
THORN! LOOK OUT!
WAKE UP NOW.
DRAGON! THORN WAS ATTACKED BY ROCK JAW! I THINK SHE MIGHT BE HURT!
SHE WAS HURT VERY BADLY.
IS SHE - - ? I MEAN IS SHE - - ?
SHE IS ALIVE. . .
. . . BUT JUST BARELY. YOU MUST HURRY OR SHE WILL DIE.

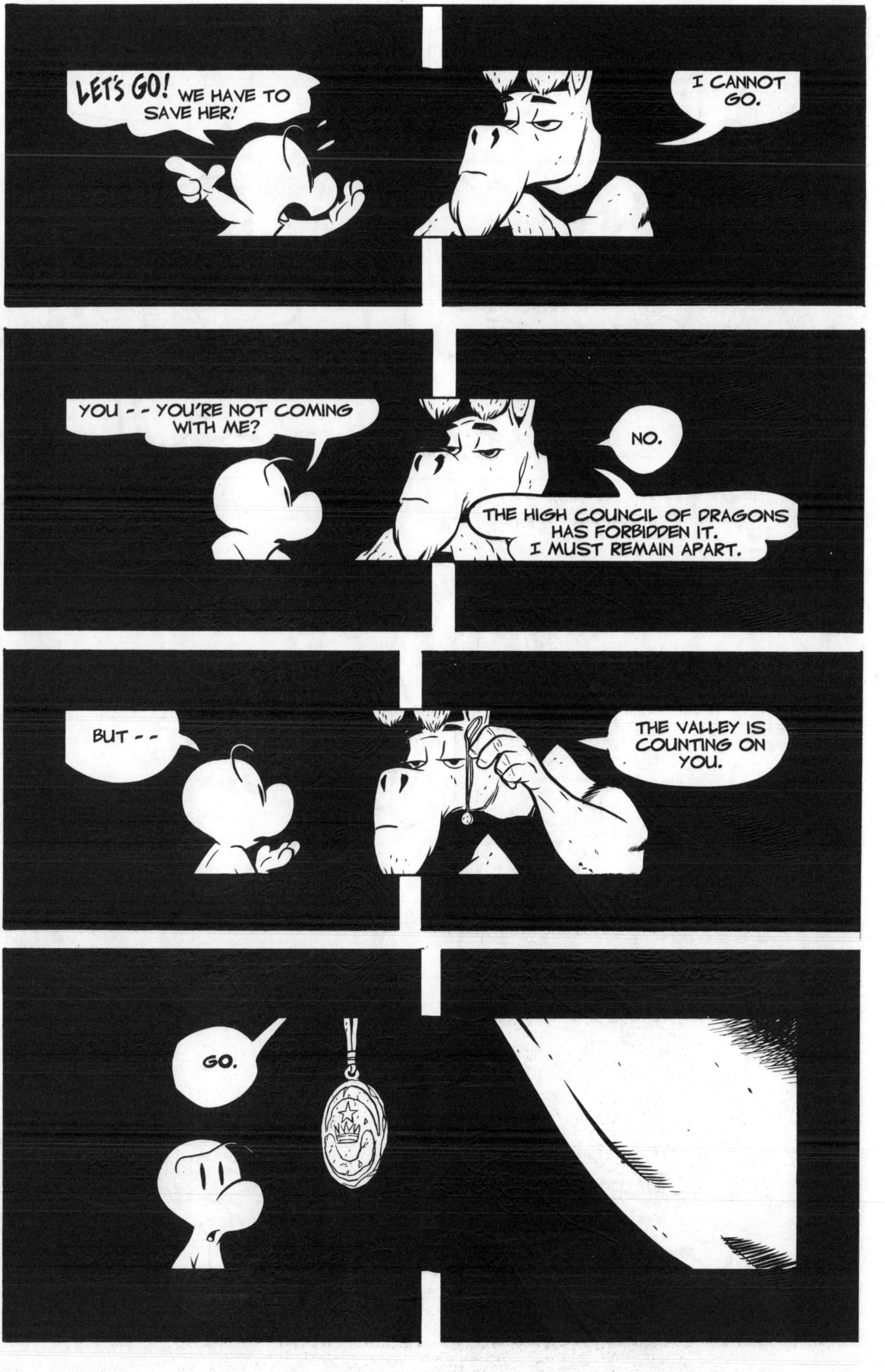
LET'S GO! WE HAVE TO SAVE HER!
I CANNOT GO.
YOU - - YOU'RE NOT COMING WITH ME?
NO.
THE HIGH COUNCIL OF DRAGONS HAS FORBIDDEN IT. I MUST REMAIN APART.
BUT - -
THE VALLEY IS COUNTING ON YOU.
GO.

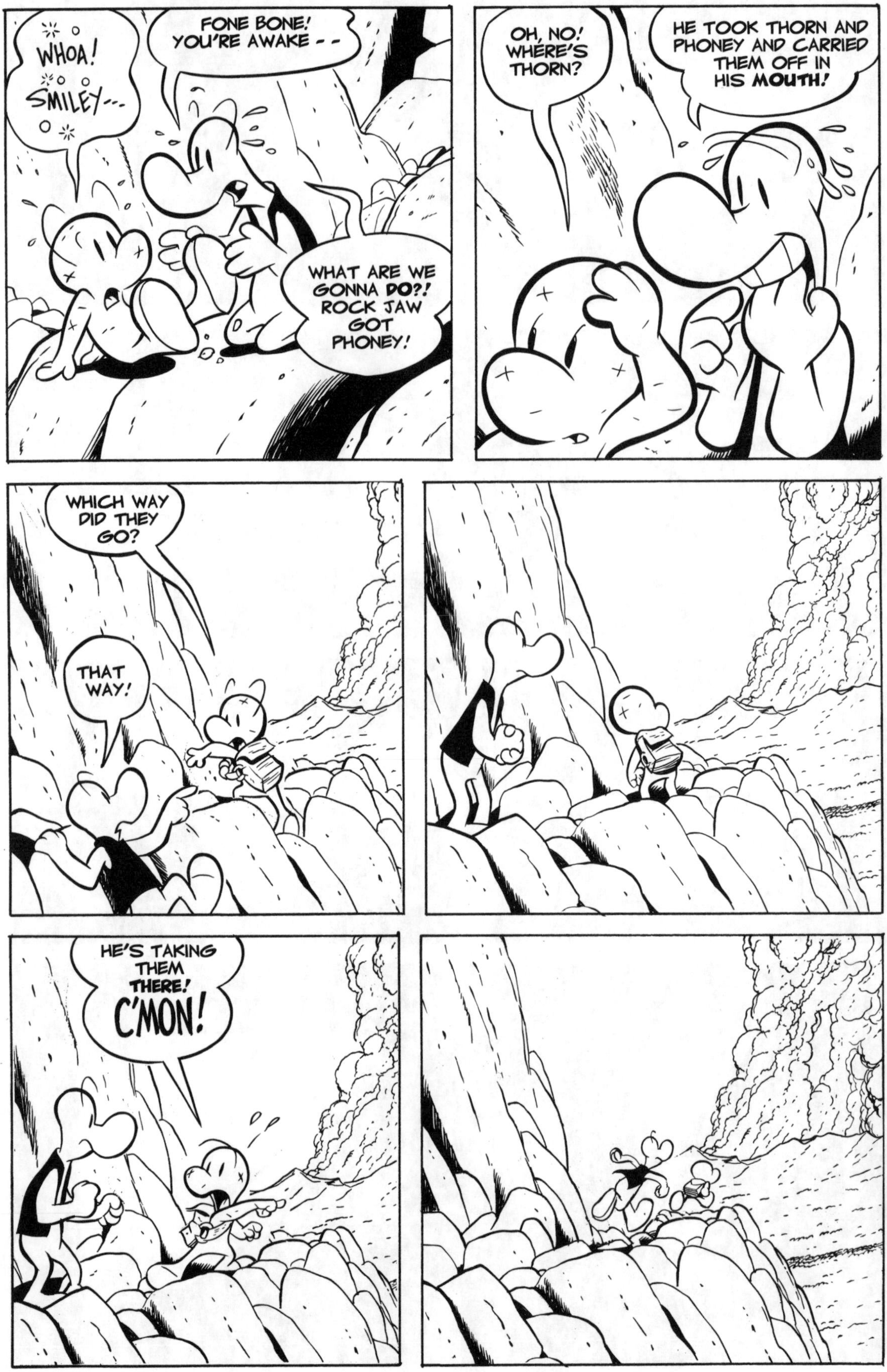
WHOA! SMILEY---
FONE BONE! YOU'RE AWAKE --
WHAT ARE WE GONNA DO?! ROCK JAW GOT PHONEY!
OH, NO! WHERE'S THORN?
HE TOOK THORN AND PHONEY AND CARRIED THEM OFF IN HIS MOUTH!
WHICH WAY DID THEY GO?
THAT WAY!
HE'S TAKING THEM THERE! C'MON!

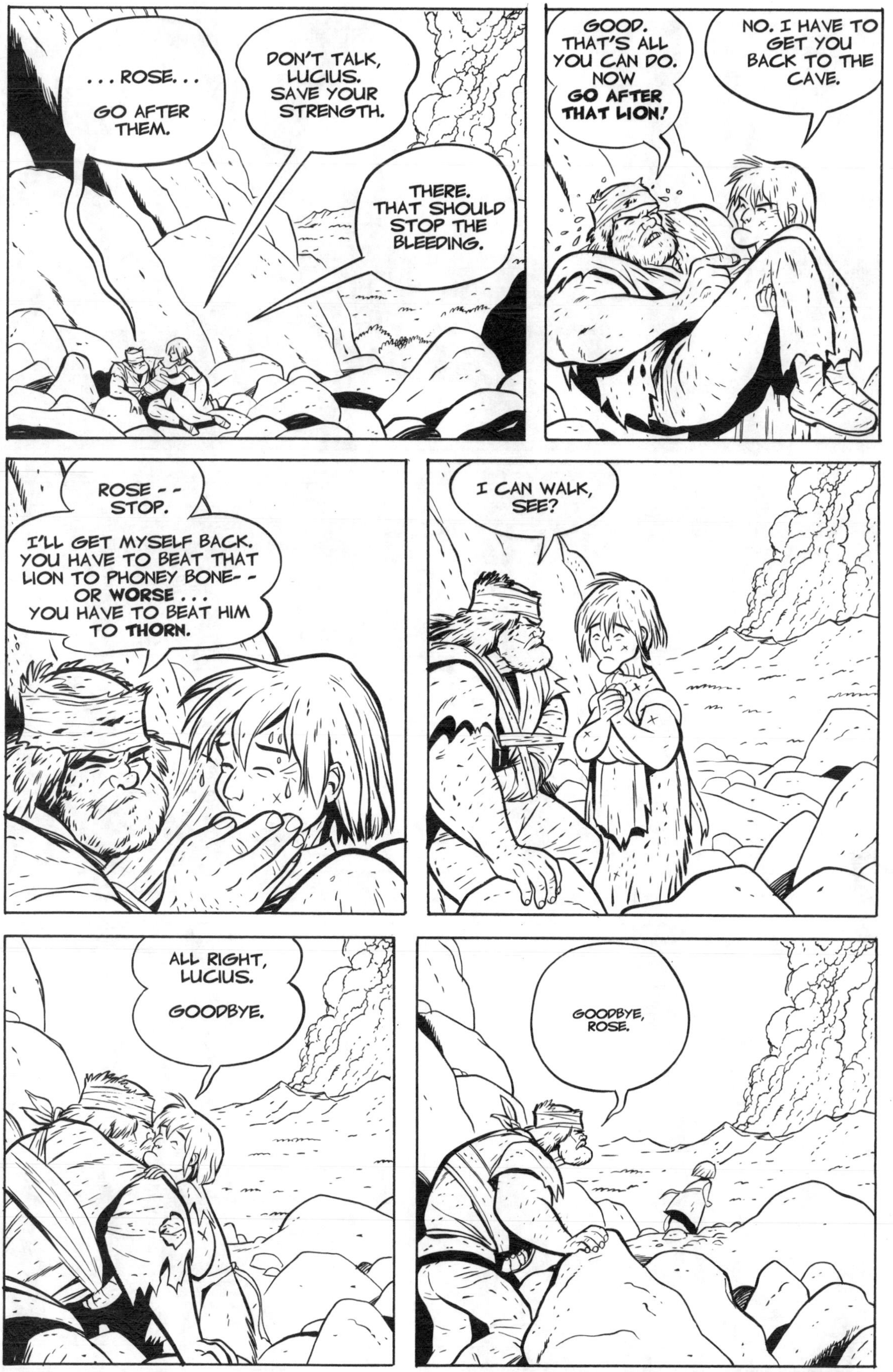
. . . ROSE . . .
GO AFTER THEM.
DON'T TALK, LUCIUS. SAVE YOUR STRENGTH.
THERE. THAT SHOULD STOP THE BLEEDING.
GOOD. THAT'S ALL YOU CAN DO. NOW **GO AFTER THAT LION!**
NO. I HAVE TO GET YOU BACK TO THE CAVE.
ROSE -- STOP.
I'LL GET MYSELF BACK. YOU HAVE TO BEAT THAT LION TO PHONEY BONE-- OR **WORSE** . . . YOU HAVE TO BEAT HIM TO **THORN.**
I CAN WALK, SEE?
ALL RIGHT, LUCIUS.
GOODBYE.
GOODBYE, ROSE.

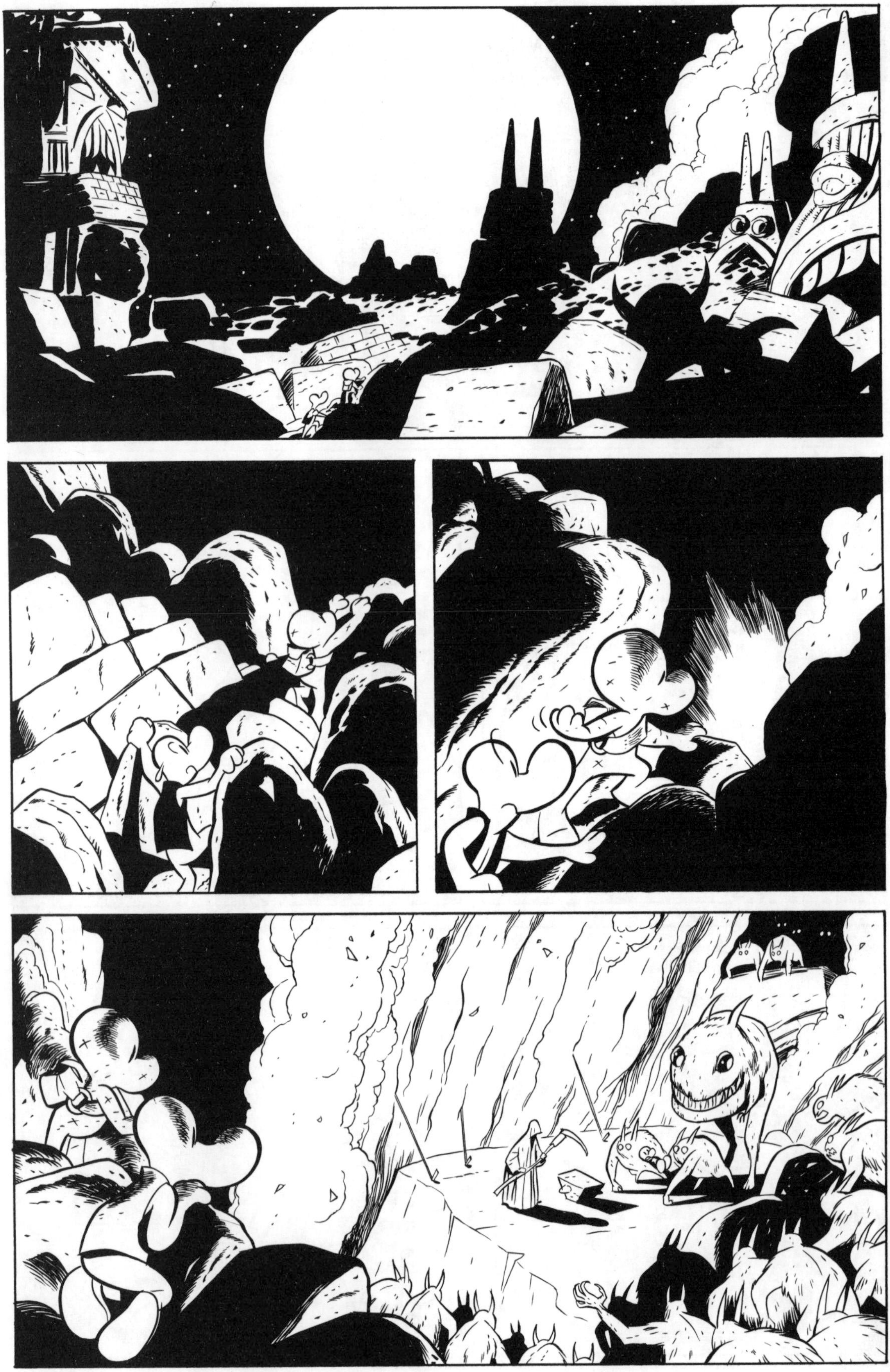

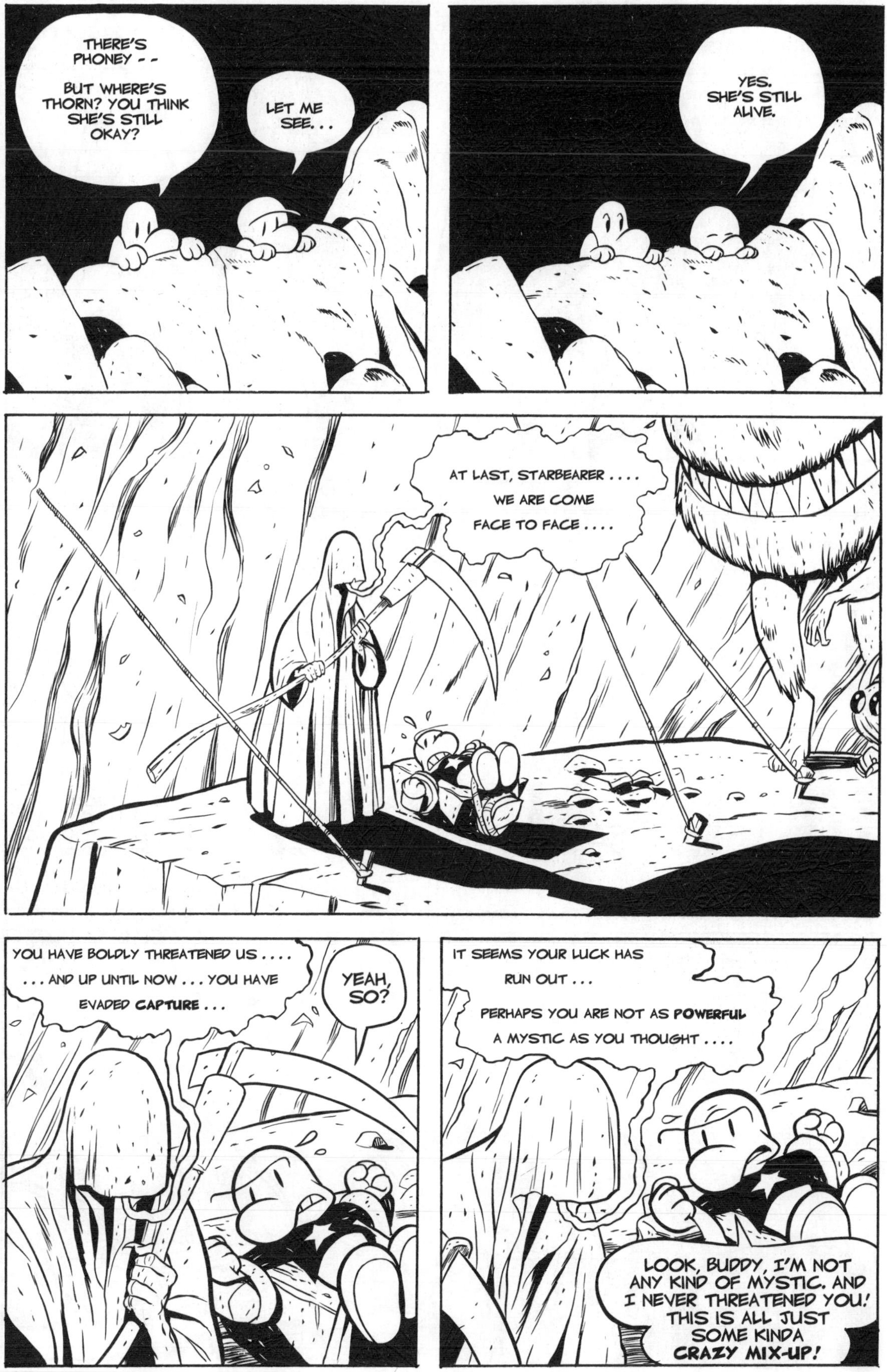
THERE'S PHONEY - - BUT WHERE'S THORN? YOU THINK SHE'S STILL OKAY?
LET ME SEE...
YES. SHE'S STILL ALIVE.
AT LAST, STARBEARER.... WE ARE COME FACE TO FACE....
YOU HAVE BOLDLY THREATENED US.... ...AND UP UNTIL NOW... YOU HAVE EVADED CAPTURE...
YEAH, SO?
IT SEEMS YOUR LUCK HAS RUN OUT... PERHAPS YOU ARE NOT AS POWERFUL A MYSTIC AS YOU THOUGHT....
LOOK, BUDDY, I'M NOT ANY KIND OF MYSTIC. AND I NEVER THREATENED YOU! THIS IS ALL JUST SOME KINDA CRAZY MIX-UP!

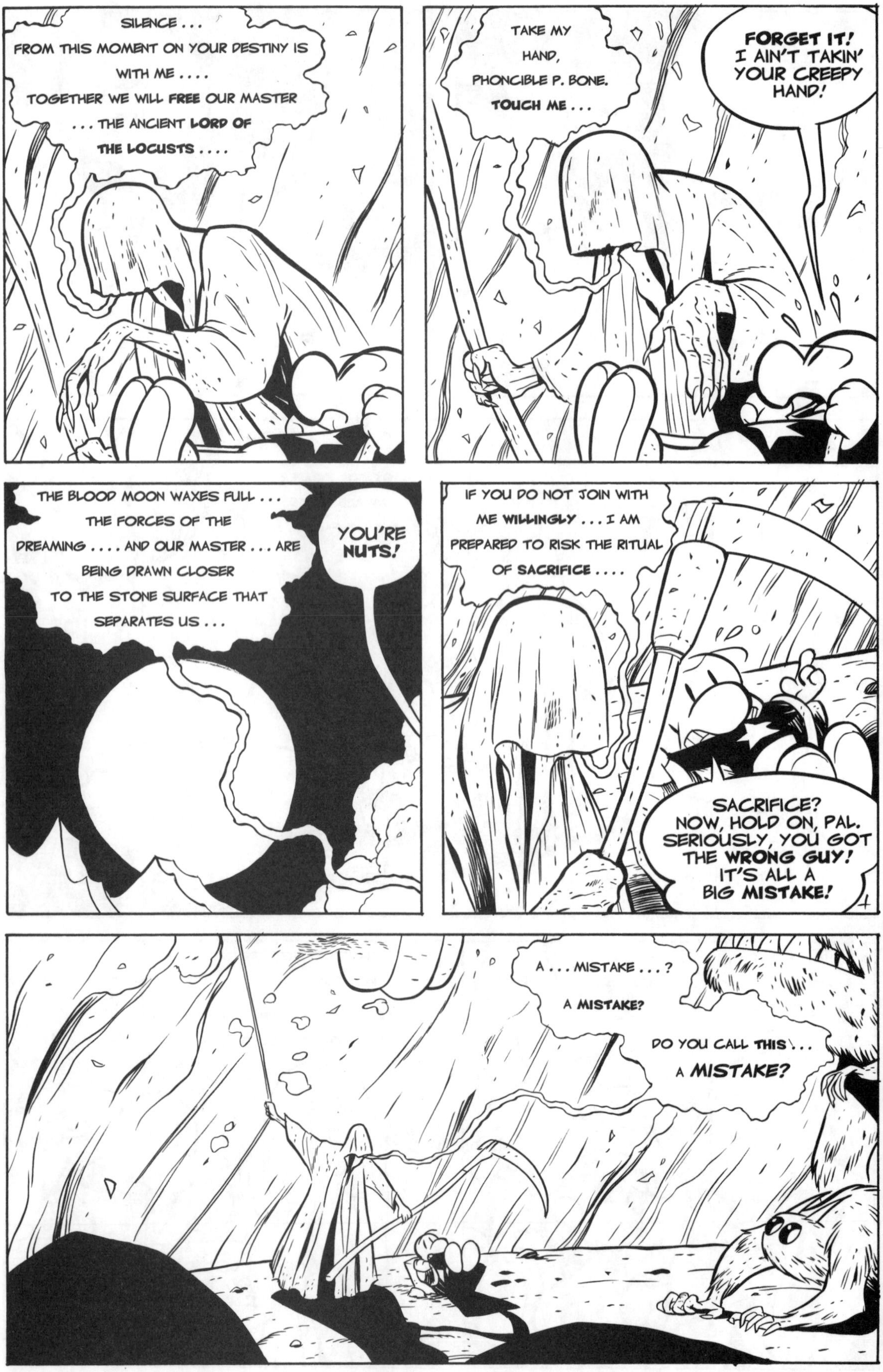
SILENCE . . . FROM THIS MOMENT ON YOUR DESTINY IS WITH ME . . . . TOGETHER WE WILL FREE OUR MASTER . . . THE ANCIENT LORD OF THE LOCUSTS . . . .
TAKE MY HAND, PHONCIBLE P. BONE. TOUCH ME . . .
FORGET IT! I AIN'T TAKIN' YOUR CREEPY HAND!
THE BLOOD MOON WAXES FULL . . . THE FORCES OF THE DREAMING . . . . AND OUR MASTER . . . ARE BEING DRAWN CLOSER TO THE STONE SURFACE THAT SEPARATES US . . .
YOU'RE NUTS!
IF YOU DO NOT JOIN WITH ME WILLINGLY . . . I AM PREPARED TO RISK THE RITUAL OF SACRIFICE . . . .
SACRIFICE? NOW, HOLD ON, PAL. SERIOUSLY, YOU GOT THE WRONG GUY! IT'S ALL A BIG MISTAKE!
4
A . . . MISTAKE . . . ? A MISTAKE? DO YOU CALL THIS . . . A MISTAKE?

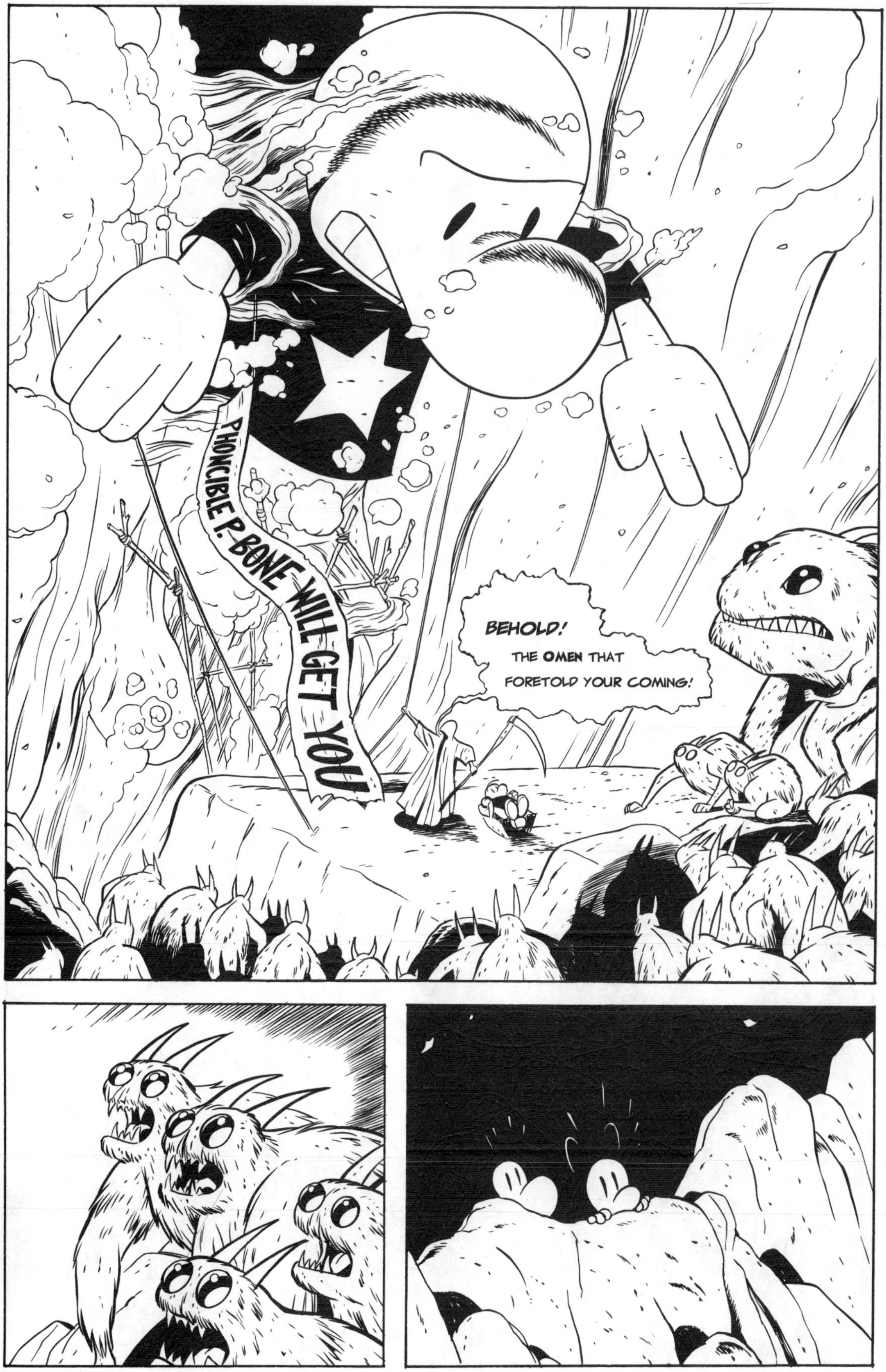
PHONCIBLE P. BONE WILL GET YOU
BEHOLD! THE OMEN THAT FORETOLD YOUR COMING!

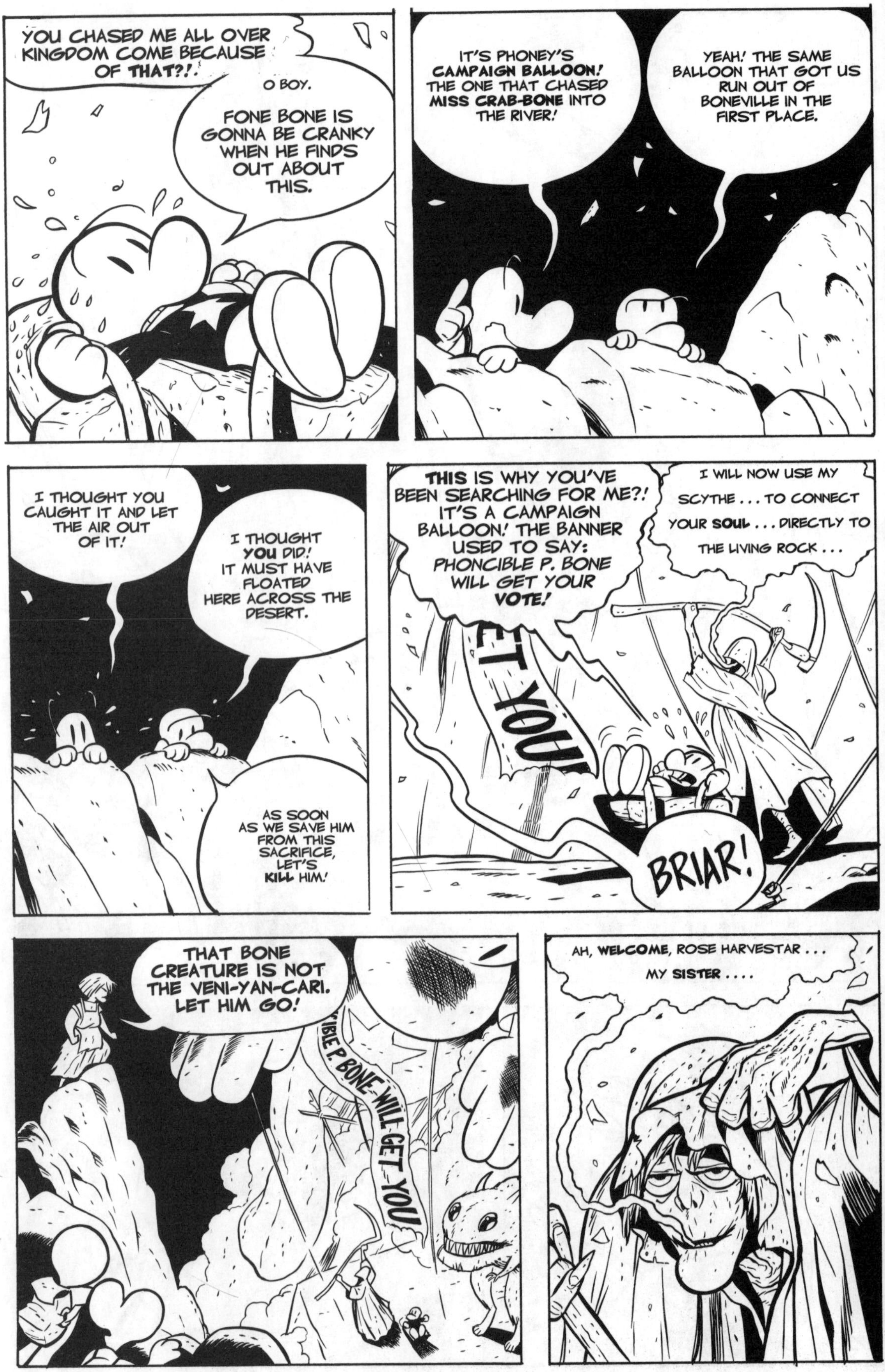
YOU CHASED ME ALL OVER KINGDOM COME BECAUSE OF THAT?!.
O BOY.
FONE BONE IS GONNA BE CRANKY WHEN HE FINDS OUT ABOUT THIS.
IT'S PHONEY'S CAMPAIGN BALLOON! THE ONE THAT CHASED MISS CRAB-BONE INTO THE RIVER!
YEAH! THE SAME BALLOON THAT GOT US RUN OUT OF BONEVILLE IN THE FIRST PLACE.
I THOUGHT YOU CAUGHT IT AND LET THE AIR OUT OF IT!
I THOUGHT YOU DID! IT MUST HAVE FLOATED HERE ACROSS THE DESERT.
AS SOON AS WE SAVE HIM FROM THIS SACRIFICE, LET'S KILL HIM!
THIS IS WHY YOU'VE BEEN SEARCHING FOR ME?! IT'S A CAMPAIGN BALLOON! THE BANNER USED TO SAY: PHONCIBLE P. BONE WILL GET YOUR VOTE!
I WILL NOW USE MY SCYTHE . . . TO CONNECT YOUR SOUL . . . DIRECTLY TO THE LIVING ROCK . . .
ET YOU
BRIAR!
THAT BONE CREATURE IS NOT THE VENI-YAN-CARI. LET HIM GO!
P. BONE WILL GET YOU
AH, WELCOME, ROSE HARVESTAR . . . MY SISTER . . . .

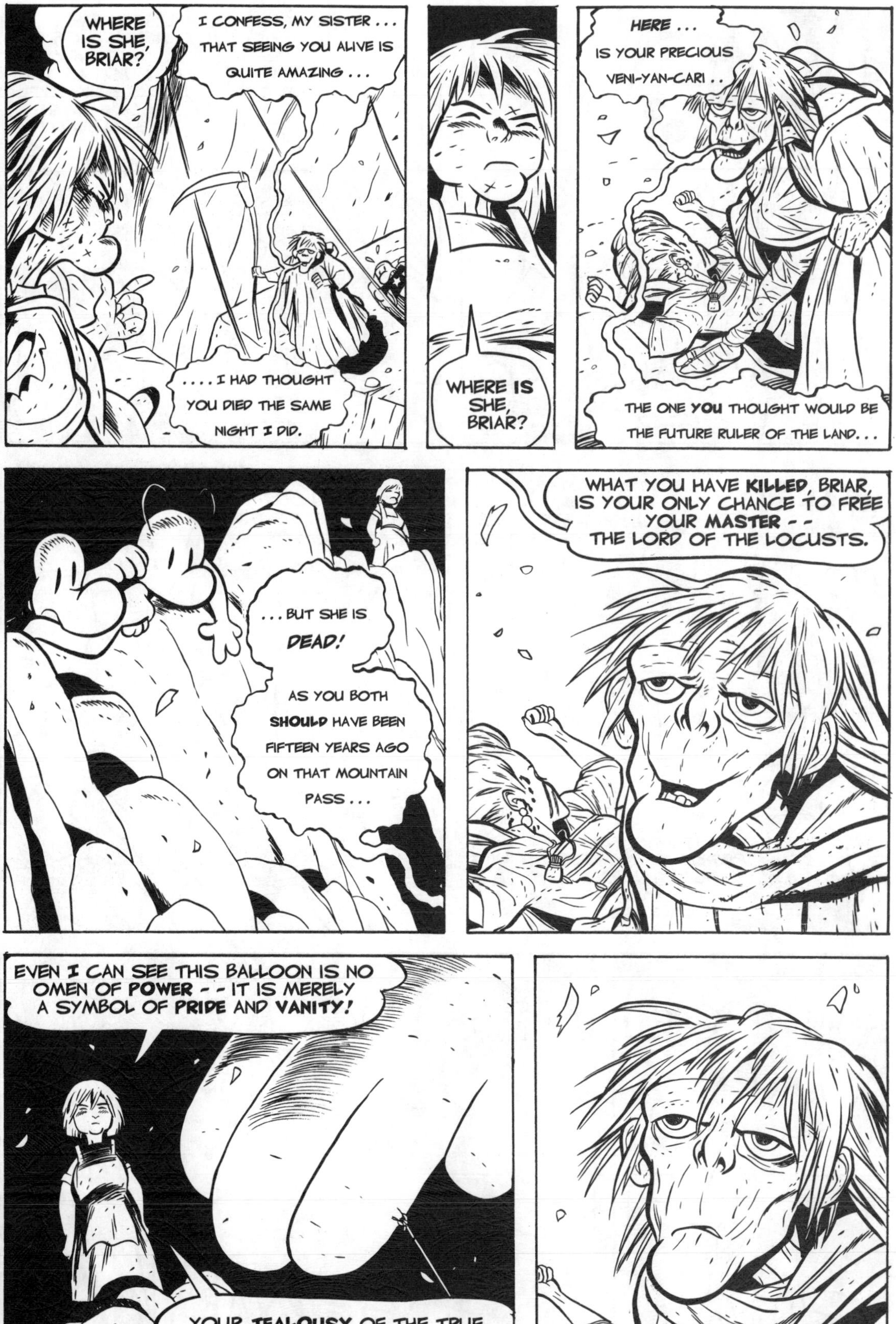
WHERE IS SHE, BRIAR?
I CONFESS, MY SISTER . . . THAT SEEING YOU ALIVE IS QUITE AMAZING . . .
. . . . I HAD THOUGHT YOU DIED THE SAME NIGHT I DID.
WHERE IS SHE, BRIAR?
HERE . . . IS YOUR PRECIOUS VENI-YAN-CARI . .
THE ONE YOU THOUGHT WOULD BE THE FUTURE RULER OF THE LAND. . .
. . . BUT SHE IS DEAD!
AS YOU BOTH SHOULD HAVE BEEN FIFTEEN YEARS AGO ON THAT MOUNTAIN PASS . . .
WHAT YOU HAVE KILLED, BRIAR, IS YOUR ONLY CHANCE TO FREE YOUR MASTER - - THE LORD OF THE LOCUSTS.
EVEN I CAN SEE THIS BALLOON IS NO OMEN OF POWER - - IT IS MERELY A SYMBOL OF PRIDE AND VANITY!
YOUR JEALOUSY OF THE TRUE VENI-YAN-CARI HAS BLINDED YOU - - AND YOU HAVE BADLY MISCALCULATED, MY SISTER.

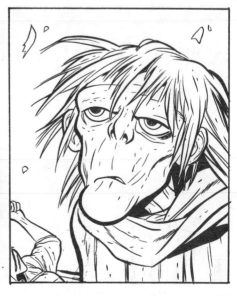

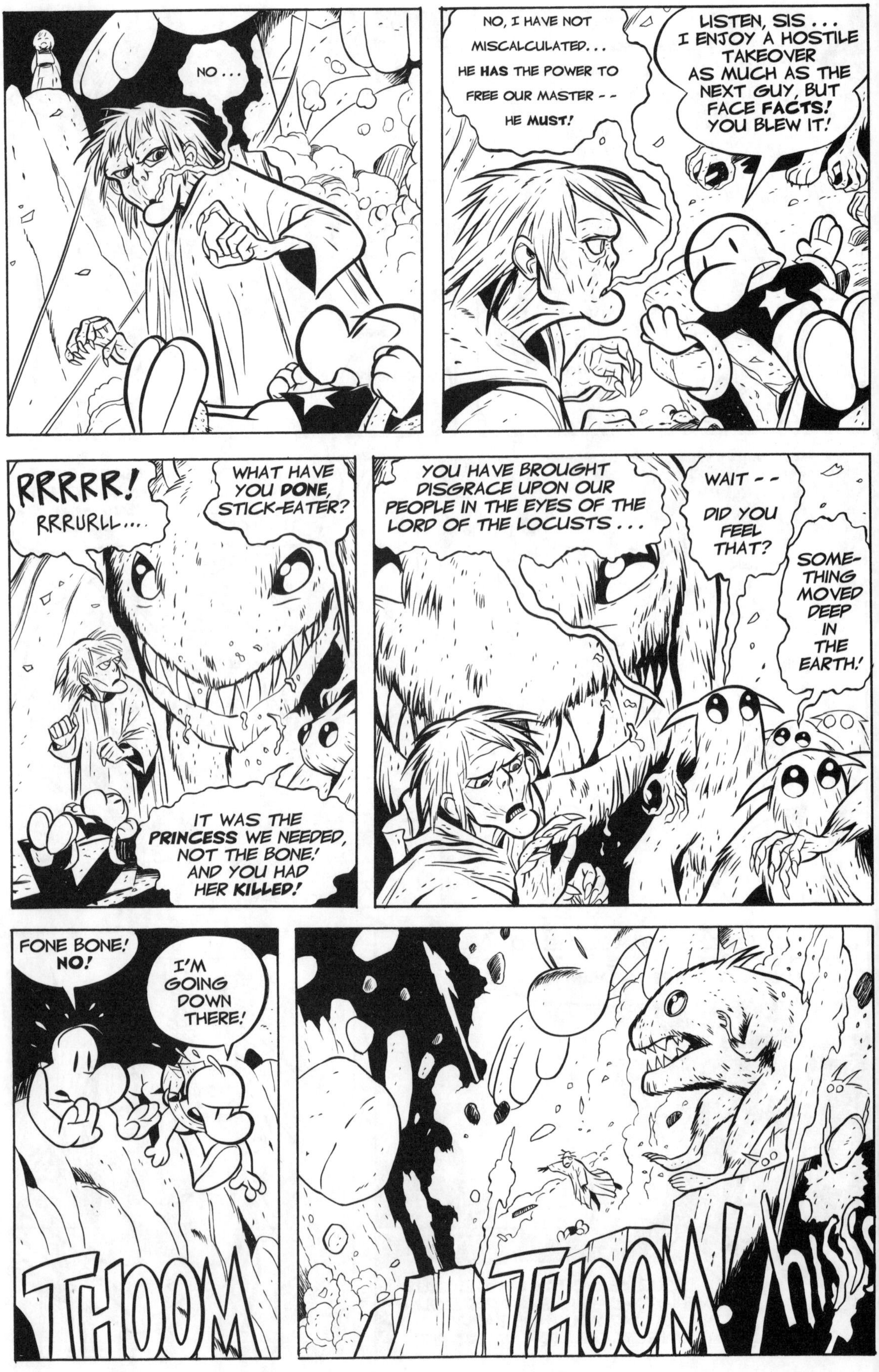
NO . . .
NO, I HAVE NOT MISCALCULATED . . . HE HAS THE POWER TO FREE OUR MASTER - - HE MUST!
LISTEN, SIS . . . I ENJOY A HOSTILE TAKEOVER AS MUCH AS THE NEXT GUY, BUT FACE FACTS! YOU BLEW IT!
RRRRR! RRRURLL . . .
WHAT HAVE YOU DONE, STICK-EATER?
IT WAS THE PRINCESS WE NEEDED, NOT THE BONE! AND YOU HAD HER KILLED!
YOU HAVE BROUGHT DISGRACE UPON OUR PEOPLE IN THE EYES OF THE LORD OF THE LOCUSTS . . .
WAIT - -
DID YOU FEEL THAT?
SOME-THING MOVED DEEP IN THE EARTH!
FONE BONE! NO!
I'M GOING DOWN THERE!
THOOM
THOOM!
hiss

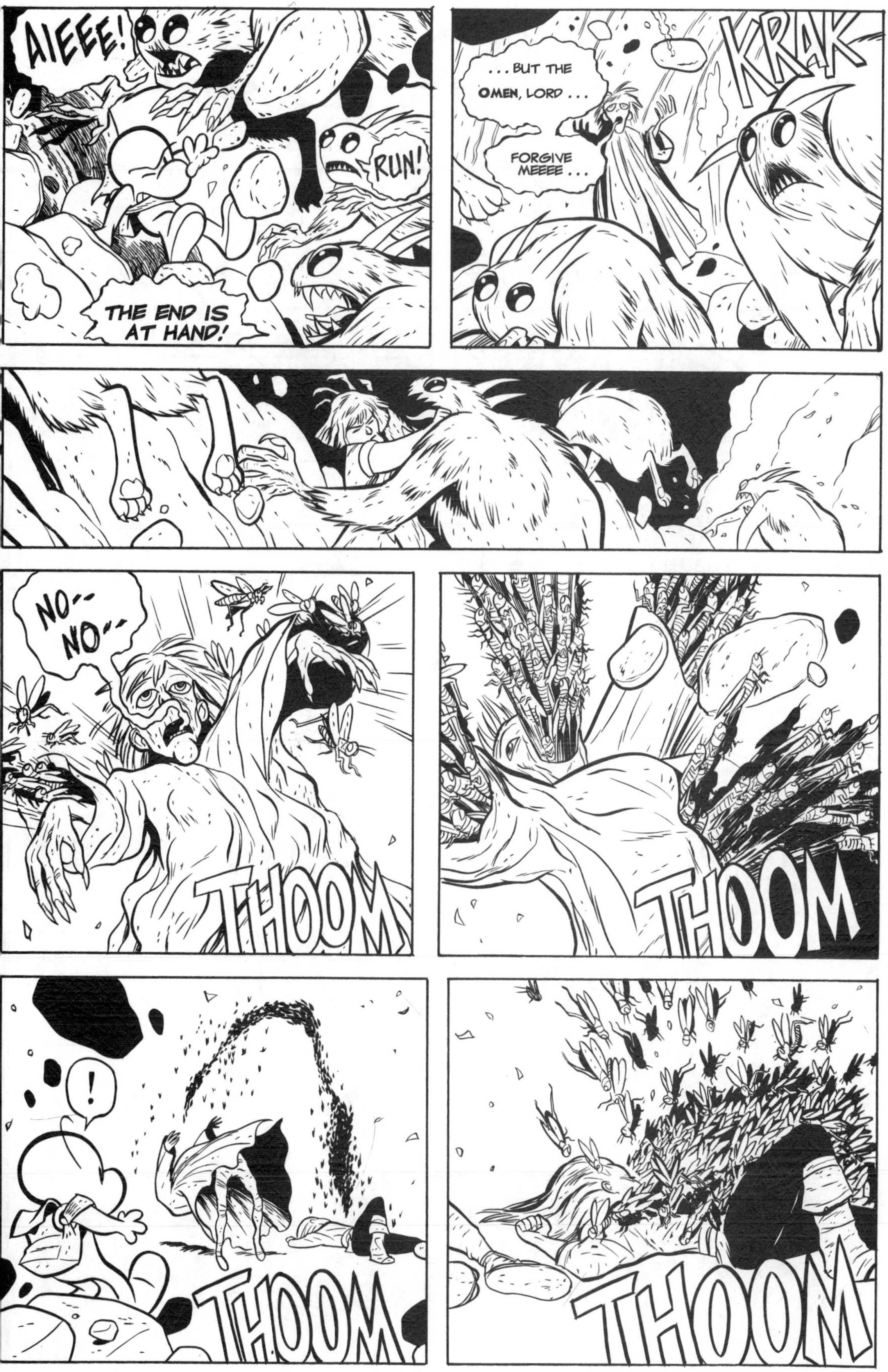
AIEEE!
RUN!
THE END IS AT HAND!
. . . BUT THE OMEN, LORD . . .
FORGIVE MEEEE . . .
KRAK
NO-- NO--
THOOM
THOOM
!
THOOM
THOOM

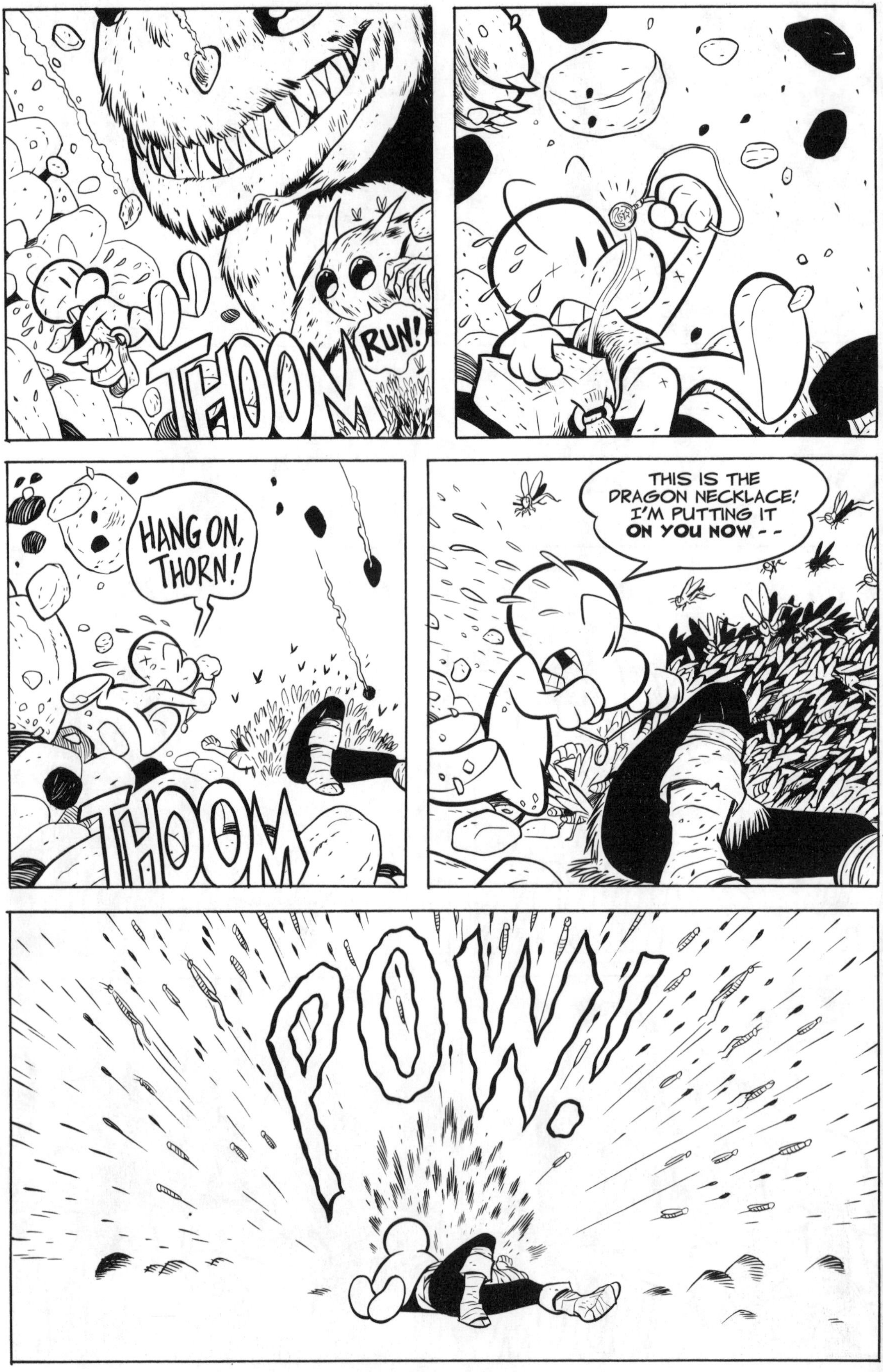
THOOM
RUN!
HANG ON, THORN!
THOOM
THIS IS THE DRAGON NECKLACE! I'M PUTTING IT ON YOU NOW - -
POW!

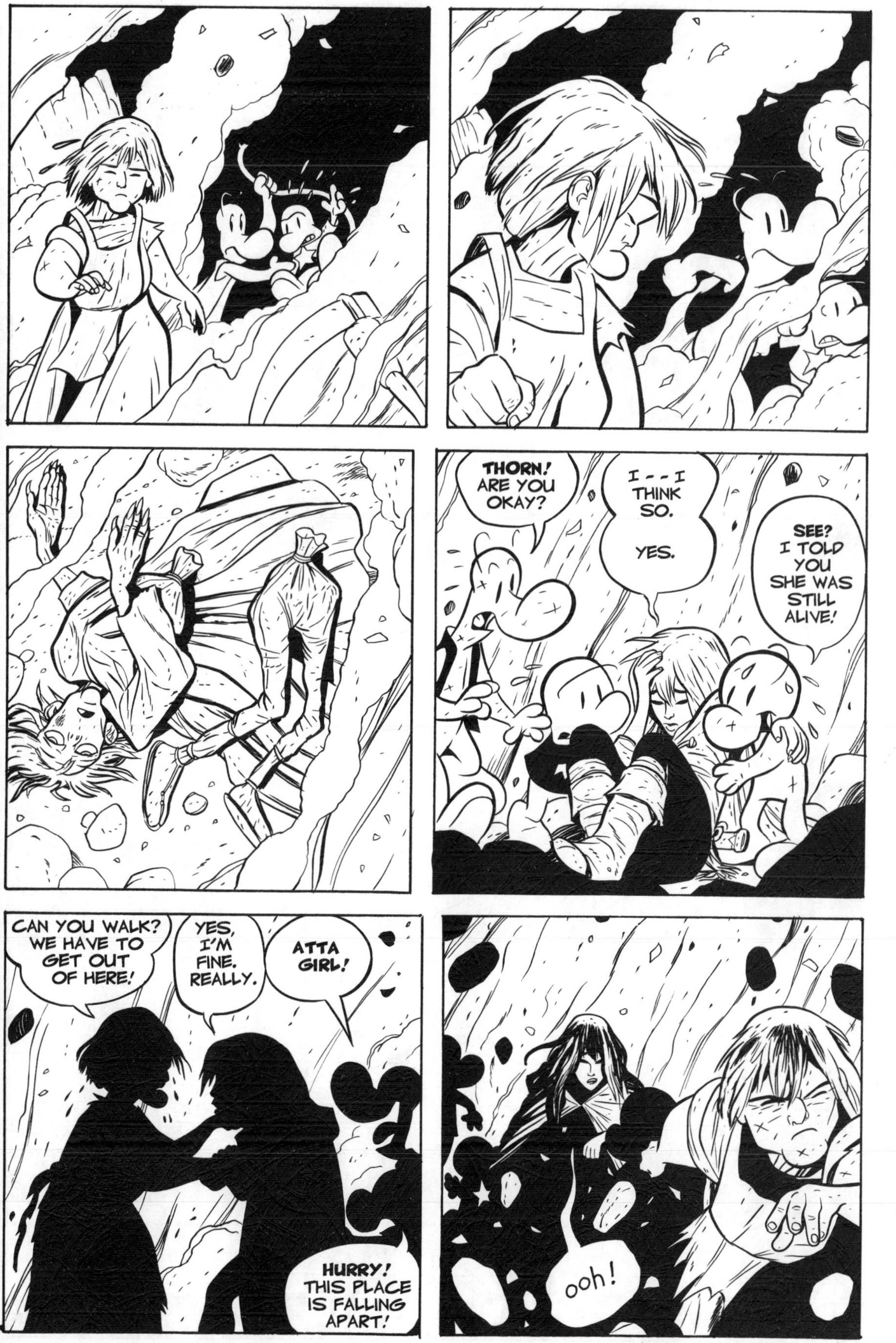
THORN! ARE YOU OKAY?
I - - I THINK SO.
YES.
SEE? I TOLD YOU SHE WAS STILL ALIVE!
CAN YOU WALK? WE HAVE TO GET OUT OF HERE!
YES, I'M FINE. REALLY.
ATTA GIRL!
HURRY! THIS PLACE IS FALLING APART!
ooh!

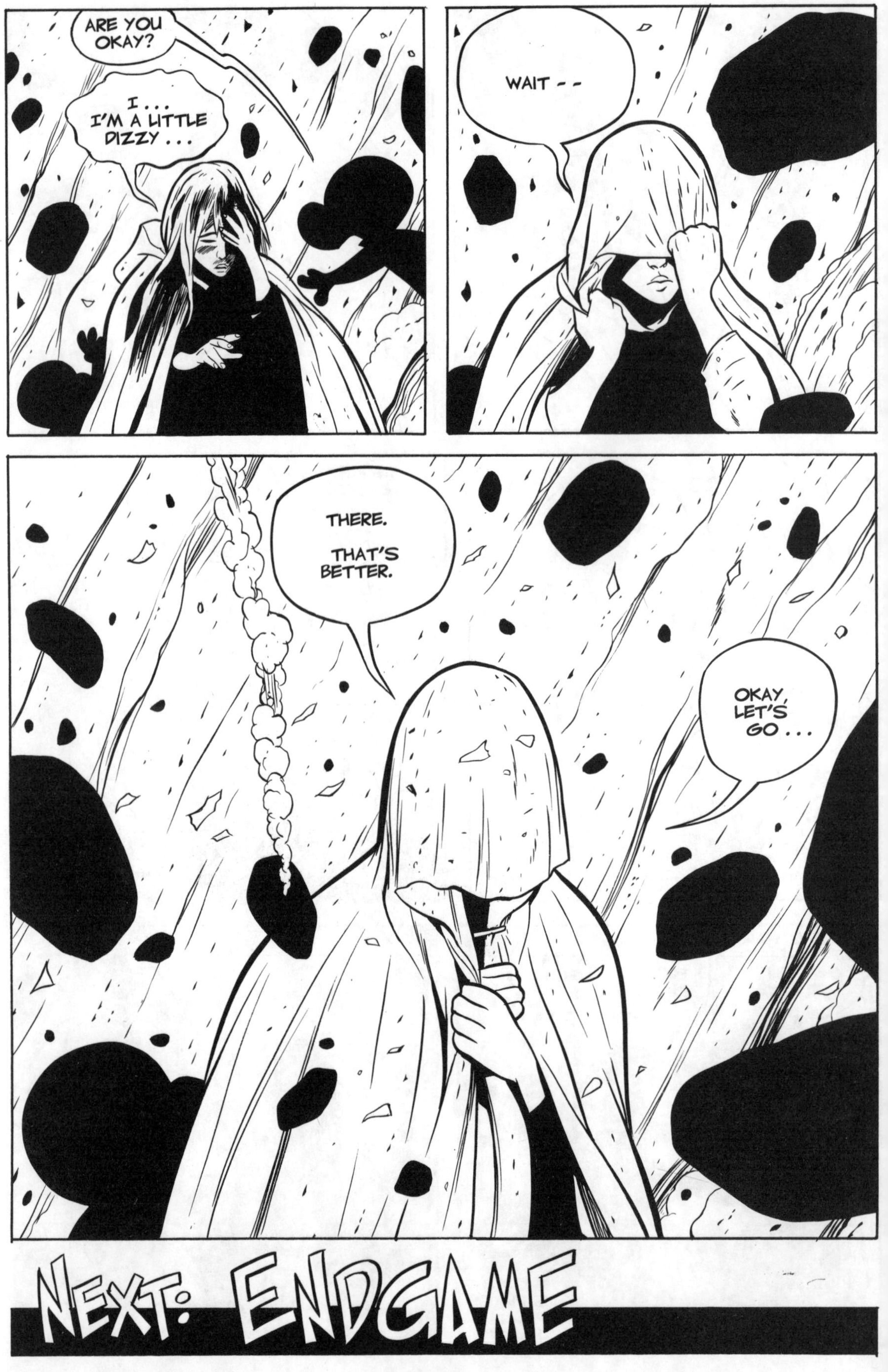
ARE YOU OKAY?
I... I'M A LITTLE DIZZY...
WAIT --
THERE.
THAT'S BETTER.
OKAY, LET'S GO...

NEXT: ENDGAME

END
OF
PART TWO

Stupid, Stupid Rat Creatures (on-line jargon) *n.* exclamation of disapproval from the wonderful comic **Bone.** Often customized to suit the occasion, most often along the lines of: *Stupid, stupid end-users! Mac's bug must load before all other systems extensions!*

- Random House dictionary of CYBERSPEAK

You **just** finished the **latest** adventure in the **award winning BONE** saga!

You can join in the adventures of the *BONE* cousins and their friends in the next book, *BONE Volume Seven: Ghost Circles*

BONE is currently printed in thirteen languages around the world, and has won all of comics' major accolades, including Eisner Awards for Best Cartoonist, Best Humor Publication, as well as France's Angouleme Alph-Art Award, the National Cartoonists Society's Best Comic Book two years in a row, and the Harvey Award (named for Harvey Kurtzman, the creator of MAD) for Best Cartoonist four years in a row.

Look for all these great *BONE* titles as well as *BONE* comic books and merchandise at your local comic book store!
Or call: **1-800-SMILEY-2** for a free catalog!

BONE Vol. One: Out From Boneville ($12.95 softcover, $19.95 hardcover)
BONE Vol. Two: The Great Cow Race ($14.95 softcover, $22.95 hardcover)
BONE Vol. Three: Eyes of the Storm ($16.95 softcover, $24.95 hardcover)
BONE Vol. Four: The Dragonslayer ($16.95 softcover, $24.95 hardcover)
BONE Vol. Five: Rock Jaw, Master of the Eastern Border
($14.95 softcover, $22.95 hardcover)
BONE Vol. Six: Old Man's Cave ($15.95 softcover, $23.95 hardcover)

CALL 1-800-SMILEY-2 to order by credit card.
Or write to: Cartoon Books, PO Box 16973, Columbus, OH 43216
Or visit us on the web at: www.boneville.com

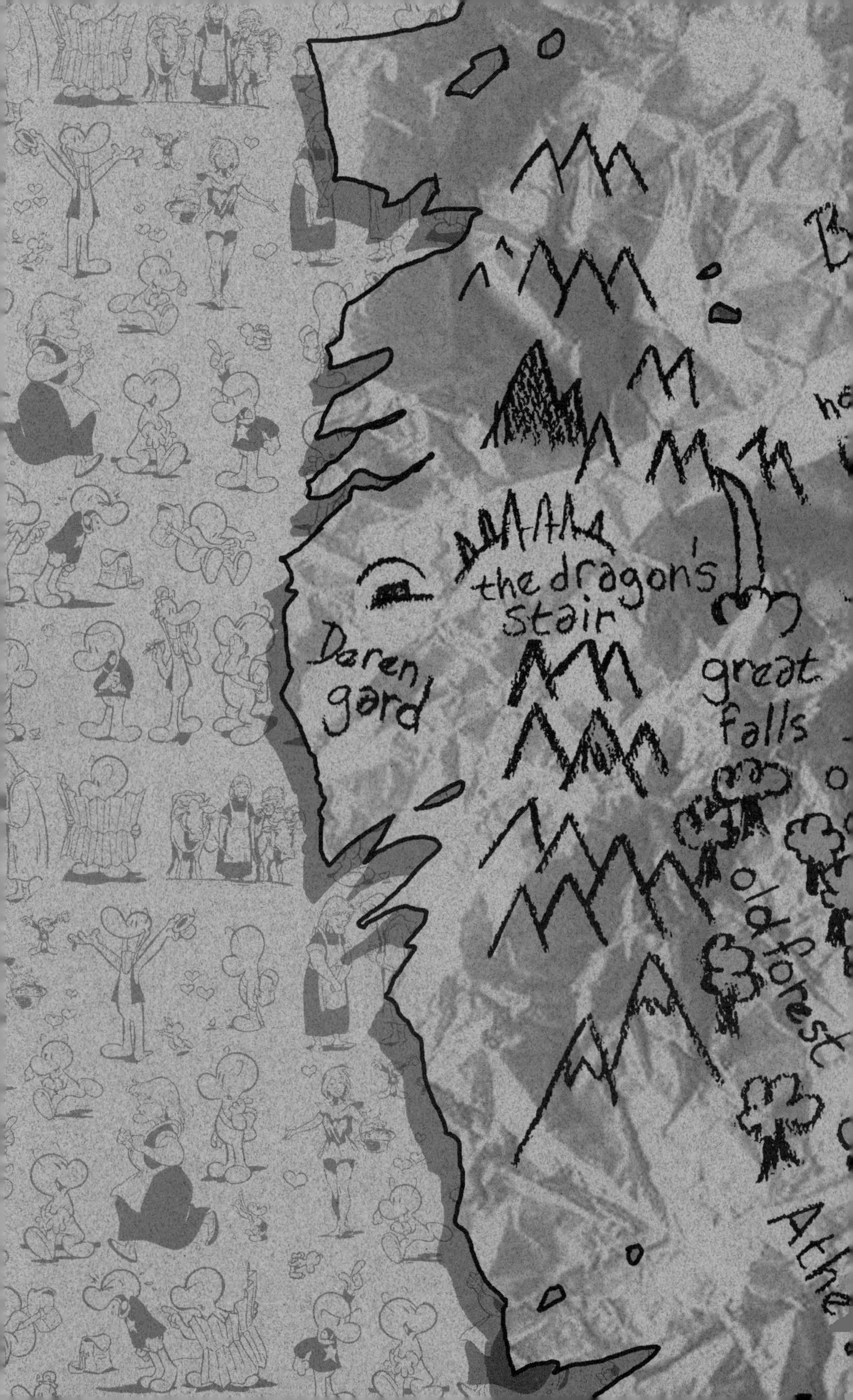
the dragon's
stair
Daren
gard
great
falls
old forest
Athe